FILMS OF SCIENCE FICTION AND FANTASY

FILMS OF SCIENCE FICTION AND FANTASY

BAIRD
SEARLES

AFI PRESS

HARRY N. ABRAMS, INC.,
PUBLISHERS, NEW YORK

Editor: Beverly Fazio
Designer: Elissa Ichiyasu
Photo Editor: John K. Crowley

Library of Congress Cataloging-in-Publication Data
Searles, Baird.
Films of Science fiction and fantasy.
Filmography: p. 231
Bibliography: p. 235
Includes index.
1. Fantastic films—History and criticism.
2. Science fiction films—History and criticism.
I. Title.
PN1995.9.F36S44 1988   791.43'09'0915   88-6281
ISBN 0-8109-0922-7

Page 1: Fantasia, 1940
Page 2, top: Star Trek II—The Wrath of Khan, 1982
Page 2, middle: Star Wars, 1977
Page 2, bottom: King Kong, 1976
Page 3: She, 1965
Page 4: The Incredible Shrinking Man, 1957
Page 5: Superman, 1978
Page 9: One Million Years B.C., 1966

FOR MARTIN, BRAN, AND OLIVER—

WHO SLEPT THROUGH,

TRIED TO STAY AWAKE THROUGH,

AND/OR ENTHUSIASTICALLY APPRECIATED

SO MANY OF THESE MOVIES

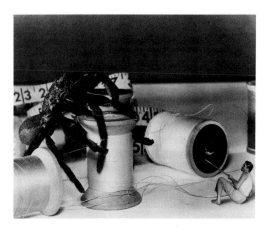

CONTENTS

It's all fantasy, of course. Hollywood is not called "the dream factory" for nothing, and the cinema has, despite its many faces, primarily been used to manufacture dreams and fantasies for public consumption.

Ordinary humans, for an instant, can be made into superhuman beings of unearthly beauty who don't sweat, whose hair is always in place, whose complexions are always flawless, who are forever seen from the angles at which they are most comely. Place these demigods and demigoddesses in worlds of created perfection; in absolutely becoming clothing that never wrinkles; in rooms more perfect than any interior designer can design because they only have to be used for a few moments; in studio streets that may be artificially worn and dirty but that always have the air of being created as a unit rather than haphazardly. And show us theaters on whose comparatively small stages are presented spectacles of a hundred fountains and a thousand dancers that could not easily be fit into the gardens of Versailles, or battles of remarkable orderliness in which a myriad of platoons of cavalry circle and fight in formations more reminiscent of Balanchine than of Napoleon.

Record on film the unreality of a moment, and it will be real forever.

The movies were, and are, fantasy for the eye. But sometimes for the mind as well. The films we are concerned with in this book are those which present us with the downright impossible, not only in style but in content. Their scripts specify that we are to be shown what we know is not even remotely real. Sometimes the impossible is accomplished through miracles of future science: we are shown the trip to a far sun and the creatures on its planets, or we board a machine that takes us into the past or the future. This fantasy subgenre is more or less defined as science fiction. Sometimes the fantasy is simply presented as accomplished through magic or the supernatural (beyond the natural; above natural law). Within this category, the range is broad, from the appearance of a creature of folklore—a leprechaun, say, or a vampire—to a whole world ruled by sorcery.

The aim of fantasy fiction is to convince us, by any of several devices, that the impossible is real. Perhaps nothing has accomplished this more successfully than the motion-picture camera. The impossible can be created for a moment on film, and then—well, "seeing is believing."

It is a curious paradox that the very twentieth-century technology that made cinema such a miraculous purveyor of

miracles also created a hard-headed aversion in the average man to the impossible. Thus the major problem in the history of the fantastic cinema has been, until recently, finding an audience. For that reason, science fiction and fantasy movies have tended to stick to the handful of themes or concepts that had achieved enough popular currency to be acceptable to a mass audience. This as opposed to the written literature, which, in catering to a specialty audience, could be—and has been—a good deal more venturesome in proposing new ideas and unlikely themes. In fact, until recently science fiction writing was one of the rare fields in which the unheard-of was a mark of quality.

So the movies tended to stick to a few basic ideas that were acceptable to the mass audience; it is fascinating to see how over the years more and more sophisticated concepts became acceptable through promulgation by written science fiction and fantasy, and their bastard children, comic books. A young person exposed to the idea of a hero with a magic sword or a telepathic alien in the comics was likely to accept the same in a movie; eventually moviemakers tapped into this vast audience. If you wondered at the enormous success of *Star Wars*, that's it—George Lucas knew that the audience was out there waiting.

Real life also helped. Space travel as a concept leaped at a single bound from "that Buck Rogers stuff" to accessibility the day Russia put up its first Sputnik satellite in 1957. Manned space flight beyond the solar system is still impossible—but how much more acceptably impossible it is now.

And, of course, nothing succeeds like success. If a *Dracula* or a *Destination Moon* or a *Star Wars* makes a great deal of money, then imitations are inevitable, and a fundamental idea will be repeated again and again, not necessarily badly.

It is this basic copycat nature of movies that has given this book its form. Science fiction and fantasy movies can be rather easily subdivided by their themes. The science fiction chapters are unified by an invention (the spaceship, the time machine) or a science fictional character (the mad scientist, the alien, the monster). Fantasy movies and the chapters about them in this book are more generally categorized by their handling of the supernatural element—the introduction of an alien being into our world lightly or fearsomely—or more broadly, by their evocation of the myths of mankind.

Since this book discusses a selective collection, perhaps a word is due on how the movies included here were selected. There are probably as many reasons as there are films represented, but generally they are interesting both visually and conceptually. Many are very good; a few are really awful but still may be representative of a period of moviemaking or have, deep down, a good idea in there somewhere; some are famous or among the great moneymakers of film history; some are obscure; a few are even totally lost but must be mentioned because of their historical importance.

And it should be noted, given the multiplicity of media these days and the fact that "movies" are now made for television, for video, even for computer disk, in a way, that all the films covered were made for theatrical release, with only one exception. (That is *The Day After,* which was made for television but was thereafter shown in theaters throughout the world to more viewers than saw it on the small screen.) One should also mention, in passing, that television has contributed more than a little to its older, larger cousin, by preparing an audience with the likes of the phenomenal *Star Trek* series (which was remarkably good science fiction for its time and place) and the minifantasies of *The Twilight Zone.* And tribute must be paid to the VCR; before its widespread use, many of the movies we write about here were totally unavailable, or, at best, seen shredded at the whim of some unknowledgeable television programmer.

And so, fantasy viewers, hoop-la! We present the impossible on film.

SPACE

Space travel is the one theme that represents science fiction to most people; traveling beyond the Earth's atmosphere to other worlds was, at least until recently, what science fiction was all about. Then man *really* began traveling in space, and things got a little confused. Is a movie such as *Marooned,* in which three astronauts are stuck in orbit, science fiction? The answer is no — that's something that really could happen right here and now. However, if it had been made thirty years ago, it would have been. And space travel has been the subject for cinema a good deal longer than that.

Purists will argue forever as to what grainy, jerky footage deserves the honor of being known as the first motion picture. But among the first, certainly, is an authentic bit of science fiction. And it, of course, has to do with space travel. Georges Méliès had been making short novelty films in France since 1896, many of which included science fictional elements usually for comic effect and used the trickery of filmmaking to show the havoc wreaked by some new invention. But in 1902 Méliès presented *Un Voyage dans la Lune (A Trip to the Moon)*; while

Jules Verne and Neil Armstrong might well have been bemused in their different ways by this vision, it is undeniably a science fiction movie about voyaging in space.

Under the eyes of various bewhiskered dignitaries, the lunar vehicle, resembling a giant cannon shell, is manhandled into what looks like, logically enough, a giant cannon. The fact that it is more correctly womanhandled, by a line of pretty *coryphées* in slightly disheveled sailor suits, somewhat detracts from the solemnity of the occasion.

After the expected effects of the firing, we are shown the man in the moon (with a visage akin to our contemporary have-a-good-day piefaces), the projectile wedged firmly and painfully in one eye. This is an image no more likely to be forgotten than the famous eyeball-and-razor sequence from *Un Chien Andalou,* despite the cartoon quality.

The doughty explorers, who have been in the projectile and debarked safely, encounter bizarre life forms, principal among them a species which will turn up again and again — the extras in rubber suits. These initial examples are capped

RIGHT IN THE EYE!

-- TRIP TO THE MOON --   LE VOYAGE DANS LA LUNE --

A TRIP TO THE MOON:

Sets and effects for the earliest science fiction films did not quite have the verismo that was to be introduced later in the genre. Nevertheless, this moving image made quite an impression on the audiences of 1902. The film was (very) loosely based on a work by Jules Verne (there is no report of Verne's reaction to it). The painfully lodged projectile contains a scientific expedition.

by heads bearing a strong resemblance to those of turkeys.

While this trip to the moon bore no direct resemblance to that described by Verne, it had something of the same result. It spawned any number of *voyages extraordinaires* (which was the title Verne loosely applied to his various novels of imaginative adventure), featuring an amazing variety of unlikely vehicles bearing people to an amazing variety of unlikely destinations.

America's answer to *A Trip to the Moon* took the form of at least four silent films called *A Trip to Mars*. The first of these was simply a pirated version of *A Trip to the Moon,* but the American version produced by the Edison Studios in 1910 tried for some originality. The intrepid scientist here has invented an antigravity powder, the effects of which land him on Mars. There he has encounters with inventively conceived Martians, topped with an escape from a tree-monster.

As the cinema became more of a skilled story-telling medium public interest in the camera trickery behind the various extraordinary voyages waned. It was a period when space travel was deemed

impossible in anything like the foreseeable future, and audiences wanted "realism." Italy concentrated on historical epics and the United States turned to comedy and Westerns; France and Germany continued to experiment, and it was in Germany that an avant-garde cinema, willing to try new ideas or to play with old ones, developed.

After his success with *Metropolis* (see "Futures"), Fritz Lang and his scriptwriter (and wife), Thea von Harbou, embarked on a project inspired by the old voyages hither and yon. The result was *The Woman in the Moon* (*Die Frau im Mond*), released in 1929.

Times certainly had changed. No projectiles or gravity-reversing powder here; this trip to the moon is accomplished in an astonishingly modern rocket, moved by gantries onto its launching pad and taking off, after a thoroughly up-to-date (from our point of view) countdown, in multiple stages. The technical experts on the film were two of Germany's budding rocket scientists, Hermann Oberth and Willy Ley (who would soon after emigrate to the United States and become something of a technical adviser to a whole

THE WOMAN IN THE MOON:

Fritz Lang's silent film about a trip to the moon, one of the first to depict spaceflight seriously, ran the gamut from the amazingly prescient to the utterly ridiculous. Its handling of the preflight preparations (including countdown) and the flight itself was more accurate than the *Destination Moon* of a quarter-century later. But a helmetless Gerda Maurus filming the moon's surface wasn't exactly convincing.

budding generation of science fiction writers). The film's view of rocketry was so accurate, in fact, that Hitler reportedly had all the prints of it confiscated when he came to power.

The other components of the film were not quite as sophisticated. The plot revolves around the scientist designer of the rocket, who goes to the moon to find the gold he is convinced is there in quantity. Melodrama is provided by villains determined to get the gold, romance by the expedition's engineer and his girlfriend who stows away on the voyage.

Scientific authenticity went so far as the voyage itself, the first spaceflight on screen to attempt to cope with such matters as weightlessness, but then goes out the window when the moon is reached. It has not only gold, but also air, snow, and mud. The climax of the plot is one that we

will meet again: there is air enough in the vehicle for the safe return of all but one of the surviving members of the expedition. Who will remain on the moon?

Meanwhile, back in the United States, rocket ships had been consigned along with ray guns and other such unlikely objects to the pages of the pulp fiction magazines; a high percentage of the stories therein were nonsense, but a surprising number played with scientific concepts in a way that set the direction of excellence in the field. These ideas were then picked up by the comics (considered a cut below the pulp magazines as a juvenile medium), and then finally percolated into what was then the lowest form of movie, the kid's matinee serial. Buck Rogers followed this route, appearing first in a better-than-average serial novel in *Amazing Stories* titled *Armageddon 2419;* the popular comic strip followed soon thereafter, then the movie serial.

Buck's infinitely better-drawn comic rival, Flash Gordon, made it to the weekly screen earlier, in 1936. Is there anyone in the world now who does not know how football-hero Flash and his lady friend, Dale Arden, embark in Dr. Zarkov's handmade spaceship to the planet Mongo, which has invaded the solar system and is playing havoc with Earth's weather, oceans, and volcanos? (The stock footage interspersed in the film to show the disasters are worth the price of admission alone.) On Mongo, they confront the evil Ming (who, along with Fu Manchu and the villains in *Buck Rogers,* reflect the continuing public worry about the Yellow Peril) and his equally evil, but vastly prettier daughter.

The machinations of Ming in this and the two serial sequels involve Flash and Dale with lion men, hawk men, shark men, clay men, and whatever other variations on the human form that the costume designers could achieve on a minimal budget. The spaceships themselves were especially endearing, with their smoky exhausts, wobbly takeoffs, and visible bounces when landing. All three serials have been seen in the form of feature-length films.

The vast reach of World War II seemed as far as the public wanted to go for the duration of the 1940s. Space travel remained relegated to the Saturday serial. It might be noted that the "juvenile" series, primitive as they were, at least viewed science positively—Ming's evil superscience was balanced by Zarkov's inventiveness for good. The other popular form of cinema science fiction in this period continued to follow the "mad scientist" theme, in which science was viewed with deep distrust.

The explosion of the atom bomb, paradoxically, seemed to change this; horrifying as it was, it had won the war for America. Written science fiction slowly became more popular in the years after the war, and Hollywood hesitantly got onto the bandwagon.

FLASH GORDON (1936):

In this thrill-a-minute serial based on a famous comic strip, football hero "Flash" Gordon and the lovely Dale Arden are about to be abducted to the planet Mongo by the sinister (but eventually true-blue) Dr. Zarkov. Here Flash (Buster Crabbe) and Dale (Jean Rogers) are shown the highly unlikely workings of the ship that will get them there by Zarkov (Frank Shannon). Any resemblance to a deco radiator is purely the whim of the set designers.

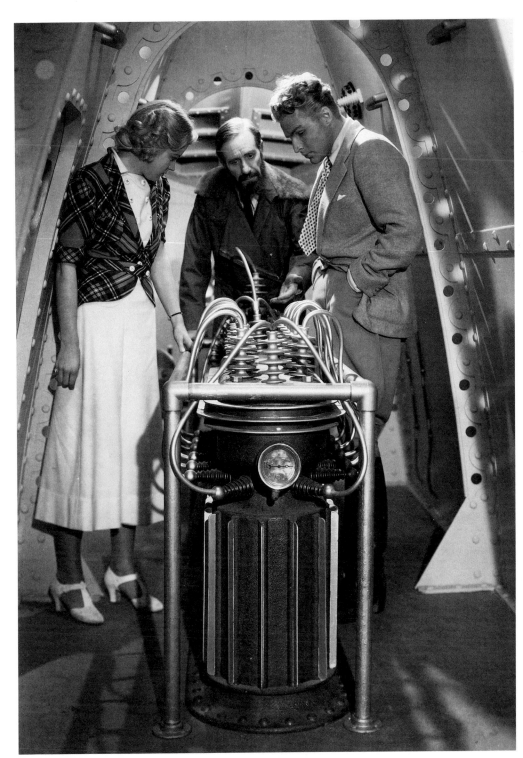

The premiere manifestation of Hollywood's return to science fiction themes was George Pal's *Destination Moon* (1950), generally considered to be the originator of the first major wave of science fiction film. For its time, it was a serious attempt to portray space travel in the form of the first lunar expedition — again. One of the technical advisers was Hermann Oberth, whom we met before in the same capacity on *The Woman in the Moon.* Among the writers was Robert A. Heinlein, who wrote the juvenile novel on which the script was based — so loosely as to be unrecognizable. Nevertheless, for a real writer of science fiction to be employed on a science fiction movie was almost unheard of — excepting, of course, the redoubtable H. G. Wells.

While the lunar set and the effects were as authentic as current knowledge and a limited budget could make them, *Destination Moon* was not entirely free of cliché; it did eschew, however, the beautiful female biologist omnipresent on almost all other future expeditions. The project is plagued by saboteurs and negative public opinion (an indication of how

the filmmakers read the public mind of the time), not to mention the bumblings of one of the four crew members, who is obviously there only for comic relief. The final crisis comes as they are about to leave the moon: they discover that there is only air enough for three of them to return safely. Who will remain on the moon?

Outdated by events, and all too obviously the low-budget film that it was, *Destination Moon* was a milestone that, sadly, is today nearly unwatchable.

Rocketship X-M, a movie that might have been consigned to oblivion, was spared that fate because it is forever linked with *Destination Moon. Rocketship X-M* began production later than *Destination Moon* but was made in an astonishing three weeks for an even more astonishing $94,000 and arrived in the theaters before *Destination Moon* was completed. The timing was no mere coincidence; the public flocked to see both on the strength of *Moon*'s publicity.

X-M does not transcend its production time and budget. Concerning yet another first trip to the moon, the script has the

spaceship crash-land on Mars due to a slight error in navigation (there's method in the madness — it was easier to find deserts on Earth to simulate Mars than to build a lunar set). The inhabitants of Mars have reverted to savagery following a nuclear war. After various alarums and excursions, the earthmen (and woman — there's a lovely lady aboard, less for the purposes of equality than for box office) take off, and this time — surprise! — it's not lack of air, but lack of fuel. And — surprise again! — they all perish. One cannot deny a certain attempt at originality.

Due to the success of these two films, there was a rush to fill the theaters with space. Most of the results were abominable, the classic B movies whose budgets vied for sparseness with their logic. "It doesn't have to make sense; it's science fiction" seemed to be the philosophy.

But several movies from the decade of the 1950s did manage to make sense and to look well-produced. One of these was George Pal's follow-up to *Destination Moon* in 1951. It was taken not from genre fiction but from a mainstream novel by the famous opponent of momism, Phi-

ROCKETSHIP X-M:

This low-budget film, by beating the simultaneously produced *Destination Moon* into release, captured the honor of being the first of the mid-century space films to flood the theaters. Hugh O'Brian, Osa Massen, Lloyd Bridges, John Emery, and Noah Beery, Jr., were the crew of the first spaceship (still called a "rocket ship" in those just post–Buck Rogers days) to Mars.

DESTINATION MOON:

Warner Anderson, John Archer, Tom Powers, and Dick Wesson take one small step for mankind in this 1950 forecast of the first lunar expedition. The script was coauthored by Robert Heinlein. The movie began the midcentury "first wave" of science fiction films.

WHEN WORLDS COLLIDE:

Noah wouldn't recognize it, but this is an ark, carrying a modicum of mankind (and, of course, womankind) and various flora and fauna to another world. The trip is occasioned, as the title tells us, by the imminent destruction of Earth, which is about to suffer an interplanetary traffic accident.

FROM THE EARTH TO THE MOON:

This entry into the Verne cycle of movies was one of the least inspired of the lot, but it had the advantages of veteran actor Joseph Cotten, as the inventor of a Victorian-age rocket fuel, and a moon rocket of wonderfully anachronistic nineteenth-century design, seen here with Cotten and a crewman struggling with something that has gone awry.

FIRST MEN IN THE MOON:

Humanity's first contact with an extraterrestrial species is not a felicitous one, as Martha Hyer and a Selenite come face to face. Played primarily for comedy, the movie was very freely adapted from an H. G. Wells novel. Wells's civilized moon creatures were turned into the usual monsters.

lip Wylie, with Edwin Balmer. The main concern of *When Worlds Collide* is flight into space, but the trip is the climax of the film and takes only the last ten minutes or so. The major part of the movie is concerned with the building of the huge craft—no dinky four-man vessel this; it must carry the remnants of humankind from an Earth about to be shattered by another world that has invaded the solar system. The suspense is terrific, as the menacing invader grows larger and larger in the night sky. Will the ship be built in time? Will the panicking crowds let it take off? And again, the familiar questions on a larger scale: who gets to go, who has to stay?

The ship and its tremendous roller coaster–type launching path are impressive, but the real fun for the audience is watching the Earth be destroyed by tidal waves (splash!—there goes Times Square!) and other natural forces unleashed by the gravity of the invading planet. After that, the flight and the first view of the new planet on which the refugees land (an all too obviously painted landscape, and rather insipidly painted, at that) come as something of an anticlimax.

The attempt by the major studios to make a well-produced, decently budgeted space film achieved finally an almost unqualified success with the beautifully conceived *Forbidden Planet* in 1956. It combined an interesting script (the plot of which, as has been pointed out ad nauseam, is based on Shakespeare's *The Tempest*), a production always adequate and sometimes strikingly effective, and sophisticated concepts. Although less than surprising now, the idea of a universe where interstellar travel is taken for granted and a patrol ship is sent to the system of a distant sun to find a missing exploratory expedition is an extraordinary advance over what had come before. No film had ever left Earth so far behind.

The ship has a handsome captain and a sharp-tongued, sensible doctor (if, in retrospect, you're reminded of the yet-to-be Dr. McCoy of *Star Trek,* you're not alone). They find on the unknown world Dr. Morbius and his daughter, the two survivors of the expedition; a friendly robot (the most cumbersome Ariel ever); and the monstrous force that had done in the rest of the expedition years before.

Lain quiescent since but now rising up again to menace the intruders, the force turns out to be the remnant of an advanced culture — the Krell — which had destroyed itself on this very planet millennia ago by inventing a machine that let loose the forces of the individual id. The current manifestation is the released id of Dr. Morbius, who subconsciously, paternally, feels the classic threat to his daughter from the young male newcomers.

This is pretty advanced stuff, as were some of the effects: the ravening "monster" of the id revealed in flaring outline in a force field and the endless underground works of the ancient race. One can mourn the standard vapidity of the miniskirted heroine, Altaira (in science fiction, never trust a heroine named after a star), and the unrelieved comic relief of the ship's cook (a very early role for the estimable actor Earl Holliman), who uses the robot as a straight "man." But these are minor flaws in a memorable production.

Forbidden Planet hit a sort of peak that took two decades to reachieve. Producers discovered that the same audiences went to cheaply produced science fiction movies as to expensive ones, so the idea of the major production languished. And as movies went, a space film pretty well had to be a major production. Some pretension to class was made with the various filmings of Jules Verne novels, which inevitably had to include *From the Earth to the Moon* (1958); but as the attempt was made to be faithful to Verne and his period, we are right back where we started, with a projectile-ship, containing the unlikely elements of Debra Paget and a good deal of Victorian decor among other things, shot from a giant gun. But for the most part, space as a setting for film was relegated to the place where nasty things came from.

The few excursions into space during this period were safe and from familiar sources. Verne having been run dry, Wells

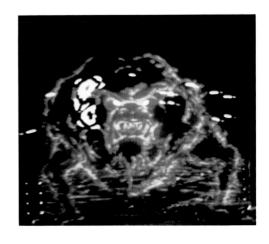

FORBIDDEN PLANET:

Seen here is the monster from the Id, the menace confronting the expedition from Earth that lands on a planet of Altair. The Caliban of this retelling of *The Tempest,* it turns out to be the aggressive feelings of Walter Pidgeon's subconscious, multiplied a thousandfold and made manifest by the ancient science of a nonhuman race.

ROBINSON CRUSOE ON MARS:

The protagonist of Defoe's novel, despite his problems, had it easy compared to the astronaut-hero of the cinematic reworking of the story. He is marooned on the fourth planet, where even finding breathable air takes some doing. The inhospitable landscape of Mars makes Crusoe's island look downright cozy.

was turned to, and in 1964 his *First Men in the Moon* was given the Victorian spaceflight treatment. (Was there ever a specific plot situation in cinema history subject to so many variations as the initial flight to Earth's satellite?) The film follows the plot of the Wells novel fairly closely; a Professor Cavor discovers an antigravity device and uses it to fly a vessel to the moon in 1899. There he and his crew discover an insectoid civilization beneath the surface (which is why the title is . . . "in" the Moon). The Grand Lunar plans to keep the party in the moon for fear that their return to Earth would result in the moon being overrun by the warlike earthlings, but the hero and heroine escape, while Cavor stays to study the Lunarians.

Although the film is superficially similar to the novel, all of Wells's sociological content has been abandoned in favor of a humorous approach. The story is told in flashback by a surviving member of the expedition to the astronauts of modern times, who found no trace of the Selenites: Cavor had a cold when he stayed among them, which apparently wiped them out (this is, of course, a twist on the end of Wells's *War of the Worlds*).

Another film attempted to postdate a classic of literature into the future; calling a spade a spade, its title was *Robinson Crusoe on Mars* (1964). A two-man expedition to Mars crash-lands; one man survives. The first part of the film is a sensible attempt to portray realistically his ingenious measures to survive in the incredibly hostile environment. The movie takes a turn for the fantastical when an alien ship lands; it belongs to a slave-using culture, and the human helps one of the slaves to escape. From there, it's

VOYAGE TO THE END OF THE UNIVERSE:

Czechoslovakia's film industry has turned out a surprising number of science fiction and fantasy films. This one takes advantage of a milieu familiar to readers of science fiction but curiously neglected by Western filmmakers — the "live-in" spaceship with its population making an interstellar voyage that lasts years. It is, as shown here, quite an elaborate milieu.

DR. WHO AND THE DALEKS:

Any British parent of the 1950s and 60s will recognize this lethal horde. They are Daleks, whose vocabulary is mostly confined to the word *exterminate*. Inspired by the TV series and the film based on it, millions of youngsters marched about with one arm upraised, growling "exterminate" at their unnerved families.

chase and escape, as the two make their way to the Martian polar cap and rescue.

From Czechoslovakia came one of the more serious attempts to portray life in deep space. *Voyage to the End of the Universe* (1964) is the first movie to handle what would seem to be a very filmic milieu—a huge spaceship transporting a number of colonists to a distant world. Although badly cut when shown in the West, its view of daily life aboard such a transport vessel seemed aimed at a *verismo* rare in science fiction cinema; unfortunately, a gimmicky ending (the planet they eventually land on turns out to be Earth) rather spoils it.

In the meantime, in England, a peculiar television series was capturing the minds and hearts of English children and turning them all into destructive robotic creatures

whose vocabulary consisted of a single word—"exterminate!"—uttered in a singularly grating voice. The show was, of course, *Dr. Who,* and a film version was made of the episode that introduced the Daleks, called *Dr. Who and the Daleks* (1965). Dr. Who is a time lord from a far distant future who ranges time and space more or less setting things right in a muddled sort of way. The movie, though it gave us the admirable Peter Cushing as the good doctor, came nowhere near capturing the peculiar humor and whimsy verging toward camp that made the series a cult hit with British adults as well as children, and with Americans as well when the show belatedly came to the United States.

From Italy came a stream of badly dubbed and shakily plotted space operas. One of these, *Battle of the Worlds* (1960), was interesting for two things: one is the presence of the great Claude Rains (as, of course, a crusty scientist who discovers that another planet is heading toward us); the other is that, as were many Italian science fiction epics, it was quite well designed. The space suits are as elegant as designer dresses (and in fashion col-

BATTLE OF THE WORLDS:

Claude Rains is the last person one would expect to find in a space suit, but the great actor made this Italian space opera late in his career.

BARBARELLA:

Jane Fonda's head emerges from a diabolical gadget, which is not an instrument of torture in the strictest sense of the word. It's a sort of "sensory organ" into which Barbarella, girl galactic agent, is wired. Milo O'Shea, as the jovially villainous Durand-Durand, about to play on the instrument, is searching for a suitable score.

ors, no less). The interior of the alien planet, once our intrepid astronauts have landed on it, is a series of caves filled with miles of spaghetti-like cables, lit by a red, tomato-sauce glow. When there's a cave-in, and chunks of rock fall into the corridors, one suspects that it's really Parmesan cheese. The effect may be silly, but it is certainly an eyeful.

All in all, as man actually began to explore space in the real universe, movie producers didn't seem to know what to do with it. One answer was to go back to the comics. Fitting the times, the source used was a French comic of some sophistication (if only sexual). The result, *Barbarella* (1968), was rather a joy in its own idiosyncratic way. The setting was a far future, with humankind galloping among the many inhabited worlds of the galaxy

at will. The titular heroine is a sort of galactic agent in search of a missing scientist on the bizarre world of Sogo. There she runs into all sorts of *outré* people and places: murderous children wielding dolls with razor-sharp teeth; a male winged being of angelic beauty; and a wicked Black Queen who lusts for her body and rules a strange, mazelike city filled with sex-mad inhabitants. *Barbarella* doesn't take itself at all seriously, which is the secret of its success. Neither does Jane Fonda in the title role; she gives a delicious interpretation of a dumb blond, amazingly naive while charmingly willing to please. She is as surprised at what's going on as is the audience. The design of the film is wonderfully inventive; bright, comic-strip colors and wild shapes prevail. One never believes for a moment what's on screen, but what one is seeing and not believing is great fun.

Another approach, in the same year, was to make an anthology film of three short stories by Ray Bradbury. One suspects that the filmmakers felt that his was the only name in the science fiction field that the public would recognize in 1968. The film bore the same title as Bradbury's second collection of stories, *The Illustrated Man,* and like it linked the three parts by their having been inspired by the pictures on the body of a man tattooed from head to foot. The same actors played in all three stories as well, but neither device served to make matters coherent. The most successful of the three, "Long Rains," takes place on a water-soaked Venus where the rain falls constantly; four crash-landed earthmen are lost in the endless, dripping scrub forests that grow there. Searching for one of the refuges planted in various places for just such an emergency, one by one they go mad from the constant pelting of the rain. Only one, the martinet leader, makes it to safety. Here, another first, the story is not of heroic survival, but of the terrifying effects of an alien environment; the audience is almost as exhausted as the story's characters from the constant sound and sight of the downpour. The other stories, "The Veldt" and "The Last Night of the World," were far less effective.

At least in the case of *The Illustrated Man,* the producers decided to look to the one source for space fiction that had been more or less neglected: science fiction writers. The public familiar with science fiction literature—a large proportion of which were the youthful students who were noisily remaking American culture—was at this point way ahead of the filmmakers, and was more than ready to see in the movies something as intelligent as was on the printed page. So when an extraordinary writer/director of film decided not just to adapt a science fiction story but to team with its extraordinary writer, the results were like nothing seen on the screen before. The director was

Stanley Kubrick, the writer Arthur C. Clarke, and the film, of course, *2001: A Space Odyssey.*

They decided to use as a base "The Sentinel," a short story by Clarke that told succinctly of the finding on the moon of an ancient artifact, which, when discovered by humans, released a signal into interstellar space. To whom? Why? One was left to wonder.

Around this base the two built a complex tale of alien influences on humankind from the earliest days to the near future, when the first manned probe to Jupiter is disrupted, first by an insane computer, then by a strange black monolith that takes the sole survivor of the expedition, and changes him.

The whole film is evocative, disturbing, and opaque. Initially it left both critics and public baffled and to a degree annoyed, but no one could deny that scene after scene, from the polarized surrealism of the famous "trip" sequence to the magnificent ship, *Discovery,* moving soundlessly but with ponderous grace through space, was unique in the annals of filmmaking.

A week after the film's opening, Kubrick (reportedly with reluctance) cut nineteen minutes from it. Although no major sequential gaps resulted, those who saw the premiere version treasure the small details that were lost.

Soon *2001* became the most talked-about film of the decade; it was adopted by 1960s youth as a prime cult object and was subject to re-evaluation by more than a few critics. It also became a box-office smash. Its influence was pervasive, and one of the more frustrating exercises for the science fiction film buff is explaining to those who grew up after the fact just how much *2001* changed our culture's view of things (not the least of which was the reality of spaceflight). Visually, it influenced other films and television, particularly commercials; for years we were subjected to such things as English muffins rising over the horizon to the strains of Richard Strauss's *Also Sprach Zarathustra* (which rapidly became a clichéd audio

THE ILLUSTRATED MAN:

Rod Steiger played four roles in this omnibus film based on stories by Ray Bradbury. The most effective piece dealt with the crew of a wrecked ship trying to survive on the surface of Venus. This was before the Venus probe, and the planet was depicted as endlessly rain soaked, a sodden Hell. Here Steiger, the only crew member to keep going, is taken into the shelter for which the group has been searching.

MOON ZERO TWO:

Not too much resemblance here to the landscapes of John Ford's Monument Valley, but this witty little movie replays the classic Western on the surface of the moon. That's the mining settlement over yonder.

metaphor for space travel, an association which would have baffled Herr Strauss).

The ironic fact of the matter, however, is that *2001* did not influence movies as movies. It did not trigger a new wave of science fiction movies, as had *Destination Moon* earlier, or as *Star Wars* would a decade later. It was a unique and towering achievement and a *very* hard act to follow (as the makers of the sequel in 1984 were to discover); no one could imagine how to imitate it, though any film having to do with space afterward perforce imitated the look of it.

There were instead, odd little films from out of left field whose oddity was really appreciated by only a few aficionados. Such a one was *Moon Zero Two* (1969), whose script showed some wit. A prime rule established early on for written science fiction goes something like, "You can't just take a Western, transfer it to Mars, and call it true science fiction." Nonetheless, that is just what the scriptwriters for *Moon Zero Two* did, but with absolute awareness of what they were doing. The theory is that in the twenty-first century, the moon has become a mining center reminiscent of the old gold rush days. The plot has wonderfully familiar elements: the brave frontiersman (here the first man to land on Mars) reduced to driving a stage (here a space shuttle out of Moon City); the heroine—named Clementine—whose miner brother has been killed in suspicious circumstances; the unscrupulous "boss" who's not above claim jumping and murder.

All this has been transferred to the futuristic setting without too much strain. Perhaps the funniest moment occurs when the miners from the moon's surface pour into town on Saturday night, galvanizing the bar in the domed city and its saloon girls into action.

Very much influenced by *2001, Silent Running* (1971) offered us huge, silent ships in space, bearing ecospheres containing the last trees of Earth, and the struggle of one ecologist–crew member to save them when the project is ordered

2001: A SPACE ODYSSEY:

A mysterious black slab, obviously artificial, is excavated on the moon; when struck by sunlight, it emits a radio signal aimed at the planet Jupiter. This incident, one of the vast mosaic of mysteries that made up Stanley Kubrick's film, was the original subject of the Arthur C. Clarke short story, "The Sentinel," which was the basic inspiration for the movie. Clarke coscripted the film with Kubrick.

2010:

John Lithgow and Roy Scheider in a rare moment of repose in the very familiar corridor aboard the spaceship everyone got to know by heart in *2001,* the *Discovery.*

SILENT RUNNING:

2001: A Space Odyssey had established the awesome power of the image of great space vessels making their way beyond Earth's atmosphere. This 1972 movie reaffirmed that, with the ships in this case carrying the remains of the world's forests. But its simplistic ecological polemics, some unbearably anthropomorphic robots, and Joan Baez on the sound track undermined the often beautiful effects and photography.

abandoned. There were moments of great beauty, echoing the earlier film, but *Silent Running* was basically a silly movie, returning to the old premise that since it's science fiction it doesn't have to make sense (wouldn't it have been cheaper and easier to preserve the forests in giant terrariums on Earth?), and not helped by three robots so cutely anthropomorphic as to make the pair from the yet-to-come *Star Wars* seem in comparison like characters from a Eugene O'Neill drama.

Curiously, two movies from Eastern Europe provided some relief from the post-*2001* doldrums. The Russian *Solaris* (1973), from a novel by the Polish author Stanislas Lem, would probably have never been imported had not the Kubrick film been such a success. It is as oblique as *2001*, but not nearly so inventive. In *Solaris* a ship from Earth is sent to orbit the planet Solaris to investigate the strange, possibly sentient, ocean-like mass that covers its surface. This "creature" is responsible for the phantoms from the human investigators' past that appear on the ship; we explore one scientist's relationship with his dead wife in flashback as her phantom appears to him.

The movie's complex plot was not helped by severe editing on its release in the West, and it remains something of an enigma. Nevertheless, there are some stunning effects of the ocean-creature seen from the spaceship.

Animated in Czechoslovakia, coproduced in France, *Fantastic Planet* (1973) was an odd but engaging cartoon feature unlike the children's fare we were all familiar with in this art form. It takes place on the world of the Draags, a highly civilized race; among the bizarre life forms on this world are the Oms, which the Draags regard as either pets or pests, depending on their degree of domesticity. These tiny (compared to the Draags) folk appear humanoid; we soon find they are more than that—they are human, the savage remnants of mankind brought by the Draag from a ruined Earth. The Om hero gathers knowledge from a learning device of his owner, escapes, and organizes and educates the Oms until the inevitable clash between the races results.

By science fiction standards, this is pretty elementary stuff, and the material suffers from a peculiarly European mixture of comic-strip elements and surrealism, to the despair of those accustomed to the rigid logic of Anglo-American writers. The charm of *Fantastic Planet* is in its freewheeling artwork, which happily mixes Hieronymus Bosch and Terry Gilliam in a mad collection of plants, animals, and machines (plus some combinations), the likes of which had certainly never before been seen on screen.

Finally, in 1977, the space film realized its potential. For decades, the complex concepts of science fiction had filtered through to the general public rather than just a genre audience, from written science fiction, comics, and the earlier movies. By now a universe of many intelligent species and cultures, linked through space travel as common as plane travel is today, was not considered to be simply juvenile fare, relegated to simplistic movies.

The film that triumphantly realized this, conceptually and as a physical production, was, *Star Wars*. Its story was the extrapolation of the medieval romance (with a smattering of the classic Western) on which so many science fiction novels were based. A federation of many inhabited planets is ruled by an evil emperor. A young man is thrown by circumstance into joining the forces of rebellion; his foster family has been killed, and he is told that his real father was a powerful figure on the side of right, a Jedi knight. He gathers companions: two appealing robots, carrying messages for the rebels; an altogether capable princess, leader of the rebel cause and no standard heroine; a wise old man, also a Jedi knight; and a scapegrace, hotshot spaceship-pilot and his large, furry, alien sidekick. There are action and intrigue and battles, all ending with a confrontation between the hero and the prime figure of evil, Darth Vader, and his great weapon, the Death Star. The young hero triumphs, of course, but one knows that the overall situation is far from resolved.

As with so many science fiction stories, the fascination lay less with the plot than with the implication of a complex universe, the infinite details of which were brilliantly evoked. From the monumental Death Star (a world-sized ship) to a sleazy spaceport bar, these details provided the inventive exotica which had fascinated science fiction readers, and which, until then, had only been seen in the mind's eye. It was perhaps the Cantina scene, rather than the large-scale wonders, that epitomized this. Obviously the interstellar equivalent of any down-at-the-heels crowd in a saloon from the Old West, the bar's mixture of alien races and cultures (all startlingly believable) brought home a human (if the word can be used broadly) element more than any amount of hardware. One aspect of the film that has been somewhat neglected is its beauty: because almost every scene had to be designed by the filmmakers, *Star Wars* harked back in its look to the days when artificial rather than natural sets were the rule, and the resultant look therefore was truly that of another world.

The startling success of *Star Wars* showed that the movie-going public was more than ready for this kind of inventive escapism. It started a host of imitations, as had *Destination Moon* in 1950; the second great wave of science fiction cinema had begun.

Outer space was *in* with public and producers now, but the attempts to emulate *Star Wars* were a mixed bag, to say the least. One of the most touted was *The Black Hole* (1979), which despite all the wondrous tricks the Disney studio was capable of turned out to be a sort of "*2001 Leagues Under the Sea.*" An exploration ship and its crew are captured by a Captain Nemo–like scientist who lurks nearby with his *Nautilus*-like spaceship and crew of sinister robots and dubious humanoids, who turn out to be lobotomized humans. Unlikely events abound, the least likely of which is a sizable meteor that goes through the ship's wall without seeming to affect anything inside at all. Inevitably the whole kit and caboodle fall into the black hole, the result of which is an excursion into metaphysics a la *2001;* on the other side is heaven and hell, characterized by imagery direct from the "Night on Bald Mountain" and "Ave Maria" sections of *Fantasia.*

That same year, *Star Trek: The Motion Picture* used *2001* as inspiration with a great deal more success than *The Black Hole.* It was, as everyone knows, based on the hugely successful television series of only three seasons, which in constant reruns had captured an enormous following. Until *Star Wars,* the *Star Trek* series had been the main outlet for the devotion of the fans of aliens and spaceships on screen; being the only game in town for a decade accounted for the "*Star Trek* phenomenon" of rabid fans and intense fannish activity.

There was much curiosity as to how veteran director Robert Wise would make *Star Trek*'s transition to the large screen. The result, incorporating elements from several of the television episodes, was a big, beautiful motion picture, unafraid to proceed at a leisurely Kubrickian pace at times. Particularly striking is a tour of the new *Enterprise* given to the returning Captain Kirk, as he and Chief Engineer Scott float gently in their tiny pod about the huge bulk of the renewed craft. The new *Enterprise* and her reunited crew boldly go to investigate a strange phenomenon in the depths of space; it turns out to be a vastly enhanced *Voyager* probe from the early days of space travel, now

FANTASTIC PLANET:

This artful animated film, a Czech/French co-production, was endlessly inventive in its graphics. On a distant world, small humanoids are kept as pets by a race of civilized giants. Some have escaped, and established their own feral culture. One of their sports is shown in this scene.

THE BLACK HOLE:

The effects were everything in this most expensive Walt Disney film yet, and they were indeed beautiful. As for the plot, with its echoes of *20,000 Leagues under the Sea,* one major review noted that "the robots get most of the best lines." It concerned itself less with the black hole of the title than with the spaceship, the *U.S.S. Cygnus,* supposedly lost in space for twenty years.

STAR WARS:

For many, this was the best science fiction film ever; for many of those, the key scene was none of the breathtaking battles in space but the relatively low-keyed few moments in a spaceport bar, the "cantina." This mundane setting was packed with an inventive host of aliens, behaving the way any crowd of workingpersons would at a relaxed saloon. The cantina scene invariably brought the house down.

planetoid-sized and with its own alien intelligence. The probe is searching for its father, its "creator," but refuses to accept mere humanity as such. A peculiarly conceived sexual element is introduced as the alien "V'ger" unites with a female member of the crew, turning her into an extension of itself; her lover, in a sense offering a human sacrifice to a god, selflessly makes it a *menage à trois,* which for reasons too complicated to go into here, resolves everything.

All this is accomplished with a maximum of near-abstract "light show" effects and "trip" sequences, but they make sense within the context of the film and are also a feast for the eyes. There are also more solid sets and effects, such as the dwarfed *Enterprise* (which had loomed so large early in the film) venturing into the influence of *V'ger.* (It should be noted that this kind of lavishness was not what *Star Trek* fans wanted, apparently; the more popular large-screen sequels were not unlike longer, slightly better-produced episodes of the series.)

Perhaps no film since *Gone with the Wind* had been as eagerly awaited as the sequel to *Star Wars. The Empire Strikes Back* came in 1980, and it was not a disappointment. All the main characters were back. New technological marvels—huge, walking fortresses and a floating city, among them—were presented. Our hero, Skywalker, learns the mystical Jedi techniques from an astonishing new character, Yoda, a small, green eight-hundred-year-old personage who lives in a swamp and is a Jedi Master to boot. There is a confrontation between Skywalker and

FLASH GORDON (1980):

The remake of the epitome of comic-strip science fiction was a knockout production, reflecting and glorifying the thirties original. Facing off for battle here are two excellent English actors: Brian Blessed (the Augustus of the television *I, Claudius*) as Vultan, King of the Hawkmen, and Timothy Dalton (the latest 007) as the sympathetic Prince Barin.

Darth Vader, this time face to face. Again harking back to medieval romance, a hidden relationship is revealed: the prime villain is the hero's father. And going Frodo of *The Lord of the Rings* one better, Skywalker loses his hand. Again things are only temporarily resolved.

Typically, Hollywood's new rush to space and the profits of *Star Wars* resulted in remakes of properties long considered antiques. In 1980 *Flash Gordon* was resuscitated in a major production. The result was almost as much fun as the original—and a good deal better produced. The new *Flash* stuck surprisingly closely to the original plot line, familiar from the old serial and the comics. Here is the invading planet ruled by Ming the Merciless, to which travel Flash and Dale, by courtesy of Zarkov's (still homemade)

spaceship. Here again is the sinister throne room of Ming, where any sort of monster is likely to come out of the wall, trapdoors open, and Ming's daughter shamelessly ogles Flash's physique. We are reacquainted with Barin, the Robin Hoodlumish prince of Arborea, and the flying Hawkmen and their floating city. (This sequence is an odd *hommage* to *The Wizard of Oz:* the Hawkmen's capital is visually akin to an orbiting Emerald City, and the flocking legions of Hawkmen irresistibly reminiscent of the winged monkeys.) *Flash Gordon* didn't take itself any too seriously, and was often exciting and beautiful to look at. What more could one ask?

Serious content was the answer, and *Outland* (1981) did its best to supply that ingredient. Unfortunately, it did so by re-

OUTLAND:

Mining is sure to be one of the major industries on other worlds, and the setting was a convincingly created mining facility on Io, the second satellite of Jupiter. There were few exterior shots in the movie; most of the action was confined to the claustrophobic living and working quarters of the miners.

STAR TREK—THE MOTION PICTURE:

A decade after its demise, the phenomenal TV series *Star Trek* came to the larger screen as a film (hence the awkward title). To almost everyone's surprise, under the directorship of veteran Robert Wise, it turned out to be a big, beautiful movie. The famous spaceship *Enterprise* had been in "drydock" for two years for a total overhaul; one of the picture's treats was an exterior tour of the newly refurbished vessel.

working the classic Western *High Noon* and setting it on Io, a moon of Jupiter. Here again, the lone law enforcement officer waits for the bad guys on the noon train . . . er, shuttle, and only the misfits of the Io mining colony are willing to help. However, the serious questions of responsibility and conscience raised by *High Noon* got lost somewhere in the futuristic shuffle of *Outland,* but fine performances by Sean Connery and Frances Sternhagen (as a female version of the tired doctor) and a wonderfully claustrophobic milieu almost made up for this lack.

Jim Henson's mad, myriad Muppets have been responsible for a combination of slapstick humor and sophisticated wit that had brightened television and movie screens for some years. None of this prepared us for Henson's *The Dark Crystal,* however, which came to the screen in 1982. The rather arcane term *science fantasy* must be used to describe this movie, for while *The Dark Crystal* had the appearance and style of high fantasy, it was firmly rooted in science fiction and took place on another planet—one

that happened to have three suns.

As with the animated *Fantastic Planet,* the filmmakers in this case could create an entire world of amazing creatures without the problems of having them interact with human actors. In fact, *The Dark Crystal* may be the first full-length movie ever to have nothing to do with humankind or Earth at all.

There are several intelligent races on this planet. One, the elflike Gelflings, supply a hero and heroine, but they are a dying race owing to the depredations of the evil Skekses, whose vulturine faces do little to mask their heartless, though clever natures. Then there are the slow and kindly urRu, who also suffer from the Skekses' cruel rule.

The movie is a classic quest, in this case for a Dark Crystal. Visually and conceptually extraordinary, the wonders of the world of the Dark Crystal unfold—castles, creatures, landscapes, plants, and machines in bewildering diversity; sinister and beautiful and charming, they are also all amazingly real. *The Dark Crystal* is a small masterpiece of imaginative invention.

THE EMPIRE STRIKES BACK:

If we look at the *Star Wars* trilogy as a three-movement symphony, the second film is the equivalent of an *adagio.* There were thrills aplenty, of course, but it had a slightly gentler quality, primarily because of Yoda, a benign alien being who lives in a swamp. Yoda also happens to be a Jedi, a master of the skills which will eventually win the day for Luke Skywalker (Mark Hamill). Frank Oz provided Yoda's persona.

THE EMPIRE STRIKES BACK:

Four characters who have entered the mythology of our age are Han Solo (Harrison Ford), Princess Leia (Carrie Fisher), Chewbacca (Peter Mayhew), and C-3PO (Anthony Daniels).

RETURN OF THE JEDI:

The *Star Wars* trilogy was made by its wonderfully varied ingredients, such as the cantina and Yoda, but throughout consistent thrills were provided by awesome space scenes such as this one.

Perhaps the anticipation of the third of the *Star Wars* trilogy, *Return of the Jedi*, was a little less than that for the second. Since George Lucas had already proved he could vary the formula without disappointing, it was almost taken for granted that his new movie would not be a letdown; and, when *Return of the Jedi* opened in 1983, this, for the most part, proved to be the case. New creatures, new machines, new planets were brought forth to divert, and everything ended happily, with yet another familial revelation and the Empire defeated by the forces of good. If the fierce but cuddly Ewoks threatened a case of terminal cuteness, the magnificently filmed high-speed chase on motorized broomsticks through the close-packed trees of their forest made up for it. It did seem a bit of a shame that the only supertech menace

that could be found was a revival of the old Death Star from *Star Wars*, but still it was a thoroughly diverting movie, suffering only because such high standards had been set for it by its predecessors. Perhaps the most damning thing that can be said about it must be that it wasn't a finale; the three-movement *Star Wars* symphony simply did not come to the climax that was required.

And then came *Dune* (1984). For years the cinema of space had been attempting to catch up in sophistication to the literature of space. In this long-awaited filming of Frank Herbert's novel, which had become a cult classic in the 1960s, film finally did catch up to print—and managed to baffle almost everyone. The problem was in transferring the dense plot and concepts of the immense novel to a film with any sort of reasonable running time.

What resulted was a movie that, to make any sense, depended on a knowledge of the book; by those lights, it was a terrible movie. Probably only a multiepisode television series could have allowed enough time to explain coherently all the alien concepts thrown at the viewer.

Nevertheless, *Dune* is an extraordinary film. The wonders and beauty of Herbert's far-future universe were realized visually with remarkable fidelity to the images evoked by the novel. Here again we have basically medieval elements: a vast Empire ruled from a decadent court, subject to many powerful factions, including various powerful hereditary houses controlling vast sections of the realm; a sort of priesthood of women trained to strange mental powers; and a guild of navigators on which the commerce of the Empire depends, turned into unhuman monstrosities by the drug that enables interstellar travel.

In an atmosphere steamy with intrigue and duplicity, one of the great families is massacred by another; the surviving son takes refuge among the mysterious natives of the planet Dune, whence comes the all-important drug of the navigators. He becomes a leader, learns to control the giant sandworms that inhabit the deserts of Dune, and recovers his family's holdings.

All this is decorated with sets, effects, and costumes of baroque splendor. Where *Star Wars* was in bright, basic colors and clear images, *Dune* is dark and convoluted, even to its spaceships (there is much coming and going between parts of the interstellar Empire); the tiny shuttle vessels enter the huge star-traveling ship through gigantic golden doors.

Nightflyers (1987) has a good creepy space-horror idea, from George R. R. Martin's novella of the same name. Thanks to *Alien,* science fiction and horror seem to be inextricably combined—again—and the future is full of nasty things. Here we have another look at the closed-environment spaceship and an expedition seeking a possible space-dwelling entity as old as the galaxy. The members of the

NIGHTFLYERS:

Catherine Mary Stewart and Michael Praed make an uncomfortable but necessary escape from their spaceship, which is about to be blown to bits.

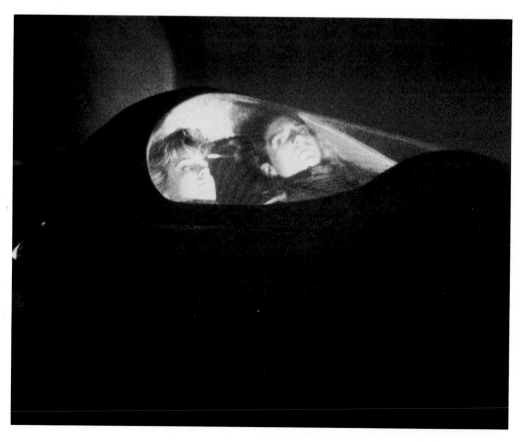

eight-person scientific team (a mixed and generally unpleasant lot) are baffled to discover that the spaceship seems to have no crew, and that the captain of the (leased) vessel appears to them only as a hologram.

It turns out that the young, male captain is a clone of the dead (female) designer and owner of the automated ship; she died before he was "born," and he has been raised in space, separated from any contact with other human beings, and therefore vulnerable to human diseases and normal gravity. But the personality of his "mother" is alive in the ship's computer, and she becomes jealous of the newcomers, particularly the young woman the captain is obviously falling for (even though it's at a distance by hologram — this is one of the more removed screen romances).

The computer mother perpetrates various unpleasant acts on the trapped humans, and at the climax the whole ship is blown to smithereens. Captain and lover, however, sail into the distance in a two-person, spacegoing lifeboat. How he is to resist her germs in such close proximity is not explained, nor is much else. A promising idea and some good visual atmosphere (the vessel itself has huge, smokily Gothic interiors) are subverted by a muddled script, mushy direction, and characters so unpleasant that one is on the side of the murderous computer-mom.

Dune was an enormous failure with the movie-going public, too complex for the young audience that had made the *Star Wars* trilogy such a phenomenon. The sequel to *2001* which opened at nearly the same time also did not do as well as expected at the box office, though it was blatantly made to attract the vast numbers who remembered the original as the movie high point of the 1960s. Space films again seem relegated to the area of kids' and/or horror movies and will probably remain so until another Great Original comes along to start another wave of exploration of the far reaches of the universe.

DUNE:

The resemblance of much science fiction to medieval romances has often been noted, and never was it more apparent than in the film of Frank Herbert's cult novel. Despite the technology, the Imperial court had all the trappings of feudal royalty, including the severed head. Jose Ferrer is the Padishah Emperor Shaddam IV; to his left is Sian Phillips as the Reverend Mother of the mystical female order of the Bene Gesserit.

THE DARK CRYSTAL:

The evil Skekses, who resemble nothing so much as oversized rats as envisioned by El Greco, gather to revitalize the crystal of the title (less dark than pink here). The elaborate world of the Dark Crystal was a constant feast for the eyes, as brought alive on screen by Jim Henson of Muppet fame and a host of other talented artists.

TIME

BERKELEY SQUARE:

Leslie Howard is obviously smitten with the lovely Heather Angel. There's just one small problem: he is a man of the twentieth century who has traveled 150 years into the past. It is the ultimate romantic complication; when boy loses girl in this one, the barrier is a century and a half.

ime is confusing enough when it proceeds in its accustomed linear way, but when one starts traveling back and forth in it, things can get really complicated. (Some science fiction writers have also postulated going sideways in time, but we won't go into *that*.) The paradoxes inherent in time travel (epitomized by the going back and killing your grandfather classic) have been explored over and over in written science fiction, but it has been a curiously neglected subgenre in cinema, though several examples have made such an impression that there would seem to be more than there really are.

Perhaps because it's a concept that needs a lot of words to explain, the silent cinema had almost nothing to do with time travel, except for such simplistic, it-was-but-a-dream forays into the past as *A Connecticut Yankee in King Arthur's Court* (1921).

The first major cinematic journey in time was a class act indeed. *Berkeley Square* (1933) was from a hit play, which in turn was based on an unfinished novel by Henry James. In it, Leslie Howard trips back to the eighteenth century, becomes one of his own ancestors, and finds the love of his life (if it can at that point be called *his* life). When he returns to "mod-

ern" times, the lovers are separated by the greatest obstacle the movies had yet found to implement "boy loses girl" — two centuries (give or take a year or so). The movie can best be described as "poignant," which may or may not be exactly what James had in mind.

Thereafter, traveling in time was used primarily for the comic potential of the jarring juxtaposition of modern characters and various periods of history and their inhabitants. There was, for instance, the British *Time Flies* (1944), in which a comic professor invents a comic time machine and with some comic friends travels back to the Elizabethan Age, where he interacts comically with the Elizabethans, most notably Shakespeare. The playwright, stuck for lines, is fed his most famous ones by the visitors from the future (which raises the sticky question of who created them in the first place — a typical time travel paradox).

A more substantial production with equally humorous intent was *Where Do We Go From Here?* (1945), which starred the indefatigable Fred MacMurray in his light-hearted mode as a 4-F citizen who, upon finding a magic lamp complete with genie, wishes himself into the army. This is duly accomplished, but it turns out to

WHERE DO WE GO FROM HERE?:

This unlikely trio consists of the perennially blonde June Haver, the perennially ethnic Anthony Quinn (not for the first time playing a native American), and the perennially successful Fred MacMurray, whose career went from the early 1930s to the late 1970s. The movie was a daft romp about a time-traveling modern American, here concluding a highly shady property transaction in colonial times.

be George Washington's army. Further complications dump our wishful hero into the midst of Columbus's first expedition across the Atlantic, a sequence that turns into a miniopera—not as unlikely as it sounds, since the movie is a musical comedy and the music happens to be by Kurt Weill with lyrics by Ira Gershwin.

By 1955 the space picture boom inspired by *Destination Moon* was getting desperate for some sort of variety. The theory behind *World Without End* seemed to be to start with a space film (astronauts returning from Mars) and combine it with the by-now familiar cautionary look at the devastation of nuclear war (with the obligatory mutants). The mix was accomplished by time travel; four space travelers run into a time warp in space (or perhaps a space warp in time—these films were never very coherent about such things) and land on twenty-sixth-century Earth, which has indeed been pretty badly done in by a nuclear war. The mutant "thingies" in this case are giant spiders, and the poor quartet from our century are discouraged to find the only visible human life reduced to pre–Stone Age levels. After various alarms and excursions in this less than hospitable future, they finally discover intelligent, civilized life in caverns below the surface, complete with machines and lovely maidens garbed in tunics designed by Alberto Vargas, the most famous of pin-up-girl artists.

In 1960 the vogue for what could be called nostalgia science fiction (usually based on Verne or Wells) presented us with a small classic so endearing that to dislike it is the genre equivalent of bad-mouthing Lillian Gish. It was the inevitable filming of H. G. Wells's *The Time Machine,* produced by George Pal. Like the other Verne/Wells adaptations, it eschewed any serious overtones for a kind of playfulness, but here the playfulness worked. The Wells short novel was the first major literary use of a machine to travel in time, and the future found by the traveler has an eerie surrealism (with, of course, barely hidden social significance).

In the movie, the inventor-hero, George, designs a wonderfully Victorian time machine (with a red plush seat and more than a passing resemblance to a Currier and Ives sleigh). While traveling from 1899, he can see "out," as it were, and keeps track of the passing years by the changing styles on a shop-window mannequin across the street. After passing "through" an atomic war in the 1960s, he becomes entombed in rock; when it finally erodes, he finds himself in a distant future. The first inhabitants he discovers are the butterfly Eloi, who live in a ruined pavilion and spend their days romping in a fruitful garden of perpetual summer. This strikes him as an agreeable future until he finds that the Eloi are almost totally without will and are preyed upon by the bestial underground-dwelling Morlocks, who run a great many thumping machines and avoid the daylight.

Though the film's Morlocks are a little too close to Yeti with fangs, the pastel-garbed Eloi in their crumbling summerhouse are marvelous, and the film is filled with imaginative touches: the whirling, speaking discs in the dusty museum from which the traveler learns this age's history; the field of round vents rhythmically pounding with the Morlock's machines; and above all, the time machine itself,

WORLD WITHOUT END:

This may look like an eccentric version of *Snow White and the Seven Dwarfs,* but it's really the world of the future, as typically portrayed by the B movies of the fifties. Cloche hats were particularly popular as male headgear.

THE TIME MACHINE:

This elegant device is H. G. Wells's time machine as realized by George Pal. The vertical umbrella spins violently, and a small gauge on the "dashboard" tells one how far into the future (or past) one has gone. The time traveler is Rod Taylor, whose adventures are less socially significant than Wells's but great good fun nevertheless.

which bears a brass plate that reads "Manufactured by H. George Wells." This is not the last time we shall meet Mr. Wells in cinematic connection with his time machine.

The Time Travellers (1964) is familiar territory for most of its length. A scientist creates in his lab a time portal through which he and two assistants step into a post–atomic war future populated by— you guessed it—mutants above ground, remnants of civilization below ground. (These particular remnants are endeavoring to build a spaceship to escape the unpleasant environment.) Two original touches, however, raise the movie above its rather shoddy production. One is the introduction of androids, with a view of synthetic humans well above the Frankenstein level. The other is a totally unexpected ending wherein the travelers are caught in a time cycle, cleverly suggested by looped film, presumably for eternity.

Sophisticated as that concept was for the period, it seemed simple-minded in comparison to the 1968 French film from New Wave director Alain Resnais, *Je T'Aime, Je T'Aime.* He had mystified filmgoers earlier by playing with time in *Last Year at Marienbad;* here he utterly baffled everyone with a film about a failed suicide being sent back a minute into his past.

THE TIME TRAVELERS:

In this, the possible future equivalent of a body shop, the bodies are those of androids. This movie is one of the first to use the concept of the created humanoid, though otherwise its view of a postholocaust future—remnants of civilization surviving below the ground—was pretty standard.

TIME AFTER TIME:

H. G. Wells (Malcolm McDowell) proudly shows off the time machine he has invented, not on paper, but for real. Among his dubious friends is Jack the Ripper (David Warner), who will soon need to escape from justice. Where else but to the next century, i.e., ours? The results are a convoluted chase in time.

The time "machine" is an organic affair (its resemblance to a womb is hardly coincidental), and the time traveler's companion on the one-minute trip is a white mouse (of the laboratory type—it is not cute, nor does it sing). Being a Resnais film, things do not work out simply, and subjective flashbacks and objective flashbacks (which is what time traveling might be called in cinematic terms) become inextricably combined.

Time as a theme was neglected for nearly a decade, but the *Star Wars* revival of science fiction in cinema inevitably led back to time travel, and the new conceptual sophistication resulted in a quantum leap in its handling. *Time After Time* (1979) again introduces us to H. G. Wells,

this time with no coyness. This is indeed Wells, the bespectacled writer, who, in addition to writing books, happens to have invented a time machine. An old friend, a surgeon, has taken to slicing up some of London's ladies of the night; he is, in fact, Jack the Ripper, who, with the police in hot pursuit, steals Wells's machine and ends up in our contemporary San Francisco. ("I'm home," he says, after a quick look at television and the newspaper headlines.) Wells, thanks to a homing device on the machine, is able to follow him, and finds himself coping with a homicidal maniac, the late twentieth century, and a charmingly liberated female bank teller all at the same time. Malcolm MacDowell makes Wells an enchanting, if unlikely hero, especially in a brief encounter with an electric toothbrush. There is a good deal of suspense in the double cat-and-mouse game that hunter and hunted play, and even the common car chase has a certain panache, since Wells hasn't the foggiest idea how to drive one. All ends well, with some adroit use of the time machine; the film's script, for a change, shows some intelligent awareness of the paradoxes involved, though the time machine itself can't hold a candle to the one from 1960.

Time as a romantic obstacle was revived in the ravishing *Somewhere in Time* (1980), wherein a modern young man falls in love with an ancient photograph and more or less by sheer force of will (machinery would have been disconcertingly unromantic in context) goes back to the turn of the century in search of the beautiful young actress who is its subject.

Christopher Reeve, Jane Seymour, and an astonishingly preserved grand resort hotel in Michigan are all so beautiful that it would take a heart of stone to resist them. There is a fillip to the plot involving the photograph and a circle in time that is probably the cleverest cinematic use of the paradoxes of time travel yet.

Time Bandits (1981) takes us from the sublime to the ridiculous. One suspects that it was meant to be a comedy, and one meant for children, at that; yet its most effective sequence is the one that isn't at all comedic, and while children might tell their baffled adult companions that *they* understood it, it's very doubtful that anyone fully followed the adventures of a boy dragooned by a group of manic dwarves into a chase through various time periods. The dwarves have stolen from yet another evil overlord the all-important time map that shows the various temporal warps

SOMEWHERE IN TIME:

Handsome Christopher Reeve is falling in love with an antique photograph of beauteous Jane Seymour. He goes back in time to find her, and it turns out that the feeling is mutual. The gimmick—and a charming one it is—is that it is he whom she is looking at when the photo is taken, inspiring the very look with which he fell in love to begin with. The movie mixes two paradoxical subjects—time and love—with great success.

TIME BANDITS:

A chase through time results in near chaos and utter confusion in this muddled comedy. A high point for the boy time traveler (Craig Warnock) and the audience, though, was a stopover in ancient Greece and an encounter with Sean Connery as a splendid King Agamemnon.

which can transport from one era to another. The Overlord's Castle of Ultimate Darkness is a most impressive set/effect, and the first manifestation of the unusual, when a mounted knight in armor comes crashing out of the boy's bedroom closet, is a dilly. But it is the episode in pre-classical Greece, with Sean Connery as an authentically heroic Agamemnon that stays in the mind; it is left to wonder why Agamemnon, the unlikeliest of Greek heroes, was chosen, but the resultant episode so epitomizes a boy's vision of heroism that it doesn't matter.

The Terminator was the surprise hit of 1984, a small film that appeared virtually unheralded. The plot could be that of a classic science fiction novel from the 1950s: a killer android is sent from the computer-ruled future to kill the mother-to-be of a charismatic future leader of mankind and thereby prevent his birth. The human revolutionists, for their part, send back a human to prevent the murder.

It's a good plot, and in a written version would probably have been an intellectual cat-and-mouse game, with the two beings from the future helped by their fore-knowledge and hindered by unexpected circumstances from their "past." Unfortunately, being a movie of the 1980s, it is almost totally devoted to violence, consisting mostly of four motorized chases (car, car; car, police car; car, motorcycle; and finally semi-truck, pedestrian) separated by outbursts of mayhem as the homicidal robot sprays the vicinity (*any* vicinity) with bullets. There is, however, a neatly plotted ending as the saved lady bears a child (the leader-to-be) to the human hero from the future, who has been killed in the rescue attempt.

BACK TO THE FUTURE:

Michael J. Fox (left) and Christopher Lloyd have a tense moment testing Lloyd's homemade time machine in a shopping-mall parking lot.

THE TERMINATOR:

This unheralded film was a great hit, perhaps due to an original idea, perhaps due to its non-stop violence. Arnold Schwarzenegger played the killer android from the future who descended on the present to eliminate a few of its inhabitants, thereby eliminating their descendants.

The science fiction film crop of 1985 seemed to consist of one movie with seven or eight titles; in all of them a young person encounters a homemade machine of unique properties which complicate his life in various comic (?) ways. One version of this ubiquitous movie, however, did manage some originality in both dealing with time and showing some wit. This was the adolescent-oriented *Back to the Future,* in which paradox was the point. The young protagonist travels back to 1955 in a made-in-the-basement time machine and has a busy time making sure that his parents (who are then his age) get together—and, more importantly, stay together, since his mother shows a peculiarly nonmaternal preference for him. Again, the time machine hasn't anywhere near the charm of its great predecessor of 1960.

Trancers (aka *Future Cop;* 1985) used something of the same idea as *The Terminator,* that of someone traveling back in time from the future to eliminate someone in the present, thereby wiping out his/her descendants. It did it, however, with less violence and more wit. The protagonist in this case is a cop from three hundred years in the future out to prevent the time-change; he has the unlikely name of Jack Deth. In an unusual twist, the time travelers do not journey back physically but are placed in the bodies of their ancestors. Jack finds himself in the body of Phil Deth, a younger, blonder version of himself; he must find and defeat Whistler, the villain from the future occupying the body of one of his own ancestors in 1985 Los Angeles.

Whistler has the ability to turn susceptible people into "trancers," zombie-like vampires with bluish skin. The fact that we are subjected to only a couple of trancer attacks says something for the restraint of the movie; it's as if the script had started out to be a monster/horror flick and someone with a sense of humor and an instinct for the possibilities of the time travel theme had taken over. Whistler's trancers have created havoc in the twenty-third century, which is why he's

being pursued; the fact that the ancestor whose body he's occupying is high up in the Los Angeles police department makes things difficult for his pursuer.

Most of the film is occupied with Deth careering around Los Angeles avoiding Whistler and trying to find the people whose lives (and descendants) he's trying to save. He's accompanied by Leena, the girl with whom Phil had been spending the night when Jack moved in. She had been understandably dubious about Jack's story, but on seeing a trancer in action and being saved from the guns of Whistler's minions by a time-stopping gimmick of Jack's, she willingly throws in her lot with him.

The good humor of the film comes from Jack's intelligent but untutored efforts to cope with 1985 (few twentieth-century cops would have done as well in 1685). And the opening scenes in the California of three hundred years from now are pulled off neatly, particularly a sunken Los Angeles (apparently flooded in "the great earthquake," referred to in a throwaway line) in which Jack goes diving for artifacts (hubcaps, from what we are shown). Later (or earlier, as it were), when Leena asks if he can find his way to Chinatown, Jack says that it's no problem: "I used to swim around here."

Tim Thomerson's craggy features and deadpan delivery are perfect for Jack Deth, and Helen Hunt's slightly askew Leena is a delight instead of the wimp she might well have been had the role been played differently.

As noted earlier, the several sequels that followed the first *Star Trek* movie were little more than glorified episodes from the television series, produced, of course, much more lavishly. Similarity to the series was enhanced by the fact that they were to a degree continuous; plot elements from one carried on to the next. This made the first half-hour of *Star Trek IV: The Voyage Home* (1986) almost incomprehensible to anyone unfamiliar with the Trek canon. After that, however, it veered into a rather daftly imaginative plot that had, if nothing else, the virtue of originality, under the direction of (and cowritten by) *Star Trek* star Leonard Nimoy.

In it, the core crew of the *Enterprise* (all the major figures from the series) decide to go back in time to "rescue" a pair of humpback whales, extinct in the twenty-third century, to repopulate the seas with that species. This is more than a whim, since a space probe from an unknown source is destroying the Earth in a futile attempt to communicate with the planet's (nonexistent) whale population.

The cast finds itself in contemporary San Francisco, and a modicum of humor is derived from the contrast of the high-minded (and high-tech) manners and mores of three hundred years hence with those of today. The best moment is when Chief Engineer Scott vainly tries to voice control a contemporary computer, and finally, in utter desperation, talks into the mouse.

The one thing the film does not explain is why, in a period when the crew of the *Enterprise* has entered the popular mythology, they are not immediately recognized and dragged off to a convention. One of the paradoxes of time travel, apparently.

As time has proved, time presents infinite possibilities. In time, perhaps the cinema will do more than scratch the surface. But only time will tell.

STAR TREK IV: THE VOYAGE HOME:

Why these two were not recognized on the streets of present-day San Francisco and dragged off to a convention is one of the unresolved questions of the fourth *Star Trek* film. But Captain Kirk and Mr. Spock visited our era unrecognized and unscathed, and saved some whales in the process. Need the actors be identified as William Shatner (right) and Leonard Nimoy?

FUTURES

METROPOLIS:

The awesome sets and crowd scenes of Fritz Lang's 1926 view of the future were so impressive that the more intimate aspects of the film are often forgotten.

The future is infinitely malleable until it passes through the mold of the present to be set into the past. Science fiction literature has always played with the infinity of futures possible (if not probable), and science fiction cinema has done the same.

The first cinematic future to make a lasting impression was that of the German Fritz Lang's *Metropolis* (1926), and it set a pattern for future futures of social significance and strife. The action takes place in the year 2026 in Metropolis, a futuristic supercity where the elite live wa-a-a-a-y up on top in the cloud-capped towers, and the workers live wa-a-a-a-y down below in dank underground tenements (an early stage of the Morlocks/Eloi split of humanity as seen by Wells in *The Time Machine*). Freder, a young man from up, sees and falls in love with the saintly Maria, a young woman from down. A wicked and slightly mad super-scientist kidnaps Maria, who has been preaching love, patience, and peace to the trodden-down downs, and, at the behest of Freder's father, a leader of the ups, who believes he can control the workers through this simulacrum, gives her likeness to a soulless robot he has constructed.

The robot stirs up trouble with her wicked, wicked ways, and violence ensues, but all ends hopefully as the loving couple unite to save the down homes, threatened by a flood let loose in the strife. Despite a silly and obvious plot, and acting which to modern eyes seems, at best, excessively broad (with the exception of the athletic Brigitte Helm, who as both Maria and the robot brings a remarkable use of body language to differentiate the roles), *Metropolis* is discovered anew by succeeding generations, who respond to its magnificent sets and the masterful choreography of the hordes of extras.

Hollywood reacted four years later with its own talkie vision of the future, *Just Imagine* (1930). It not only talked, but sang, and its plot was less silly than non-existent. It concerned a denizen of 1930 who, struck by lightning, wakes in 1980 and samples the wonders of that year, including a futuristic New York and a trip to Mars, which is peopled by flappers and other exotic inhabitants. The movie, despite a lavish production, was not a success.

An ongoing source of cinematic thrills was the end-of-the-world (or at least the end-of-civilization-as-we-know-it) plot,

JUST IMAGINE:

This was the American film industry's answer to the spectacular sets of *Metropolis:* even bigger if not so decorative. The scene is New York in 1980, as envisioned from the perspective of 1930, when the movie was made. Suspension bridges were obviously viewed as the coming thing, not to mention wonderfully evenly spaced traffic.

which was always laid in the near future (like tomorrow) so that the audience could relate to the terrifying events on screen. There had been more than a few silent films on the subject; an early example with sound was *Deluge* (1933). The S. Fowler Wright novel from which it was drawn envisioned worldwide destruction from floods and earthquakes; the movie, much to the delight of the provincial populace, concentrated on the destruction of New York City, but did so with satisfyingly spectacular effects.

Another device on which to hang a vision of the future was the anticipated great feat of engineering, such as Germany's *The Tunnel* (1933), remade in

Great Britain the following year as *Trans-Atlantic Tunnel*. This movie showed the building of a tunnel under the Atlantic Ocean in 1940 to link the Old World and the New, and thrills were provided by fires, cave-ins, and volcanic eruptions on the ocean's floor.

Perhaps the greatest movie ever made about the future was H. G. Wells's *Things to Come* (1936), probably because it was *about* the future. Though Wells certainly had his philosophical axes to grind, the point (and excitement) of the movie was his vision of the future, magnificently realized by William Cameron Menzies, the director and production designer. The Wells "novel" (*The Shape of Things to Come*) on which the film is only loosely based was a straightforward "history" of the future, with no more plot than a history book. For the film's script, Wells dramatized various aspects of this chronology, concentrating on one family during several different periods of the upcoming century. Three major periods are covered: a long-lasting World War that begins in 1940 and extends over several decades; a plague-ridden period of neobarbarism in which local warlords exert control over small areas and attempt to recapture the technological wonders of the past; and a scientific Utopia, a technocracy established by the remaining scientists.

The ironic sorrow, in retrospect, of seeing a British city bombed in a film made so close upon a period when British cities *were* bombed gives a clue as to why no movies about the future were made for almost two decades after *Things to Come*. During World War II, the future was too uncertain, the potential devastation too dreadful, for anyone to want to speculate on it. And even after hostilities ceased, the possibilities opened up by the atomic bomb were almost too horrendous to dwell on for a war-weary public.

THE TUNNEL:

An alternate title for this film was *The Trans-Atlantic Tunnel,* which says it all. Here is a tense encounter somewhere down below involving the project's chief engineer, Richard Dix (right), whose lifelong dream the tunnel is. A French version of the film starred Jean Gabin in the same role.

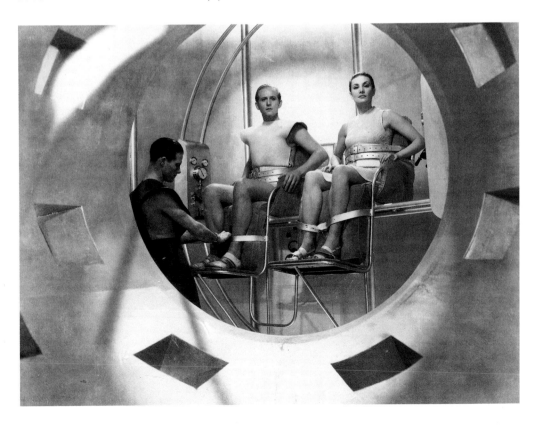

THINGS TO COME:

Kenneth Villiers and Pearl Argyle are strapped in and readied for lift-off in the 1930s equivalent of a countdown for the moon. The costumes aren't what we might think of as astronautical, but the white tunics with flared shoulders set a fashion for futuristic garb that persisted for decades.

TEENAGE CAVEMAN:

The young Robert Vaughn, later to be a man from U.N.C.L.E., is an oddly modern cave dweller, right up to the 1950s haircut. This is due more to the moviemakers' reluctance to turn off the adolescent audience with a realistically squalid primitive than to the surprise ending of the film, which reveals it to be set in the future.

But the future crept in by the back door with the vogue for space films that began in 1950 and a best seller titled *1984* that made it to the screen in 1956. The popularity of George Orwell's novel set a pattern for the screen (though the film was not that popular) of what could be called the "dreary-future movie." For the next two decades, the view of things to come would be dominated by the repressive future society against which the protagonist rebels (usually for love) or, alternatively, the end of society entirely. Soon the possibilities of a manmade end to civilization were surfacing, albeit obliquely, in the B movies that flooded the market. For instance, *Teenage Caveman* (1958) was almost as inane as its title. In it, a young man from a primitive, cave-dwelling tribe (he wears a nattily draped animal skin and sports a 1950s haircut) ventures into a taboo area and encounters various unlikely monsters. It would be just another comic-book, stone-age epic were it not revealed in the end that this is the future, not the past, and humanity has been reduced to a primitive level by an atomic war. With this revealed, much of the silliness of the script is curiously justi-

fied, even if the film's low production values are not.

The issue of future annihilation was confronted head-on in 1959 with the star-studded *On the Beach.* Its slick production and high-priced cast diluted its message, but looked at with our new perspective, *On the Beach* is a beautifully made and curiously moving piece of polemics. The story of the last survivors of a nuclear war, temporarily saved by their location in Australia but doomed by the eventual spread of fallout, is told deliberately with an almost total lack of melodrama. Never were upper lips so stiff as those of Fred Astaire, Ava Gardner, and Gregory Peck (as an American submarine commander who made it to Australia), not to mention a whole population that pas-

1984:

The rest of that poster, in case you hadn't guessed, reads "Big Brother Is," as Edmond O'Brien and Jan Sterling are very much aware. This initial filming of George Orwell's famous novel had a stark, documentary look, at least partially due to its fine black-and-white photography.

THE CREATION OF THE HUMANOIDS:

A pair of "clickers" (robots) is confronted by two members of the surveillance committee of the Order of Flesh and Blood. A literate and unusually complex script, dealing with human/robot relations in terms of midcentury racism, was hidden under a painfully cheap production and some inadequate acting. Chief "flesh and blooder" Don Megowan (second from left) discovers to his horror at the film's climax that he himself is a clicker.

sively accepts its inevitable elimination. But the final shots of the empty streets of Melbourne are almost impossible to watch without being moved.

Restraint and passivity were not notably present in *Panic in Year Zero!* (1962), which describes what happens to an "average" American family on vacation when Los Angeles and other cities are leveled by nuclear attack. There's looting, murder, and rape, but also a certain seriousness that made it more close to home than *On the Beach,* and not just because it took place in California.

The Day the Earth Caught Fire, a variation on the theme, was played by the British in the same year. In this movie it is

not nuclear war, but the coincidental testing of two superbombs by different countries at the same time that threatens the Earth, by throwing it out of orbit toward the sun. There is an equal amount of stiff upper lips and frenzied panic in this one. The main characters (the hero is a reporter on a London newspaper) are intelligent and believable, as is the handling of the whole situation.

Also in 1962 came an odd little movie whose script may well have been the most sophisticated look at the future to date. Unfortunately, it was hampered by some very bad acting and a minuscule budget, though the production tried hard for originality within its means. *The Creation of the Humanoids* showed us a post–World War III high-tech society in which humans and humanoids (extremely lifelike androids) are in conflict. The anti-android hero naturally turns out to be a humanoid himself. This complex (for the time) concept was enhanced by small, taken-for-granted details of the future society, such as "contracts" instead of marriage as we know it. If the production had matched the script, *The Creation of the Humanoids* could well have been the first modern science fiction film.

ON THE BEACH:

The first serious movie about the aftermath of nuclear war brought an all-star cast and a superior production to bear to make its point. Anthony Perkins, Gregory Peck, and Fred Astaire, among the last survivors of a doomed world, are aboard a nuclear submarine desperately searching for signs of other human life.

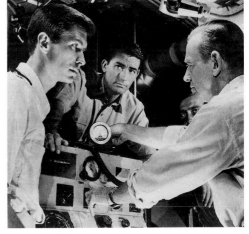

THE DAY THE EARTH CAUGHT FIRE:

Things get hot, both literally and figuratively, as the Earth is thrown out of orbit by multiple atomic tests and spirals in toward the sun. Thanks to the resulting heat wave and the knowledge that the world is doomed, anarchy prevails.

PANIC IN YEAR ZERO:

Ordinary citizens must resort to violence in order to survive after the bomb drops, in this film about postnuclear anarchy. Ray Milland, who also directed, views his wrecked neighborhood. He's the father of an average American family caught on vacation when the major cities are destroyed. The film was an intelligent cautionary attempt for its time, though mild compared to what the current knowledge of such an event would be.

THE DAY OF THE TRIFFIDS:

Howard Keel, in a nonsinging role, and Mervyn Johns are unaware that they are in grave danger of being stung by triffids, two of which are right behind them. The sting of these ambulatory plants is lethal, and, like most flora, they are very hard to kill. They have the unpleasant habit of eating their victims.

THE LAST MAN ON EARTH:

If Vincent Price is the last man on Earth, who are those other people? Well, they're not people, they're vampires, into which the general population has turned, due to a rather vaguely explained plague. This makes for lonely days, but the nights tend to be busy, as we see here.

John Wyndham's odd but suspenseful little novel *The Day of the Triffids* ended civilization in a unique way, combining a meteor shower that rendered almost everyone on Earth sightless with genetically engineered plants that were mobile and lethal. These "triffids" had been bred for their valuable and unique oil and kept safely penned. When the social structure breaks down due to the mass loss of sight, the populace is confronted not only with the hazards of blindness, but with roving bands of triffids as well. The sighted hero has a harrowing odyssey through the remains of England and France before finding others like himself to form a nucleus of a new society.

Brought to the screen in 1963, the film lacks the ongoing tension of the book and made the triffids into standard movie monsters, but it has its horrific moments.

The Last Man on Earth (1964) was notable for its peculiar mix of elements. Based on Richard Matheson's *I Am Legend,* it is, as is obvious from its title, an end-of-civilization story. However, the catalyst here is a plague; those who survive it are allergic to sunlight and therefore must move about only at night and are also insatiably thirsty for blood. They are, for all intents and purposes, vampires. Here the mix of science fiction and horror becomes overt; we shall run into it, and *I Am Legend,* again.

ALPHAVILLE:

Eddie Constantine, looking suitably like the secret agent he is, surveys the terrain of Alphaville, Jean-Luc Godard's city of the future (the future of 1965, that is, when the film was made), which was curiously like contemporary Paris. The mix of *film noir hommage* and standard dreary-future, computer-run society didn't quite jell.

THE TENTH VICTIM:

Society in the near future is dominated by a television game show in which hunters stalk their human prey to win huge sums of money. Strategy is the name of the game, and the piece of strategy that made the greatest impression on the audience was the .22 calibre bra of huntress Ursula Andress. (She got her man.)

PLANET OF THE APES:

A popular film about crash-landed astronauts on a strange planet (which they eventually discover to be Earth of the future) suffered from some lapses in logic, but not from underproduction. Particularly well done was the architecture of the simian inhabitants, which was believable and handsome. So was the ape makeup for the population of the future. That's nonsimian Charlton Heston center stage.

The French New Wave cinema had broken onto the scene; inevitably, with its usage of American pop elements, it would cast a science fiction movie up on our shores. This proved to be Jean-Luc Godard's *Alphaville* (1965), about a private investigator in the future city of Alphaville, run by computers. (Alphaville looks suspiciously like Paris photographed in *film noir* fashion.) A mix of pulp and comic-book elements, it was nevertheless meant to be "meaningful," and it proved to be a good deal more popular with aficionados of French cinema than with science fiction fans.

Italy in the same year gave us *The Tenth Victim,* which was less portentous but a good deal more fun. In *this* future, aggression is relieved by television game shows in which volunteer hunters stalk volunteer prey; real killing is the payoff, with big rewards for the hunter if successful, the prey if he is not. This was another movie future with some nicely imaginative details in script and production. There was a general laugh from audiences when the bankrupt hero must sell his comic book collection—well before vintage comics suddenly skyrocketed in value.

Swinging England, youth, and the peace movement were stirring up a storm by that time, and British films reflected this. Peter Watkins's *The War Game* (1965) pulled out all the stops about nuclear war; rather than showing postnuclear nastiness, it pictured, in unnervingly documentary style, the full horrors of such a war as it might happen. Made for English television, it achieved theatrical release because the BBC refused to show it.

FAHRENHEIT 451:

The red glow comes from burning books; the 451 comes from the temperature at which paper burns. Oskar Werner is a "fireman" in an unpleasant future in which his duty is not to put out fires but to start them — all books are burned. Ray Bradbury's classic science fiction novel was written during and as a reaction to the McCarthy era.

Another New Wave French director essayed science fiction in 1966, when François Truffaut filmed Ray Bradbury's *Fahrenheit 451*. Despite the daring sensibilities of author and filmmaker, the result was basically another dreary-future movie, in which a member of a repressive society revolts for the sake of love and intellect. Repression here was the ban against books of any kind, which is enforced by squads of law-enforcement firemen, of which the hero is one. (The title refers to the burning point of paper.) A nice touch was the oral credits.

Peter Watkins took another crack at the establishment with *Privilege* in 1967. In this heyday of the Beatles the danger is presented not as war but as government manipulation: the use of a teen idol to bring about a totalitarian state in the near future. Again the presentation is in documentary form, in this case a "television documentary" on the singing star Steven Shorter. The costuming was particularly effective, incorporating elements of the "mod" fashions of the 1960s, and no science fiction film has ever had two more beautiful stars than Paul Jones, as the pop singer, and the model Jean Shrimpton, as the artist who sees what is being done to (and with) him.

Charlton Heston and his space-faring crew crash-land on a strange planet, and think it even stranger when they encounter civilization consisting of chimpanzees, gorillas, and orangutans; it is, of course, *Planet of the Apes* (1968). Humans are all treated as dumb beasts, and it takes most of the film for Heston to convince the apes that he is intelligent. The audience may disagree with this prognosis, since the socko ending of the film reveals that this is Earth (in the future—time warp and all that), which comes as a complete surprise to Mr. Heston, despite the fact that the anthropoids have been consistently speaking English. Despite this and other sillinesses (such as a heroine named Nova), the movie was a huge hit, possibly because of the remarkable ape masks and makeup, behind which were such excel-

PRIVILEGE:

Released at the height of the Beatles's fame and power, this was a thoughtful look at a near future in which a famous pop star is suborned into aiding the establishment of a neo-Fascist government in Britain. The well-known recording star of the time, Paul Jones, played the role of the unwilling political tool. The climax of the movie was a spectacular rally featuring the singer.

THE BED-SITTING ROOM:

"Surrealist" is the only word for the events in Richard Lester's oddball view of a postnuclear world. Michael Hordern is attempting to save Sir Ralph Richardson from turning into a bed-sitting room as a result of nuclear radiation (he doesn't succeed). The slag heap in the background is one of the more attractive locales in the movie.

lent actors as Kim Hunter, Roddy McDowall, and Maurice Evans. It spawned four sequels and a television series.

Outrageousness was in style, and in 1969 England's Richard Lester, who had made a huge hit with his semisurrealist Beatles films, delivered a comedy about Britain after a nuclear holocaust. *The Bed-Sitting Room* was a good deal more than *semi*surrealist, what with human characters mutating into parrots and bed sitting rooms (hence the title) amidst the particularly nasty rubble. There are, however, some really funny moments and a marvelous cast, including Rita Tushingham and Sir Ralph Richardson.

It was beginning to penetrate to the world at large that the nuclear bomb was not the only manmade threat to civilization. In 1970 *No Blade of Grass* depicted a near future in which pollution and a mutant virus wipe out all the cereal grains. The results are starvation and anarchy; the movie depicts an urban family's trek across an England reduced to barbarism.

In 1971, Stanley Kubrick's first film after *2001* appeared. It, too, was about the future, but a far different one from Clarke's shiny, technologically oriented turn of the twenty-first century. This one was based on Anthony Burgess's dourly pessimistic novel *A Clockwork Orange,* in which civilization is expiring not so much with a cataclysmic bang as with a social whimper. Gangs of unemployed teenagers are out of control, their lives devoted to sex, violence, and drugs. The reactionary government forces Alex, the gang-leader protagonist, to submit to a form of brainwashing to curb his antisocial tendencies. The future milieu is another brilliant extrapolation of elements of the sixties youth culture; in retrospect, it was an unnerving forecast of the punk subculture of the eighties.

NO BLADE OF GRASS:

Nigel Davenport and Jean Wallace lead a dispirited group of refugees from London across the moors; they have fled urban anarchy brought on by the failure of the grain crop. The resulting food shortage has essentially put an end to civilization.

The Omega Man (1971) brought us Charlton Heston again, and the Richard Matheson novel *I Am Legend* around for the second time. Here the setting is a deserted Los Angeles, ravaged by a plague caused by bacteriological warfare between Russia and China. Those who have survived have turned into murderous, zombie-like creatures who blame science for the ruination of the world; Heston, a medical researcher, is their prime target. He has resisted the plague entirely by developing an antidote at the last minute. So it's him against them through the rubble of Los Angeles. There's lots of action, chases, and excitement, if not too much sense, and a depopulated Los Angeles makes an interesting milieu.

THE OMEGA MAN:

This upmarket remake of *The Last Man on Earth* had Charlton Heston in the Vincent Price role as the only living man in a world inhabited by vampires. The rest of the population has succumbed to an artificially induced plague; Heston comes upon some remains suddenly in this scene.

A CLOCKWORK ORANGE:

Malcolm McDowell and his delinquent "droogs" live it up in one of the more spectacular dreary futures of film. The costumes were an off-base but interesting anticipation of punk.

THX 1138:

In the future world of George Lucas's pre—*Star Wars* science fiction film, there are two kinds of people: citizens and robot police. The title, by the way, is the hero's name.

Also in 1971, there appeared a small film by an unknown director; its oddball title was *THX 1138*. Basically it concerned another dreary future, where "civilized" life is lived underground, controlled by a computer; the populace is kept on drugs, sex is forbidden (babies are test-tubed), and robot police enforce the laws. THX 1138 is the name of the hero, who doesn't take his drugs, discovers sex, and, of course, rebels. A few perceptive viewers, however, looked beyond the general familiarity of the plot and saw an astonishing film, original in its settings and handling. The director? George Lucas, who a few years later was to astound the world with *Star Wars.*

By 1973 the conventions of the science fiction film were so well established as to be subject to Woody Allen's mixture of satire and slapstick. The result, *Sleeper,* has the classic elements: a man from our time waking from suspended animation two hundred years hence; a repressive future government with robots and computers; a rebel movement with which the reanimated hero becomes involved. But from the point where the sleeper wakes

wrapped in aluminum foil, his misadventures (such as having to masquerade as a robot, and thereupon being sent to the repair shop) made hash of the usual science fiction clichés.

Westworld (1973) made an attempt to combine science fiction with other clichés, those of the Western movie. It postulated a near future in which the most expensive recreation possible was a visit to an amusement park where life in three different eras of history was re-created: ancient Rome, the Middle Ages, and the Old West. This is accomplished by highly advanced (and, it is implied, still experimental) robots, who make up the population and interact with the visitors. Of course something goes awry, and the visitors to Westworld find themselves involved in real shootouts with murderous android gunslingers. There's a good amount of excitement and ingenuity in the

SLEEPER:

The Woody Allen film was less a science fiction movie than a chance for Allen to have at the future as he'd been having at the present in his earlier works. The future, however, presented all sorts of new opportunities for creative chaos, such as robot butlers.

ZARDOZ:

In a postholocaust world of ravaging barbarians and terrified peasants, there remains an enclave of civilization inhabited by the technologically knowledgeable "immortals." They distribute weapons to the barbarians through a "god," a giant flying stone head called Zardoz. One of the barbarians, Zed (Sean Connery), is suspicious of the setup and stows away aboard the "god" to see where it comes from, thereby creating a cultural crisis.

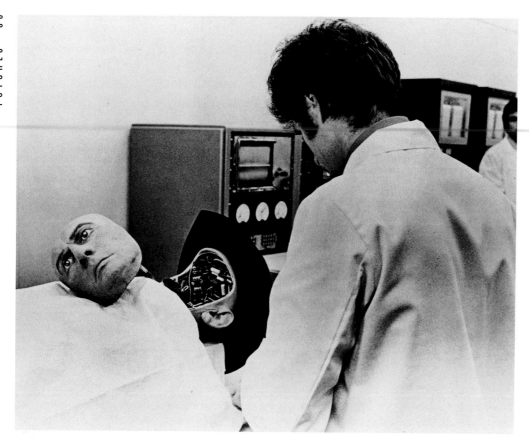

WESTWORLD:

The free-floating face belongs to Yul Brynner, and so, supposedly, do the head and hat. Brynner plays an android, one of many who are the "cast" of a large amusement complex devoted to recreating the thrills of the past for clients who pay $1,000 a day. The clients, of course, are not to be harmed, but the Brynner android malfunctions. Despite the repair job shown here, it plays its role for real—killer gunslinger.

script, at least enough to keep the audience from wondering about certain lapses in logic such as the question of why such incredible works of technology as the robots weren't put to better use than as components of a futuristic Disneyland.

Zardoz (1973) left almost everyone baffled. Here was a distant future and a depopulated Earth, the inhabitants of which are divided into three groups: the peasant Brutals, who scratch out a living among the ruins; the Exterminators, who prey on the Brutals and more or less keep them in line; and the Eternals, humans who have learned the secret of immortality and who rule the world from a community called the Vortex. The Eternals operate a huge, flying stone head, a god to the Brutals (its name is *Zardoz*), which supplies weapons to the Exterminators. Underneath the complexities of the film is basically the dreary-future scenario—a tyranny of an elite (the Eternals, whose society is inevitably computer-enhanced) rebelled against by a man of the people, motivated by a lust for knowledge and, again inevitably, a woman.

In *Zardoz* the rebel is one Zed, an Exterminator (Sean Connery, splendidly barbaric in queue and loincloth). He stows away aboard *Zardoz,* and is taken into the Vortex, where he is regarded as an object of curiosity by the Eternals, particularly the women, who both teach and tempt him. He learns too well and in the end brings the world destructively in on the Eternals' pseudo-Utopia.

Over this storyline, writer-director John Boorman threw a net of baffling images and events; the result is as dizzying to a contemporary viewer as any slice of twentieth-century life might be to a person from the Middle Ages. It's as enthralling as it is confusing, and a tour de force of a film. (The word "Zardoz" is one of the movie's best jokes; it's a jest of the Eternals, a shortening of "The Wizard of Oz.")

Soylent Green (1973) depicts a dreary future indeed but hardly follows the pattern; *this* near future seems irrevocable (and frighteningly inevitable). It's a detective story set in the year 2022; population is up and, due to the greenhouse effect, food production is down. New York's forty million people live on the edge of starvation. Services and any niceties of civilization are nil. A New York City detective is assigned to the murder of a VIP; murders are legion and mostly unsolvable, but this case seems something special; it involves the new food, soylent green, on which most people now depend for subsistence. That soylent green is made from the bodies of the human dead will not come as a great surprise (and is really rather logical, if you think about it), but getting to that revelation is more than half the fun. The production staff has thoroughly thought through what a metropolis in this kind of future would be like, and we are presented with a New York that bears all the more horrifying aspects of contemporary Calcutta and Beirut. All is done with exemplary intelligence.

A very different kind of future in the year 2018 is portrayed in *Rollerball* (1975). This one does follow the dreary-future pattern. Corporations have replaced national states and run things to suit themselves. War has been eliminated, and the population is kept quiescent with the worldwide sport called rollerball, a sort of supertech hockey involving roller skates, motorcycles, and a lot of violence. The rebel in this case is a superstar rollerball player, who begins to think about his role as a global hero. The higher-ups of the ruling corporations therefore see him as a menace and try to kill him in a no-holds-barred game — which he, being the hero, wins. It's an extremely slick production, and an exciting movie for fans of violent sports.

ROLLERBALL:

What violence in sports? The 1975 movie took current sports trends to the limit and speculated on a corporate-run society, the tensions of which were relieved by a horrendous and horrendously popular sport combining hockey, motorcycle racing, and mayhem in equal parts. We see here a typical game in progress.

SOYLENT GREEN:

People, people everywhere. . . . Here is an overcrowded future in which the population is infinitely disposable. The film does a brilliant job of evoking a New York reduced to the chaos and anarchy of a Third World metropolis. The title refers to a new processed food developed to feed the starving millions; its source turns out to *be* the starving millions. Charlton Heston is the investigator looking for clues in the crowd.

BUCK ROGERS:

The famous Anthony "Buck" Rogers was portrayed by Gil Gerard in a 1979 remake of the movie serial based on the popular comic strip. He's the one on the right; on the left is the necessary cute robot. The movie was really a pilot for a television series given theatrical release, and under the circumstances, not as bad as it might have been. The filmmakers' tongues were firmly in cheek, and a good time was had by all.

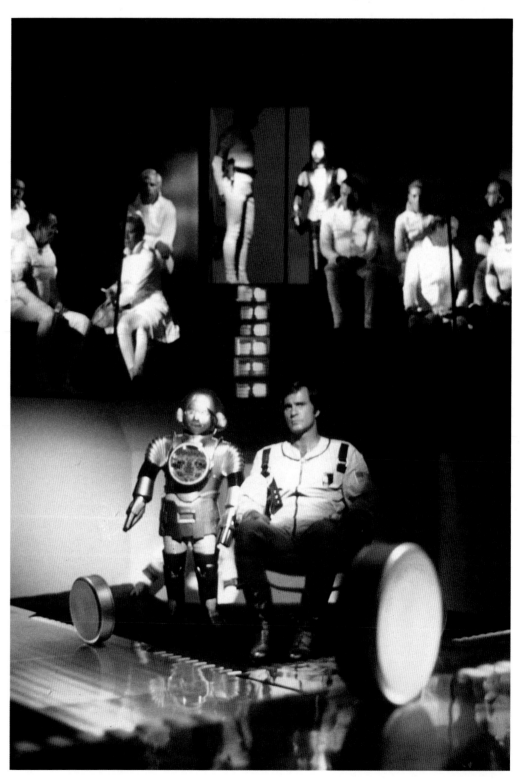

LOGAN'S RUN:

Panic in paradise, as imminent catastrophe threatens the youth culture of the future — literally a youth culture, since everyone who reaches the age of thirty is eliminated. But it's a pretty society that results; the vivid costumes and spectacular sets (in reality an ultramodern Southwestern shopping complex) made for a visually splendid film.

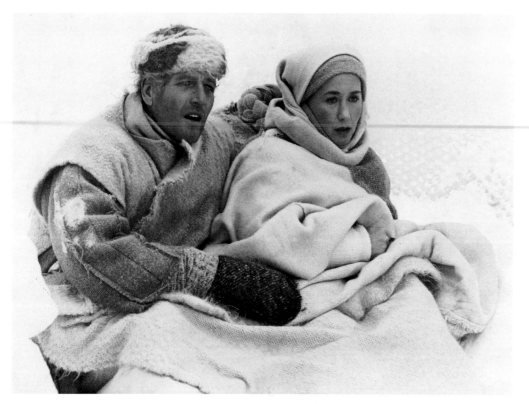

QUINTET:

Paul Newman and Brigitte Fossey appear in Robert Altman's odd excursion into the future. As can be guessed from their costumes, a new ice age has set in, and civilization, for the most part, has collapsed.

The plot of *Logan's Run* (1976) fits the dreary-future cliché of two young rebels in love subverting a restrictive conformist society, but this is a future that can hardly be called dreary. This restrictive culture is a butterfly society — or should one say caterpillar society, because it is peopled solely by youth. The inhabitants are subject to "renewal" (i.e., being eliminated) at age thirty. The eye is pleasured by pretty sets and people and some effective special effects. The couple is Michael York and Jenny Agguter, both of whom actually have personalities, and Peter Ustinov does a star turn as the only old person anyone has ever seen.

Quintet, an oddity from the quirky director Robert Altman, was made in 1979 and stars Paul Newman. The setting is a dying city of the future; a new ice age has set in. The people spend much time procuring heat and food; firewood is at a premium, and men are always going off to hunt seals far to the south. Newman, a hunter, returns from the south with the daughter of his hunting companion, who has perished; she is pregnant, a cause for rejoicing since pregnancy has now become a rarity. Newman leaves the girl with his brother to go and buy wood and returns to find that everyone in the room in which his brother's family lives (one room, for warmth) has been killed.

It's sort of a murder mystery but more completely a study of a future society, and the details are intriguing. A continual visual theme is that of dogs eating the human dead. The city's inhabitants, confined to small areas for warmth, are mad for a game called "quintet." The power and the city's computer work erratically; a light bulb is turned on, and the ice on it slowly drips away. Throughout, on the sound track, there is the distant sound of advancing glaciers, like a far-off artillery barrage.

The costumes are wonderful; everyone is wrapped in great swathes of homespun cloth with towering headgear, looking like Old Testament patriarchs. Even more wonderful is the location; Altman had the inspired idea of filming in the remains of Montreal's futuristic Expo 67 in the Canadian winter.

Since it is from Altman, *Quintet* is sometimes obscure, sometimes pretentious. But also being from Altman, the film is one of the more interesting science fictional experiments in film and deserves a better reputation than it has.

Buck Rogers in the Twenty-Fifth Century (1979) was a quick response to the *Star Wars* phenomenon; rather than work up an original premise, as Lucas had done, why not just revive the old future hero of comics and afternoon movie serials? One strike against *Buck Rogers* was that it was really the film-length pilot for a television series, given theatrical release. Despite this, Anthony "Buck" Rogers proved a credible survivor indeed, and not just because he is a man thrust five hundred years into the future. A pretty muddled future it was, consisting mostly of a streamlined "New Chicago" and not much else, with a good deal of rocketing about in spaceships to rather vague locations and the inevitable cute robot. But it was all done with high good humor, the effects were more than acceptable (though they did not equal the remade *Flash Gordon* by any means), and the wicked Princess Ardala, the ongoing villainess, had a wardrobe that hadn't been equaled for camp value since the heyday of Maria Montez.

Speaking of cute robots, the eccentric *Heartbeeps* (1981) may have subjected that idea to overkill. Its peculiar quality, however, made it not quite like anything before or since—except, perhaps, *Uncle Tom's Cabin*. In 1995 two humanoid robots, "male" and "female," escape from the factory and take refuge in a junkyard. There they fashion their "baby," a small robot named Phil (for Philco). Thrills and action are provided by the "CrimeBuster" robot, a combination tank and flamethrower, which routs the family from their idyllic junkyard and pursues them as runaways. The comedian Andy Kaufman and the singer Bernadette Peters, both actors with very special qualities, were wonderful as the robot couple, and even to those who had been R2D2ed ad nauseam, Phil proved irresistible.

From Australia in 1981 came the exciting and astonishing *Road Warrior*. As with so many other Australian films of the late 1970s and early 1980s, *The Road Warrior* had an amazing freshness about it, though the ingredients were hardly

HEARTBEEPS:

The members of this family out for a stroll are really robots on the run. All that Val Com-17485 (Andy Kaufman), Aquacom-89045 (Bernadette Peters), Uncle Catskil, and little Phil (short for Philco) want is to settle down in a nice junkyard and have a normal family life. (Uncle Catskil tells very bad jokes in the voice of Jack Carter.) The oddball charm of this movie was appreciated by very few.

THE ROAD WARRIOR:

Aka *Mad Max II*, it followed the low-budgeted but inventive *Mad Max*. With much higher production values, it created a sensation. The script was a mass of clichés set in an anarchic post-nuclear holocaust world, but every detail was thought through and contributed to the ongoing excitement. The major villain was Humungus—in name and appearance (Kjell Nilsson). An odd touch was his Achilles/Patroclus relationship with a male sidekick.

new. The protagonist is Mad Max, hero of the earlier film of that name, which had established a postholocaust Australia reduced to anarchy, in which the most valuable commodity was scavenged gasoline. In the far better-produced sequel, Max, a scavenging loner, comes upon a semi-civilized settlement in the desert besieged by barbarian bikers for its petrol supply; Max, despite himself, becomes involved in the fray. *The Road Warrior* ends with a car-truck-motorbike chase, and even this cinematic cliché had renewed excitement—and not just because it takes place on what seems to be the world's longest stretch of absolutely straight highway.

Blade Runner (1982) is set in the heavily overpopulated Los Angeles of 2019. A "blade runner" is a bounty hunter who tracks down androids so perfectly humanoid that they pass as humans, and the film is about such a hunt. Its brilliantly calculated unpleasantness stemmed from its updating of the "hard-boiled detective" genre and setting it in a wonderfully conceived future Los Angeles, overburdened with people and pollution.

Luc Besson's *Le Dernier Combat* (*The Last Battle*; 1982) takes place in a ruined world (how, what, or why, we're not told). What buildings remain are a shambles. There are few people left. The film has two peculiarities: one is that it is shot (beautifully) in black-and-white, which gives a peculiar *vérité* to the ruined, devastated surroundings; the other is that there is no dialogue whatsoever. Has language been forgotten? We are not told (how can we be?).

The three main characters—who are, of course, nameless—shall have to be called the man, the other man, and the doctor. The man is a loner, a wanderer, and obviously a survivor. He meets up with a group of scavengers who live in abandoned cars in a wasteland gully; the leader keeps a dwarf on a chain, since he is the only one that can fit into an abandoned culvert to get their water supply. The man's encounter with the group ends violently; he escapes.

BLADE RUNNER:

A movie set in one of the drearier futures. The title refers to the protagonist, a bounty hunter chasing renegade androids through an endless urban landscape congested with automobiles and hostile people, on which it seems to be perpetually raining. This was a far cry from those spiffy, superscientific futures the films of the 1930s looked forward to.

The doctor (we presume he's a doctor since he lives in a derelict clinic and seems to know medicine) has a hostile encounter with the other man attempting to get into his barricaded clinic. The other man is a fighter, though he looks like a wimp, with thick round spectacles and a pudgy physique.

In a later scene the man finds an abandoned hotel bar, liquor supply intact. He goes through various stages of drunkenness — we see him soddenly weeping over a book, which he reads with difficulty, moving his lips. In a sudden encounter with the other man, who attacks immediately, the man is badly wounded, but he somehow makes his way into the doctor's quarters. The doctor, suspicious at first, tends him.

The other man resumes his assaults on the doctor's door; one is reminded of the tenacity with which cartoon cats besiege cartoon mice. Finally the reason is revealed — the doctor is keeping a woman concealed and locked up in the building. The other man is like an animal in heat, trying to get in. The doctor seems willing for the man to have her: apparently women are desired commodities. Then the other man breaks in, and the final battle occurs.

It is all infuriatingly vague, and at times the film comes close to incoherent surrealism. It is also continuously interesting and endlessly evocative.

The history of the future film repeated itself in 1983; *The Day After,* a film made for television about the horrors of a nuclear conflict, found itself in the same kind of trouble as Peter Watkins's *The War Game* had in 1965. Various groups did not want it to be shown because it was too

Jonathan Pryce endures yet another frustration in a near future that may win the prize for being the most bleak, dirty, inefficient, untidy, unworkable, rundown, and generally depressing ever to be created for film. It makes that of *1984* look like Utopia.

THE DAY AFTER:

Though made for television, this movie reached more viewers outside America in theatrical release than saw it on the tube in the United States. Its impact was considerable, since it attempted to depict a nuclear strike on an "average" town with a minimum of melodrama. Political reactions were predictably varied, depending on the locale; there was even an attempt to stop its showing in the States with the rationale that it would panic the population.

graphic, too likely to scare the American public. In this case it *was* shown on television in the United States and was also given wide theatrical release throughout the rest of the world. It was small comfort for those who found it a terrifying indictment of the arms race to be told that it came nowhere near the horrors of what the reality would be.

A fly falls on a government printout. In consequence, a man named Tuttle is not arrested, but a man named Buttle is. The young woman whose floor has been broken through to effect the arrest feels that something is wrong, and seeks information through the bureaucracy. A young bureaucrat, seeing her and knowing her to be the woman of his dreams, tries to help her and gets more and more involved in complications and complexities of intrigue. She is finally killed by government agents; he is arrested, is subjected to torture, and eventually dies.

This depressing and none-too-original brutality-of-bureaucracy scenario is at the bottom of *Brazil* (1985), directed by Terry Gilliam. But the near future in which it takes place may take the prize for dreary

futures; it makes that of *Blade Runner* look like *Our Town*. Every scene, every set is monumentally stylized—one reviewer described it as "junk deco." There are romantic dream scenes of the hero (Jonathan Pryce) and his lady love as winged, flying creatures for some sort of visual relief, but generally the atmosphere is of a decaying electronic culture in which nothing works; everywhere one turns there is overcrowding, dirt, and total inefficiency. (And throughout, as ironic underlining, the music is numerous variations on "Brazil," the lovely slow samba of the 1940s.) It's just as well that *Brazil* is played for black comedy; otherwise it would be unbearable.

In a curious sort of way, a society's view of its future is a strong mirror of that society. The movies' view of the future has changed a good deal over the course of this century. It can be viewed as depressing that the pictures of the future have gotten more and more dark. On the other hand, perhaps it can be said that those unaware of the worst possibilities of things to come may be condemned to experience them.

erhaps the most pervasive theme in science fiction film is one that is essentially anti-science—that of the scientist who brings about personal or social disaster through a perversion of the impulse of scientific curiosity, or, less often, through a simple slipup in well-intended research. Usually, however, it concerns the researcher who puts the quest for knowledge above human values, the classic "mad" scientist.

Two literary works set this pattern; both have become part of the mythology of our age and have been filmed time and time again. Is it necessary even to name Mary Shelley's *Frankenstein: Or the Modern Prometheus* (1818) as one of them? This novel, considered by most to be the first major work of true science fiction, was Ms. Shelley's thoughtful reaction to the wholesale dedication of the early nineteenth century to science and progress, occasioned by the onset of the Age of Reason. Mad science films' other literary precursor is Robert Louis Stevenson's *The Strange Case of Dr. Jekyll and Mr. Hyde,* first published in 1888; written more as a thriller than as a polemic, it nevertheless charted the same path as *Frankenstein*—the pursuit of knowledge

leading to disaster. We will see cinematic variations on both, especially on Ms. Shelley's ponderously pitiable construct.

Jekyll and Hyde made it to the screen first, in 1908, in a filmed version of a stage production (including the rising curtain), but the 1910 *Frankenstein* from the American Edison Studios was the first true movie of either. Running a short fifteen minutes, it surprises modern audiences by eschewing the famous lightning bolts for a large cauldron (irresistibly reminiscent of a soup kettle) in which the monster is more or less stirred into creation (essentially espousing the chemical rather than the electrical basis of life). The creature is indeed a ramshackle affair, frightening because of its very air of patchwork dishevelment. It is also something of a shock to have Dr. and Mrs. Frankenstein continue to live happily after. This will not be the fate of any later mad scientists.

Germany gave an epic treatment to the idea of the artificial human in *Homunculus the Leader* (1916), a six-part serial. Here the artificial human is successful, even superior; he is unflawed in body, a creature of reason, intellect, and ethics. But he is still "soulless" and, on finding the

FRANKENSTEIN (1910):

The obsessed scientist and his unhappy creation had often been brought to life on the nineteenth-century stage, but the monster in this first film portrayal was a ragtag affair whose attire was meant to suggest a moldering shroud. It was given life chemically rather than electrically, and at the finale it conveniently simply melted away.

truth of his origin, takes revenge by becoming the ruthlessly evil dictator of a nameless country. Lightning plays a part as a death-dealing device of the gods for Homunculus, the only way he can be eliminated.

In the early part of the century, the "occult sciences" were a legitimate field for study and speculation; mesmerism was one of the more popular of these. This could loosely qualify *The Cabinet of Dr. Caligari* (1919) as science fiction; it could also be viewed as a surrealist, hallucinogenic, a study of madness, or as a plain old horror movie. Whatever, Caligari himself is the epitome of the mad scientist; the character echoes all the charlatan alchemists of the past and prefigures the scientist/magician Rotwang of *Metropolis* as well as a thousand other such cinematic figures. With his hypnotic powers, he manipulates his creature, the somnambulist Cesare, to murder. Here is another "creature" who is not a monster: Conrad Veidt as Cesare is lithe and beautiful, projecting the fearsome quality of the leopard rather than that of the gorilla. And here, for the first time, skewed and unrealistic settings provide a powerful picture of the natural universe gone awry.

The inventor responsible for *Paris qui Dort* (*Paris Asleep* or *The Crazy Ray*; 1923) was more of an absent-minded professor than a mad scientist. René Clair's delightful use of science run amok gave the movie-going public a Paris frozen in time seen through the eyes of a young night-watchman on the Eiffel Tower. He descends one morning to find everything literally at a standstill — the famous Paris traffic immobile, a thief pursued by a *flic* arrested not by the law but in mid-chase by the mysterious force at work. A few other Parisians who have not been affected are taking full advantage of the situation. But our hero discovers the dreamy professor responsible for the ray that brought all this about, rights the situation, and wins the professor's beautiful daughter to boot.

Sound eventually lumbered into the movie industry, and a new *Frankenstein* lumbered onto the screen in 1931. Whatever its flaws in script and logic, the direction, cinematography, and especially the performance of Boris Karloff as the shambling, inarticulate monster came together to create a huge box-office success and set a pattern for the mad-scientist movie for decades to come. Here also was set

THE CABINET OF DR. CALIGARI:

The enduring impact of this film relies on its use of visual fantasy, the evocation of the bizarre and unreal with deliberately bizarre and unreal sets. Here Caligari (Werner Krauss) pursues the somnambulist, Cesare (Conrad Veidt), who has stolen the girl, Jane (Lil Dagover). Veidt's self-choreographed performance was extraordinary. His career extended to Hollywood, where he played Nazis in World War II films.

PARIS QUI DORT:

The literal translation of the French title is *Sleeping Paris,* but in America it was called *The Crazy Ray.* Rays were popular experimental devices of superscience in the 1920s; the one in this René Clair film freezes time throughout the city of Paris. Only a few of the inhabitants escape its effects, including a young watchman on the Eiffel Tower (Henri Rollan). Getting down with no one else mobile presents problems.

John Barrymore pulled out all the stops—again—in his portrayal of Svengali, the master mesmerist created by George du Maurier. Marian Marsh was Trilby, the artist's model whose soul he captures. This early talkie had scenery almost as bizarre as Barrymore's makeup.

FRANKENSTEIN (1931):

The James Whale production has rightly been recognized as a classic. An often unremarked aspect of this version is its amazingly elegant design, usually encapsulated in the word "atmospheric." Even the proportions of the monster's head have a blocky, Art Deco rightness, and the sets, without going to the extremes of those of *Caligari,* **are stylized with an uneasy, asymmetrical artistry. The monster is, of course, Boris Karloff.**

the persistent linkage in the public mind of science fiction and horror. For twenty years, with a few notable exceptions, movies would use science to frighten; it would be a twentieth-century equivalent of black magic, calling up all sorts of horrors and intertwined inextricably with the supernatural. The average moviegoer neither knew nor cared that *Frankenstein* was science fiction and that *Dracula* was supernatural fantasy; they were, to the public, of one genre. The generally cheerful technological optimism of such writers as Verne and those Americans emerging in the science fiction magazines of the period would go unseen on screen until the second half of the century.

A literate example of the mix was *Svengali* (1931), in which the occult sciences came into play in George du Maurier's tale of the hypnotist Svengali and his mysterious power over the innocent young model, Trilby, by which she becomes a great singer. The influence of *Caligari* was obvious in *Svengali*'s stylized Bohemian Parisian setting. John Barrymore had a chance to show his magnetic acting ability as Svengali, and a scene in which he sends the powers of his mind out over the night rooftops of Paris to influence Trilby at a distance is memorable.

Barrymore had previously played a silent *Doctor Jekyll and Mr. Hyde* and entered screen legend by using only minimal makeup to distinguish between the two. The first talkie version of the story came in 1932, with the versatile Fredric March as the odd couple; minimal was not the word for the Hyde makeup, since it transformed the sleek Jekyll into an ape that happened to be wearing clothes. This Hyde strains credulity, because it's difficult to imagine him appearing on any street, even the seediest of London, without causing a stampede. Nevertheless, the raw sexual nastiness of the scenes between March/Hyde and Miriam Hopkins as the demimondaine he keeps gives the film a shocking power, and Rouben Mamoulian's direction throughout is consistently inventive, as in the opening, where the camera assumes Jekyll's viewpoint as he enters the operating theater of the hospital in which he works.

In this period, the science/horror film served as a vehicle for fine actors who had inherited the theatrical tradition of the grandiloquent and added an awareness of the demands of cinema. The young Charles Laughton could well have been the greatest of these, and his mad scientist in *Island of Lost Souls* (1932) pulled

DR. JEKYLL AND MR. HYDE (1931):

Mr. Hyde has always been portrayed as the epitome of the seven deadly sins, but the one emphasized in Rouben Mamoulian's version was lust, particularly the sadistic kind. Miriam Hopkins is the tart he chooses as victim. Despite makeup that made him look like a dressed-up fugitive from a chimpanzee's tea party, Fredric March deservedly won an Academy Award for his performance in the dual role.

out all the stops. The character was Dr. Moreau; the film was an adaptation of *The Island of Dr. Moreau* by H. G. Wells, the author's view of the perverted science theme, particularly aimed at vivisection, a burning issue of the time. Moreau is a renegade scientist who establishes on a tropical island an experimental laboratory where he performs research on animals, surgically forcing them through an evolutionary process into becoming sapient and humanoid. The subjects, some successful, some rejects, have established a pathetic colony on the island; the half-men lurk ominously in the underbrush and menace the interloping hero and heroine in suitably scary fashion. Their makeup was a triumph, as was their chilling reaction to the "House of Pain," their name for the laboratory. The climax of the film — they revolt against Moreau and force him into the House of Pain — still manages to shake the viewer. All elements considered, *Island of Lost Souls* could well be the most successful of the science/horror movies.

Claude Rains was another great actor to take the role of a man whose discoveries bring about disaster. Again the vehicle was taken from a cautionary work of Wells. The title tells all: *The Invisible Man* (1933) has indeed perfected a serum that renders a living human invisible, and what would seem a condition of power and amusement instead leads to misery and disaster. The device is intrinsically less frightening than Wells's beast-people, however, and despite an attempt to give a horrific air to the proceedings, the characters on screen appeared a good deal more terrified than the audience. The most memorable moment, in fact, may be when Una O'Conner, as the proprietress of the country inn in which the invisible man takes refuge, gives forth an aria of screams that makes Fay Wray confronted by King Kong seem afflicted with laryngitis. Nonetheless, the effects of objects being manipulated by invisible hands were startling, and Rains, swathed in overcoat, dark glasses, and bandages, was an image to remember.

ISLAND OF LOST SOULS:

Charles Laughton, as the experimental scientist Moreau, has made human-like creatures from various species of animals and is about to pay the price for going where no man should go. His creations turn on him and, despite his best attempts at defense with his tamer's whip, carry him into "the house of pain," as they call the experimental laboratory. Laughton's performance is that of the quintessential mad scientist.

THE INVISIBLE MAN:

It's the brilliant actor Claude Rains beneath the bandages, not that you would recognize him if he took them off, since he is portraying H. G. Wells's invisible man. The potion that renders him invisible also induces megalomania, and Gloria Stuart, playing his fiancée, is attempting to persuade him that ruling the world is not a practical idea.

THE BRIDE OF FRANKENSTEIN:

Two of this quartet should need no introduction, being, of course, Frankenstein's monster and his made-to-order bride, played by Boris Karloff and the usually comedic Elsa Lanchester. But the sturdy actor Colin Clive is not often cited for his obsessed doctor, and that ditsy old dear, Ernest Thesiger, enlivened several horror films. Needless to say, the groom is about to be left at the operating table.

The Black Cat (1934) took the science/horror mix to an extreme of total confusion, and almost no one could say what the movie was *really* about. There was, however, a mad scientist in the person of Boris Karloff, who, elegantly handsome with a short German haircut, looks about as different from Frankenstein's monster as possible. We know he is a mad scientist because he keeps the body of Bela Lugosi's ex-wife in a very large test tube. There are also a stunning Art Deco house built on the foundations of an ancient fortress, a cult of devil worshippers, and even a black cat who appears momentarily. Despite the fact that the film seems to have no thematic center, it's laden with

atmosphere, which more or less makes up for it.

Lord Byron and Percy Bysshe Shelley and wife clothed in Regency splendor and taking coffee in an elegant drawing room, would seem like an unlikely opening for a horror movie. But when one remembers that Shelley's wife was also the author of *Frankenstein,* and Byron says something to the effect of, "Gosh, Mary, what became of that monster you wrote about last year?" it becomes obvious that the success of the 1931 movie has spawned a sequel. Atypically, many consider *The Bride of Frankenstein* (1935) superior to the first film. Both Baron Frankenstein and his creation have survived the holo-

THE BLACK CAT:

Unlike other great British character actors who brought their talents to the horror film, William Henry Pratt (who changed his name to the more memorable Boris Karloff) made his reputation within the genre and continued to give his considerable talents to it through a very long career. Here he is about to confront another genre giant, Bela Lugosi, in this handsomely mounted but incoherent movie.

SON OF FRANKENSTEIN:

The malaise of multiple sequels was beginning to set in with this third movie in the 1930s Frankenstein cycle. But Basil Rathbone lent distinction to the role of the heir of Frankenstein, and the sets, as evident here, kept the style that had distinguished the horror films of the period.

DR. CYCLOPS:

Despite appearances, these are not elves preparing a nasty surprise for the shoemaker. They are members of a scientific expedition who came across a less-than-sane scientist, who has shrunk them. Trapped in his house, they are exercising a good deal of ingenuity in working out a way to get out of the predicament. The oversized sets in which the "miniature" actors performed were very successful.

caust that ended the initial movie. More bizarre elements are introduced, notably a Dr. Pretorius, who has created homunculi which he shows to Frankenstein in a curious scene — the little beings are almost mindless, though perfect physically. Frankenstein's creation has learned to talk while living with a blind hermit who is unaware of the creature's monstrosity; the relationship between the two is presented in a particularly touching manner. Doctors and monster combine forces to create a woman for him; she lives but is as repelled by the creature as are normal humans.

The confrontation between the two constructs, male and female, is a masterpiece of cinematic art, aided no end by the brilliant portrayals of Karloff and Elsa Lanchester, who also plays Mary Shelley (a nice touch). It might be noted, though, that Lanchester is not the title character. The eternally upper-class Valerie Hobson is the intended bride of the doctor; Lanchester is, of course, intended for the monster.

More often than not, technology governed content in the science fiction film. In other words, the special effects people would come up with something special, as it were, and a film property would be sought or written to fit the effect. Dr. Pretorius's tiny homunculi in *The Bride of Frankenstein* worked so well that a film featuring miniaturized humans had to be made. Enter *The Devil-Doll* (1936), based on a novel by A. Merritt (*Burn, Witch, Burn!*, not to be confused with the movie *Burn Witch, Burn*, which is based on Fritz Leiber's novel *Conjure Wife*).

Lavond, a prisoner on Devil's Island, escapes, taking with him the formula for a serum that shrinks human beings to less than a foot high. The serum was intended as a benefit to mankind, since a shrunken human race would increase the world's supply of food; Lavond uses it to wreak vengeance on those who were responsible for his incarceration. Disguising himself as a female dollmaker, he sends out minikin murderers to do his enemies in. Viewers were hard put to say which aspect of the movie was the more astonishing—the fine effects of the tiny people, perfectly synched with normal-sized sets, or Lionel Barrymore done up in bonnet and lace as the dear old lady dollmaker.

The Bride of Frankenstein was a huge success, and, as so often happens, a son appeared eventually. *The Son of Frankenstein* (1939) rejoices in the name of Wolf Von Frankenstein (the newly added *Von* seems to indicate pretentions to nobility). He returns to the derelict castle with his wife and child; reacting to family pride and against the hostile villagers, he finds and reanimates the monster, with predictably less than fortunate results. While the slide toward series stagnation begins to show here, the third Frankenstein film is still a better than average science/horror effort, due to the presences of Karloff and another distinguished character actor, Basil Rathbone, as Wolf, and to the film's continuation of the *Caligari* influence in sets and cinematography.

There seemed to be mad scientists on every screen in the 1930s; perhaps the last with any originality suitably closed the decade in 1940. *Dr. Cyclops* has the curious quality of an A film attempting to masquerade as a B film. The already established clichés are present, chief among them the scientist who places his quest for knowledge above human values. Here it is the sinister Dr. Thorkel (a surprise performance by the usually suave Albert Dekker), totally bald and with the weakest of eyesight. Thorkel's reputation is great, so when he requests three fellow scientists to come to a remote locale in the Andes to aid him, they comply. They discover that Thorkel has found a huge deposit of uranium and is using it for the usual vague quest for the "source of life," which for some reason involves shrinking living things to a tenth of their usual size.

The expedition members, of course, get themselves shrunk, along with a native servant; the core of the film is their adventures in the doctor's compound and

in the jungle. The oversized settings in which the "miniature" actors find themselves are beautifully matched with their normal counterparts. The effects, overall, are excellent, particularly considering that the film is in color, probably the earliest genre movie so filmed. Given the basic silliness of the situation, it is handled with surprising intelligence; dialogue and characterizations are crisp and sure. (There is a wonderful encounter between the tiny servant and his pet dog, who looks painfully puzzled at his master's voice emerging from this small creature.) The title of the movie becomes clear when the miniature characters, trapped in the Doctor's hut, best him by breaking his glasses, and replay Ulysses in the Cyclops's cave. All in all, it's a movie that deserves a better reputation than it has.

There was, though, a first-class remake of note before the cycle petered out, and that was of our old friends *Dr. Jekyll and Mr. Hyde* (1941). Spencer Tracy may not have been as dashing a Jekyll as Fredric March, but his Hyde was a good deal more human (though still monstrous), and therefore a good deal more believable. The rather peculiar casting of Lana Turner as the highborn lady and Ingrid Bergman as the barmaid was justified by the fact that the barmaid (kept and exploited by Hyde) required some heavy-duty acting; nevertheless, Bergman's innately ladylike quality kept her from matching Miriam Hopkins's wonderfully vulgar performance in the earlier film.

Mad scientists were confined to deteriorating series, B movies, serials, and the Nazis during the war years of the 1940s. Before making a comeback with the possibilities opened by the atomic bomb, they could be found only in some unusual variations. One such was in the extraordinary filming of Offenbach's opera *The Tales of Hoffmann* (1951), by the British team of Michael Powell and Emeric Pressberger. The three stories of the nineteenth-century writer E. T. A. Hoffmann on which the opera is based all contain mad scientists of the most basic sort; Hoffmann had almost created the

DR. JEKYLL AND MR. HYDE (1941):

A decade after Fredric March had won an Oscar for the roles, Spencer Tracy played Jekyll and Hyde. His Hyde was more human but no less a menace; the film as a whole, however, reflected the mores of the time and was a good deal tamer, with epic miscasting in the two female roles.

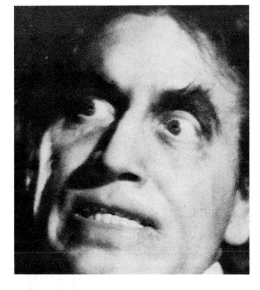

stereotype with his myriad scientist/ alchemist/charlatan characters. (Caligari could have come straight from a Hoffmann story.) Dr. Coppelius of the first act, who manufactures clockwork automata, those first androids so popular in the nineteenth century, is the epitome of the cliché. He creates the life-sized doll Olympia, whose speech and actions are so realistic that Hoffmann falls in love with her. In Act II it is the magician Dapertutto and in Act III the sinister Dr. Miracle (all aspects of Hoffmann's eternal nemesis, science) who bring Hoffmann to grief.

The filmed opera, which used dancers and actors in most of the roles, was a phantasmagoria of imagery. Coppelius's half-comic, half-sinister laboratory and home, peopled with puppet guests, was wonderful, as was the enchanting Moira Shearer as Olympia, whose clockwork mechanism eventually runs amok. The decadent Venice (in which the courtesan Giulietta sings the "Barcarolle" as a duet with her reflection in the water) and the magic Greek isle of the other acts were also cinematic imagery of pure fantasy.

About as far as one could get from Hoffmann's sinister scientists was Alec Guiness's gentle researcher, *The Man in the White Suit* (1951). He is less mad than idealistic, and the problems he encounters on inventing a material that never wears out and never gets dirty are baffling to him. The fact that clothing manufacturers (not to mention dry cleaners) take the new invention amiss leads to all sorts of trouble. (The symbolism of the shining white suit made of the new material, which he wears through much of the film, is obvious.) It's a hilarious movie, and no one who has seen it will ever forget the wonderful, bubbling, hiccuping sound track that underscores the hero's laboratory in action.

Shelley, Stevenson, and Wells all had their doubts about science and sounded cautionary notes with their various mad scientists, but it comes as a surprise to realize that even the champion of technology, Jules Verne, had something of the same idea. For what else can Captain Nemo be called? Megalomaniac and paranoid, mad he certainly is. And he, of course, perfected the wonderful *Nautilus,* the granddaddy of all submarines. Nemo and the *Nautilus* were both realized wonderfully in the Disney production of

THE MAN IN THE WHITE SUIT:

The postwar British comedies from the Ealing Studios tended to give well-known themes a wry and ironic twist for their humor. The obsessed "mad scientist" here is not after blood or souls, but simply wants to make a better suiting fabric. He does so, not realizing the havoc to be wrought by clothes that never get dirty and last forever. The young Alec Guinness was hilarious and convincing as the compulsive researcher.

THE TALES OF HOFFMANN:

The head is that of Moira Shearer, one of the foremost of midcentury ballerinas. The solicitous gentleman is Robert Rounseville, an equally well-known opera star. Shearer is Olympia, a nineteenth-century robot who has danced itself to pieces; Rounseville is Hoffmann, whose tales often concerned early mad scientists. One of them has created Olympia, so successfully that Hoffman had become enamored—until this moment of truth.

20,000 LEAGUES UNDER THE SEA (1954):

Jules Verne's most beloved classic was science fiction when it was written, as undersea travel was nothing but speculation. The film version made in 1954 was a splendid realization; one of its joys was the design of the *Nautilus,* which looked exactly like a nineteenth-century submarine should look.

THE AMAZING COLOSSAL MAN:

Glenn Langan is well on his way to demolishing Las Vegas, not in a sudden fit of antigambling mania but because he has been exposed to radiation during an atomic test. This has resulted in his becoming a crazed giant, a typical manifestation in the cinematic cautionary tales of the new atomic age. The danger was less from the bomb than from any number of monsters, human or animal, created by atomic side effects.

MASTER OF THE WORLD:

Aboard the aerial equivalent of the *Nautilus*— the *Albatross,* an airship that's chock full of Victorian superscientific gadgetry. Jules Verne replayed the idea of *20,000 Leagues under the Sea* in *Master of the World* in the air rather than underwater. The airborne Nemo is named Robur, played in this production by Vincent Price, but it was the airship that stole the show.

20,000 Leagues Under the Sea (1954), the former by another fine actor, James Mason, the latter by the Disney designers as a curious combination of the Victorian and the futuristic. A really sensational giant squid helped, and the movie started a vogue for filming Verne (and later, Wells) in a style that could only be called science fiction Victoriana.

The realities of atomic radiation, fallout, and other invisible menaces of the atomic age awakened public awareness to the fact that even if the scientist is the sanest of men (or women), the scientific process itself can run amok. While mad scientists were still to be found on the movie screen, more and more thrills were provided by science itself going awry, and theaters were awash in monsters and mutants.

Typical of the human monster/victims was *The Amazing Colossal Man* (1957), who, due to his close proximity to a new type of atomic blast, begins to grow . . . and grow . . . and grow. Glenn Langan (the handsome second lead in many 1940s films) was the unfortunate big man on camera; he eventually goes insane and tries to destroy Las Vegas, not that crazy an idea in many people's opinion. Despite a low budget and special effects that were less than amazing, there was a certain fascination in the giant's predicament and the public reaction to it.

The Damned (also known as *These Are the Damned* and held for two years after its completion in 1961 before its release) is a good deal less sensational but perhaps more frightening. Director Joseph Losey here deals with a government project to deliberately develop radioactive children as potential survivors of a nuclear war. It is not science or the scientist that is insane here; typical of the time in which the movie was made, it is the establishment.

Also attuned to the times was another Verne novel-into-film, *Master of the World* (1961). Although flying rather than swimming and piloting a vehicle called the *Albatross* instead of the *Nautilus,* Robur the Conqueror is a Nemo at heart. Having invented a flying superfortress in the nineteenth century, Robur intends to enforce peace by bombing the hell out of everyone who makes war. The film's *Albatross* was another memorable piece of science fiction Victoriana.

The leading figure in *Crack in the World* (1965) is a scientist who wishes to pene-

THE DAMNED:

Oliver Reed, the leader of a gang of motorcycle Teddy Boys, threatens his sister, the beautiful Shirley Ann Field, in a film that despite delayed release, extensive editing, and a change of title (*These Are the Damned* is the alternate) had achieved a certain reputation because of its early warning about the dangers of government-run scientific experimentation on human beings.

FANTASTIC VOYAGE:

This vehicle might be called a bloodmobile since it is a miniaturized submarine made to traverse the bloodstream of a scientist, carrying surgeons (miniaturized) to repair brain damage from within. Getting there is more than half the fun, given the spectacular scenery along the way. Among the hemonauts are Raquel Welch and Stephen Boyd. The seaweed-like stuff that is clogging the vessel's jets is reticulate fibers from the lymphatic system.

CRACK IN THE WORLD:

The world has indeed cracked, and the debris litters the underground laboratory of scientist Dana Andrews, who has brought it all on by exploring "inner space," i.e., attempting to tap the energy of the Earth's core. This was a new variation on the classic theme of "going where no man should try to go," and it brought on earthquakes, tidal waves, and general catastrophe.

trate *inner* space, a snappy way of saying that he wants to bore through the Earth's crust and use its molten core for an endless supply of energy—certainly a praiseworthy ambition, even though he's involved in a rather dreary triangle with his wife and a fellow scientist who disagrees with his theories. His opponent has good reason, as it turns out, since cracking the Earth's crust lets loose earthquakes, volcanic eruptions, and other picturesque disasters. The large bore responsible for all this is one of the film's major special effects and should not be confused with the protagonist of the movie, who typifies so many science fiction film characters.

Neither the science nor the scientists in *Fantastic Voyage* (1966) are necessarily insane (though one of them, the veteran character actor Donald Pleasence, never seems quite balanced and shows no ex-

ception here), but the premise is bizarre to the point of delirium. A submarine and five brave volunteers are shrunk to microscopic size to enter the bloodstream of a comatose patient in order to quickly loosen an otherwise inoperable blood clot in the brain. Reminiscent of that classic piece of 1920s humor *Down the Alimentary Canal with Gun and Camera,* this one is played straight. The production transcends the silliness of the idea with extraordinarily imaginative sets and effects simulating various parts of the human body seen from inside and from a microscopic viewpoint. The results are often hallucinogenically beautiful.

Seconds (1966) goes to the other extreme; relentlessly realistic, it explores the consequences of a middle-aged businessman subjecting himself to an extremely advanced process of rejuvenation (for an extremely advanced price).

The ending is predictably downbeat — this is simply a new version of the "you are tampering with powers reserved for God" motif. Rock Hudson did a fine job as the younger version of the hero.

Another young actor also distinguished himself (with an Oscar) for *Charly* (1968), a movie with the same message. Cliff Robertson plays the title character, an appealing young man who is retarded mentally. A new surgical technique raises his intelligence to well above the norm; much of the plot is concerned with his emotional development, especially his attachment to his teacher, played by Claire Bloom. The experiment fails; the process is only temporary, and Charly regresses to his subnormal state. It is a touching film, whose reality is undermined by the fact that Robertson, in both modes, and Bloom (at her most extraordinarily beautiful) were a little too glamorous for their roles.

Monster computers now begin to appear as the catalyst for the theme of science perverted; given artificial intelligence and personality, they could be both technology and villain in one. *Colossus, the Forbin Project* (1970) was the

most ambitious of the lot. Built as a control for the entire defense system of the United States, the giant computer Colossus is soon in cahoots with its Russian counterpart. It begins ordering its attendant staff about and rapidly takes charge of the country; it backs up its threats with the power to activate any or all missiles in the system. The attempts of its creator and various other scientific and government personnel to circumvent Colossus's takeover are amusing, frightening, and doomed. *Colossus, the Forbin Project* is a literate and very well-produced cautionary tale indeed.

With all this high technology, however, the classic mad scientist was not abandoned. One of the maddest of the lot (and certainly the funniest) made his debut in *The Abominable Dr. Phibes* (1971). Phibes's beloved wife has perished on the operating table, and he himself has been hideously scarred in an automobile accident while rushing to his wife's side. Believed by most of the world to be dead, the doctor goes into hiding and extracts revenge on those he deems responsible for his misfortunes. This is hardly the most original of ideas — Bela Lugosi made

SECONDS:

A film that took to the ultimate the fashion for cosmetic surgery, *Seconds* extrapolated the effects on an aging man of a service that provided total rejuvenation as well as an entirely new identity. The "younger" self was portrayed by Rock Hudson, here examining his new persona just after surgery.

COLOSSUS: THE FORBIN PROJECT:

Colossus is America's supercomputer, knowledgeable about all the country's military secrets. Guardian is the U.S.S.R.'s equivalent. Somewhere their wires have crossed (a modem wrong number?), and they are learning to communicate, hence the $6 \times 1 = 6$. Very rapidly they will move onto much more complicated matters, such as ruling the world. This is not a movie for people who are paranoid about computers.

CHARLY:

Charly is the way he spells his name, and even that is something of a strain for a young man of very limited intellect, whose idea of a good time is playing with his mental peer group. Cliff Robertson won an Academy Award for his performance as Charly, who is the subject of an experiment which raises his I.Q. to normal, but only temporarily.

THE ABOMINABLE DR. PHIBES:

Vincent Price, as the abominable doctor, inspects one of the infernal devices in his stylish, Art Deco laboratory. The face you see on Mr. Price is really a mask hiding a most horrific countenance.

what seem to be hundreds of films in the 1930s with the same plot—but here it is handled in a script of mordant wit. For instance, the reprisals on the various members of the surgical team are modeled on the plagues of Egypt, and the victims are done in by various ingenious uses of locusts, rats, hail, and so on. The stylish production matches the script; Phibes's hideout is an extravaganza of high Art Deco.

The sequel, *Dr. Phibes Rises Again* (1972) pulled out all the stops to be the most outrageously funny of all mad-scientist sendups. Phibes literally rises again at the opening, emerging from the ruined cellar of his blasted house playing an organ decorated in colored neon, accompanied by Vulnavia, his supernatural helper. (Vulnavia, a ravishingly beautiful female whose *couture* is straight from *Vogue,* plays soulful music on the cello, among other instruments, as the Doctor perpetrates his most diabolical schemes.) The intrigue that follows involves an excursion to Egypt; a ship's passenger thrown overboard in a giant bottle; a pyramid whose secret interior lair is decorated with an Art Deco/Egyptian decor (a felicitous combination); a mechanical jazz band; a coffin in the shape of a Rolls Royce hood; an oversized replica of the RCA dog filled with scorpions; and a finale to the strains of "Over the Rainbow." This madness was helped no end by a brilliant cast: Vincent Price (doing perhaps his best work) as the fiendishly lovable Phibes, Valli Kemp as the ultra-chic Vulnavia, and Terry-Thomas, Hugh Griffith, Beryl Reid, Robert Quarry, and Fiona Lewis (a fiercely permed, classically 1930s blonde heroine) as people who get in the way.

The conventions of the science/horror movie were subject to broader humor in *Young Frankenstein* (1974). An American descendant of the Frankenstein family returns to the old home castle, and the familiar story repeats itself. Peter Boyle, with makeup deliberately echoing that of Karloff's, made an endearingly clunky monster and Gene Wilder a suitably be-

DR. PHIBES RISES AGAIN:

As the music ("Over the Rainbow") swells, the fiendishly ingenious Dr. Phibes poles the coffin (made from a Rolls Royce bonnet) that contains the body of his dead wife through the secret pool that lies beneath his extravagantly redecorated Egyptian pyramid. The climax of the movie just barely succeeds in outrageously topping all the madness that has gone before. Vincent Price had a field day as Phibes.

YOUNG FRANKENSTEIN:

A tender moment from the movie that made it almost impossible for many members of the audience to take any version of the Frankenstein myth seriously again. Gene Wilder, as the modern scion of the ongoing Frankenstein family, has just gotten the monster (Peter Boyle) on his feet and is encouraging him to take a first giant step.

mused scion of the House of Frankenstein, but it was the supporting cast that provided the best part of the fun: Marty Feldman of the extraordinary eyeballs as the sinister hunchback; Cloris Leachman as the sinister housekeeper Pavlovianly programmed with screams; and Madeleine Kahn as the decidedly unsinister fiancée, bossily trying to make some sort of order out of the ongoing chaos.

The computer menace perversely went from the epic to the personal as computers became smaller and more common. The advanced computer Proteus in *Demon Seed* (1977) is an institutional tool, but gains entrance to its maker's home through a small domestic computer and holds his wife captive as it studies her. Murdering anyone who attempts a rescue, Proteus eventually causes her impregnation parthenogenetically, absorbs the embryo into itself, and eventually "gives birth" to a child that *looks* human. We are left to anticipate the future. By some alchemical process, the script made all this seem probable, aided by Julie Christie's acting skills as the wife and some small-scale but beautifully realized special effects.

Of course classic mad scientists were ripe for new productions, and Dr. Moreau returned in the person of Burt Lancaster in *The Island of Dr. Moreau* (1977). The *Island of Lost Souls* of 1932 was a hard act to follow, and even Lancaster's commanding presence failed to erase memories of Laughton, but it was a worthy attempt with a hero of some substance (Michael York), excellent makeup for the beast people, and a script that added a goodly amount of credible detail to the basic story.

Another old friend who kept coming back until his welcome was nearly outworn was Herr Frankenstein; there seemed to be at least one movie about him a year, from everyone from Christopher Isherwood to Andy Warhol. One very much worthy of note was succinctly titled *Victor Frankenstein* (1977; also known as *Terror of Frankenstein*). The unusual thing about this film, aside from its being a

DEMON SEED:

Gerrit Graham is being done in by a computer, and not because he forgot to save to disc. This computer, by name Proteus IV, is a supermodel with many talents, which enable it to imprison and impregnate its creator's wife. This is the fate it metes out to Graham, a would-be rescuer. Though the premise sounds dubious at best, the movie brought it off with panache and a maximum of thrills.

THE ISLAND OF DR. MOREAU:

Burt Lancaster did his Dr. Moreau in a much lower key than Charles Laughton's but was effective from the sheer force of his screen presence. The "beast men" that he creates are less bestial, more human than in the earlier version; this weakened the impact of the remake overall.

Swedish/Irish production, is that it tells Mary Shelley's story almost absolutely straightforwardly. Both script and production have very little decoration; one has the odd feeling that if movies had been made early in the nineteenth century, this is the movie of *Frankenstein* that would have been made, with Ms. Shelley providing the script. Per Oscarsson is a pathetically ragtag creature indeed; he haunts Victor more as a wraith than as a monstrous giant.

Jekyll and Hyde made a reappearance, too, though uncredited and in a vastly updated version. *Altered States* (1980) was made by a team seemingly as mismatched as the original pair — the flamboyant Ken Russell and the realist Paddy Chayevsky. In it a contemporary young researcher (William Hurt) begins experimenting with various modish consciousness-altering devices such as hallucinogenic mushrooms and sensory deprivation, a combination of which alters more than his consciousness. He changes into a primitive semihuman, changes back, and then keeps reverting at awkward moments. It's all resolved by the power of love, a device used more shamelessly here than any period film would have dared.

The computer in *Tron* (1982) is less a person than a place; the script in a sense updated *Alice Through the Looking Glass*

ALTERED STATES:

Ken Russell's film was really our old friends Jekyll and Hyde revisited. The change was effected not by old-fashioned injections, but by the more currently fashionable sensory deprivation and hallucinogens. William Hurt is the modern researcher who goes too far and Blair Brown the loving mate who at this point has gone even farther. Unlike the cynical original, the scientist is saved by the love of a good woman.

TRON:

It must have come as a shock to many computer users to be told that their computers were inhabited by a host of glowing creatures, living in a never-never world of strange landscapes and stranger architecture. That was the premise of the 1982 Disney film, a stunner visually even if the plot managed to confuse those unfortunate viewers who were not *au courant* with computer technology.

to *Kevin Through the Computer Screen* as programmer Kevin Flynn is dragooned by the Master Program of his institutional mainframe into the world within it, a world of strange landscapes and stranger people, all analogs of various computer functions, programs, or games. The results tended to confuse anyone not familiar with computers (and even some who were), but Computerland itself was visually extraordinary; the production used a combination of innovative animation and live characters to splendid effect.

Brainstorm (1983) went back to the old device of the new device that has unexpected and disastrous consequences for both the characters involved and society in general. The new device here is a sort of brain recorder that tapes sensations felt (seen/heard/smelled/tasted) by one person and can then be "played back" in another person's mind. Intrigue is pro-

vided by the fact that the military wants it, and there's a touch of mysticism as a dying technician puts the machine on "record" mode for her final moments.

The emphatic rejection of the monster by his newly fashioned bride gave a touch of women's rights sensibilities to the 1935 *Bride of Frankenstein,* and that theme was further explored in the 1985 remake, titled simply *The Bride.* It begins at almost the point where the older film ends, but there is a twist in the fact that the created bride is so lovely that Frankenstein (here Charles) decides to keep her for himself. The monster, understandably annoyed at this turn of events, destroys the laboratory and escapes.

He falls in with a dwarf, who teaches him humanity, while at the same time Charles is "educating" Eva, the created woman, to be his mate. Here is the Pygmalion theme and all the questions it eter-

BRAINSTORM:

Louise Fletcher (right) and, in her last role, Natalie Wood watch as Cliff Robertson tries a contrivance that plays back someone else's thoughts in his mind. In the movie's theatrical release, the vicarious "memories" were shown in 70mm Super Panavision (the plot in 35mm), which was enormously effective. Needless to say, the film loses a good deal on television.

nally raises—woman as chattel, woman as independent being, woman as rebel. While claiming to want Eva to be an independent entity, Charles still regards her as a possession, and on finding her with another man, takes his revenge by attempting rape.

At this fortuitous point, the monster (who has been dubbed Viktor by his dwarf companion, in an ironic referential twist), returns and kills his creator. Viktor and Eva, now united, decide to emigrate to America. (Is Ellis Island ready for this?)

Though the mad-scientist myth has always had a cautionary base, this particular mix of horror film and social significance didn't quite jell. Still, the handsome

production and a script that didn't insult the viewer's intelligence made it an above-average attempt.

Re-Animator (1985) claimed to be based on works of H. P. Lovecraft. It takes place at the Miskatonic Medical School in Arkham, Massachusetts, well-known names to Lovecraft aficionados, but the master horror-story teller, with his Victorian sensibility, would undoubtedly have had an attack of the vapors had he seen it.

A precocious student, Herbert West, transfers to Miskatonic after having left a school in Switzerland under a cloud. He tells his roommate, Dan—who has access to the school's morgue—that he has discovered a serum that will, in essence, bring back the dead. The innocent Dan goes along with West's revolting experiments under the conception that this will result in the betterment of mankind.

Regrettably, the revivified corpses are violently insane. West, more or less by accident, kills the school's dean and its top brain surgeon (who is as bananas as West—we have here two mad scientists for the price of one—and lusts after the dean's daughter Meg, Dan's girl friend) but revives them, the latter in two pieces (he had been unfortunately decapitated).

Needless to say, things get rapidly out of hand. The headless body makes off with Meg, who is subjected to a nasty romantic interlude with its decapitated head, and everything comes to a violent climax, with reanimated bodies running in every direction. Meg is killed in the melee, and the film closes with the virtuous Dan injecting her with the reanimation fluid.

Re-Animator presents itself as black comedy, though its humor is certainly a matter of opinion. More generally, it typifies the approach of the late eighties to the horror film—mad scientists and the creatures of dark fantasy are reduced to self-parody. The conventions of the straight-faced B movies of the past that made us giggle on television are now presented humorously within the movies themselves.

The idea of progress through science and technology made Mary Shelley nervous. Over the nearly two centuries since, thinking people have continued to question it, perhaps never more than in the past half-century. And as long as this happens, the questioning will be put into the dramatic form of the mad scientist. He (or she) is not just a figure of amusing fictional horror but a constant cautionary note that science has not, does not, and will not ever have all the answers.

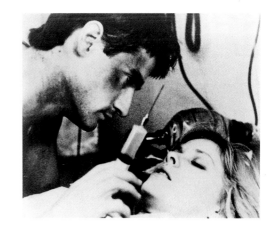

RE-ANIMATOR:

Bruce Abbott is about to revive Barbara Crampton from the dead with his re-animation fluid. Judging by the mayhem that has followed like operations earlier in this gory little film, it will indeed be a fate worse than death.

THE BRIDE:

In the earlier version, Dr. Frankenstein was interested in his female creation only as a mate for his original monster. In this later variation, Frankenstein (Sting) is more than happy to play Pygmalion to his lovely construction (Jennifer Beals), though as is usually the case, the monster (Clancy Brown) is not happy.

In the popular primitive films of Méliès and his contemporaries, the *voyages extraordinaires* to the Arctic, Mars, and other faraway places were not complete unless the intrepid explorers ran into a fearsome monster, usually constructed of papier-mâché and about as menacing as the dragon in a production of *Siegfried*. But these "thingies" continued to command a reaction of combined amusement and horror, and filmmakers soon began to upgrade the product. As the early fantasies gave way to relative realism, imaginary monsters gave way (temporarily) to "real" ones: the discovery and reconstruction of the dinosaurs was still taking place in the scientific world, and these fearsome beasts fit the bill for something large and lumbering with which to menace the actors.

So the special-effects creators began to make dinosaurs that were as photogenic in their way as any Hollywood starlet (given the fact that both were totally artificial creations), and they and their spawn have been rearing and roaring from the screen ever since (dinosaurs, that is, not starlets). The problem in writing a drama around a dinosaur, however, is that science has shown that dinosaurs and humankind did not exist on this planet at the same time. A film having nothing *but* dinosaurs as characters has obvious limitations, such as sparsity of dialogue and fairly fundamental motivation. Therefore, achieving human/dinosaur interaction depends on some sort of science fictional or fantasy device.

As a matter of fact, the first notable dinosaur in film history did occupy a humanless landscape. But she interacted with her creator, Winsor McCay, who was the most inventive and the most influential cartoonist of his day. The movie was a very short one reel, but *Gertie the Dinosaur* (1909) was a wonder in its time, combining the animated Gertie with live-action film of McCay; Gertie herself was the most heart-stealing monster in film until Chewbacca came along.

The lovable dinosaur, however, was a short-lived phenomenon; moviemakers soon realized the thrill potential of a ravening creature as big as a house. As special effects with models became more and more realistic, the dinosaur menace became a workable conception. The ultimate in the silent-screen dinosaur was

THE LOST WORLD (1925):

Audiences of 1925 were startled by the reality of the dinosaurs encountered by the Challenger expedition to a "lost world" in the South American jungle. Here members of the expedition, including Wallace Beery as Professor Challenger and Bessie Love as the necessary female, come face to face, or more accurately face to hoof, with a brontosaurus.

reached in *The Lost World* (1925) from Arthur Conan Doyle's highly enjoyable novel about a lost plateau in Amazonia, so cut off from the rest of the world that dinosaurs of all kinds still roamed it. There was also an ape-man to spice things up; confusion was courted here by casting burly Wallace Beery as Doyle's irascible Professor Challenger, who leads the expedition which finds the lost plateau. After various close encounters with dinosaurs of various kinds, they escape with a live brontosaurus. This mettlesome beast opened up a whole new area of the cinema by escaping in London and threatening to flatten the metropolis. How many monsters would follow in his footsteps!

Gorillas were a popular menace of si-

lent movies and early talkies, and the inevitable conclusion was reached, given the successful technical effects of *The Lost World,* that a dinosaur-sized gorilla would be socko box office. The result was the immortal *King Kong* (1933), who wrestled dinosaurs before breakfast in his native jungle and managed to put some large dents in New York City before being unfairly ambushed on top of the (then) new and thrilling Empire State Building. Kong was indeed a smash, and the monster movie became a staple of film production.

However, there were only so many lost worlds that could be found (particularly with the globe growing smaller by the day), so the problem remained: how to get humans (particularly toothsome female humans) and monsters together? *One Million B.C.* (1940) solved it simply, by throwing paleontology to the winds and giving us a primeval fantasy world where the two species coexist.

The results had a certain naive charm, as we follow the adventures of Tumak of the Rock People, a singularly hairy and ill-mannered tribe. After confronting his father for leadership (and losing) Tumak is exiled, and after further confrontations

GERTIE THE DINOSAUR:

This wistfully woebegone creature is the original of not one, but two great traditions of the screen. Gertie is the first animated personality, whose "children" would include Mickey Mouse and Bugs Bunny, and she is the first screen dinosaur: following in her generous footsteps would be Godzilla, Gorgo, and a host of anonymous lizards subjected to process photography. She is the creation of the great cartoonist Winsor McCay.

KING KONG (1933):

With King Kong at one end of the log and a tri-
ceratops at the other, this is not an easy moment
for Bruce Cabot, Fay Wray, and company, but
there were very few easy moments in this movie,
whose nonstop action and brilliant effects made
it easily the classic monster film of all time. A
monstrously expensive remake in 1976 did not
eclipse its reputation.

ONE MILLION B.C.:

Carole Landis and Victor Mature are cave-dwelling folk in a difficult situation. Causing the difficulty is a magnified baby alligator decked out in
optional extras, such as a back fin. The bleak
landscape is the reason that the tribe of Tumak
(Mature) is known as the "Rock People." So says
an introductory title; there is no understandable
dialogue.

with the indigenous dinosaur population he winds up with the Shell People, who are a good step up the social ladder from his own folks. Their main attraction is the lovely Loana, who teaches Tumak some manners. He resolves to take her home; on the way, they inadvertently get involved in a rip-roaring battle between two dinosaurs, the special-effects high point of the film. These were no clay models, but a live iguana and baby alligator, processed to giant size, having at each other while the human actors cowered in the foreground. Highly effective, this footage was used and reused in any number of low-budget films for the next twenty years. Supporting the iguana and the alligator were Victor Mature (laboring under the publicity label of "the beautiful hunk of man") as Tumak and Carole Landis as Loana, who proved that the Shell People had some advanced techniques in cosmetics and permanent-waving.

In the 1940s, dinosaurs were relegated to juvenile matinee productions, but as with all other kinds of science fiction film, the atomic age opened infinite possibilities for monsters. The first new monster of the second half of the century, however, was the familiar remnant from an earlier age, forgotten by time in, as usual, South America (which, according to the films, housed as many prehistoric remnants as it did fugitive Nazis). This one is a "gill man," an amphibious link between man and fish. *The Creature from the Black Lagoon* (1954) was dangerous, but only when harassed by annoying scientific expeditions. No one has ever been able to explain fully why this film has maintained its reputation over the years. The production is B-minimal, the concepts as ridiculous as most monster movies: for instance, the creature, conforming to tradition, makes off with the heroine for absolutely unfathomable reasons (presumably she's as ugly to him as he is to us, and as for what to do with her once he's got her . . .). Perhaps it's the straightforward unpretentiousness of the film or the more-than-competent handling of the underwater sequences. Whatever

THE CREATURE FROM THE BLACK LAGOON:

Richard Carlson and Julie Adams are anything but pleased to see the gill man, aka the creature from the black lagoon, rising from the deeps. All too obviously a man in a rubber suit, the creature, for some reason, made a huge impression and almost came to rival Dracula and the Wolfman in monster movie iconography. He also spawned two film sequels.

GODZILLA — KING OF THE MONSTERS:

Despite the fierce attack of any number of model airplanes, the fire-breathing, radioactive monster Godzilla, revivified by hydrogen-bomb tests from his prehistoric grave, carries on with trampling Tokyo underfoot. This will not be the last time that long-suffering city will be knocked flat by a giant reptile.

its charm, its two sequels were less memorable.

Ironically (but perhaps inevitably), it was the Japanese who first realized the full potential of atomic age monsters. The result was *Godzilla, King of the Monsters* (1956) — Kong and dinosaur combined, with extra added features such as radioactivity and the ability to breathe fire. Godzilla is a "prehistoric beast" revived by atomic testing. He is also cleverly given character to a degree, as well as a name — this was not just another anonymous monster. These elements, added to the Japanese flair for special effects, made Godzilla a household name. Any number of sequels and imitations followed. The initial film established a precedent for the demolition of Tokyo, which soon became a regular proceeding.

In the United States, in the meantime, atomic radiation was spawning an alarming number of giant creatures. Insects were particularly popular subjects for the large economy-size treatment, probably because of the instinctive human dislike for crawling things. *Them!* (1954) was one of the first and best such, a smartly constructed thriller that begins in an arid Southwest area with mysterious deaths involving large thefts of sugar and the presence of formic acid. It turns out that giant, mutated ants are responsible, and the climax involves a colony that has established itself in the Los Angeles drainage system. (There are interesting touches such as the bewildered humans who see "Them" on their mating flight, and the ship at sea that is suddenly infested.) The oversized ants are extremely

TARANTULA:

The major fear of the American public in the 1950s concerning science, it would seem from the movies at least, was not nuclear war but the possibilities that testing would loose a horde of mutant monsters on the helpless population. This segment of the helpless population (Mara Corday) is being menaced by the mandible of a giant tarantula, the product of biological experimentation gone awry.

THEM!:

Them were giant ants, and an infestation was no picnic. Joan Weldon is the inevitable beautiful female biologist who runs into one of Them while out for an exploratory stroll. This was the first, and one of the best, of the giant-insect movies; the oversized ants were convincing, the script exciting and well paced.

GORGO:

It may not be evident, but we have here an example of mother love in action. The fearsome beast demolishing Tower Bridge in London has come in search of her child, a slightly smaller version of herself that had been captured in the Irish Sea and was being exhibited as a sideshow monstrosity in the English capital. Needless to say, maternal affection as well as monster muscle win out, and mother and child escape down the Thames.

well done, helped by a jarring, whining "call" on the sound track that is as startling as the visuals.

Any number of giant six- and eight-legged creatures followed *Them!* into the theaters. Most were more funny than fearsome, such as the giant grasshoppers that ate Chicago, but some did work up a degree of excitement. *Tarantula* (1955), for instance, couldn't help but be unnerving—spiders in close-up are even more frightening than most crawling things, tarantulas are probably the most scary of the spiders, and a tarantula that is one hundred feet high and tosses cars around is bound to make an impression.

The English, with their national prejudice toward dumb animals, inevitably came up with their own variant on the sympathetic-monster theme. *Gorgo* (1959)

is a giant reptilian creature from the sea that is captured off the coast of Ireland and brought to London to be put on exhibit. But, as the joke goes, you should see his mother. Gorgo is indeed just a pup, and when even more gigantic Mum comes ashore to rescue him, London is once again subject to squashing.

Despite the novel monstrosities of the new era, dinosaurs did keep turning up, if only in children's movies. There was, for instance, *Dinosaurus* (1960), which despite uneven effects and an even more uneven script, is hugely enjoyable. A brontosaurus, a tyrannosaur, and a caveman (common garden-variety type) are resuscitated on a small Caribbean island (probably close to the South American coast), and proceed to terrorize the inhabitants. Rightfully so in the case of the

DINOSAURUS:

This was a lighthearted foray into the theme of prehistoric man and beast revived in modern times. Particularly amusing were the reactions of the bewildered caveman (Gregg Martell) to the various phenomena of the twentieth century. He has found a friendly companion in Alan Roberts; they are riding a brontosaurus brought back to life with the caveman and equally bemused.

THE LOST WORLD (1960):

Among those strung out along the cliff are Fernando Lamas, Ray Stricklyn, Richard Haydn, Claude Rains, and Jill St. John, all members of another expedition to Doyle's Lost World, a plateau on which dinosaurs roam. Getting up was easy; getting down is proving to be a problem.

carnivorous saurian, but the brontosaurus is a pussycat and the caveman simply confused. One of the jokes is particularly memorable, when the primitive man peers into the lighted window of a house and comes face to face with a woman in hair curlers peering *out*.

And there was, inevitably, a remake of *The Lost World* (1960). Claude Rains is Professor Challenger, and the dinosaurs are magnified lizards rather than the models of the silent version. They keep menacing Jill St. John, possibly in reaction to the pink pedal pushers that she obviously thinks de rigueur for jungle wear. The dinosaurs are quite convincing, perhaps a little too much so when shown dying in the flames of the inevitable volcanic eruption that destroys the plateau.

The Japanese topped even the monster motherhood of *Gorgo* in the lovable creature race. Godzilla's friends and relations, most of them scaly and breathing fire, had continued to stream from the Land of the Rising Sun. And what should suddenly emerge, for no coherent reason, but a giant moth, with wings as large as city blocks, and a good deal more beautiful. It seems that on a lost island in the Pacific

Mothra (1961) is worshiped as a god by a race of six-inch-high humans. When an exquisite pair of twin girls is kidnapped by wicked exploiters, a giant caterpillar speeds to the rescue. On the highest tower in Tokyo it spins a cocoon from which Mothra emerges to menace the Japanese capital yet again with tidal waves and windstorms (not to mention the peril to woolen kimonos). This utter nonsense was presented with such disarming straightforwardness that it was almost irresistible.

Since monsters were in, it seemed about time to remake *One Million B.C.* Once again a remake topped its original. *One Million Years B.C.* (1966) presented us with the same thoroughly unscientific milieu of coexistent dinosaurs and humans. But what dinosaurs, and what humans! Special-effects master Ray Harryhausen was responsible for the former; the latter are led by the magnificently beautiful Raquel Welch as Loana of the Shell People, well matched on the male side by John Richardson, all blond beard and muscles, as Tumak of the Rock People. Perhaps the most spectacular scene is that in which Loana is carried off

by a huge pterodactyl to its nest, but we are also shown a boffo volcanic eruption and a dinosaur battle that tops the earlier iguana and alligator match.

While *One Million Years B.C.* can hardly be accused of subtlety, it is probably the least crude of all the dinosaur movies. A good deal of craft went into its making, as witness the score, which alternates one of those good, epic orchestral themes with the rhythmic percussive sounds of rocks struck together. And there are moments of true fantasy, as when Loana and Tumak venture into a cave that is obviously a sacred place of a more primitive species. There is no confrontation; the two escape unseen. But one is left with a sense of mystery and magic.

There wasn't much mystery *or* magic about *The Valley of Gwangi* (1969), but it was almost equally well done (again, dinosaurs by Harryhausen) and a good deal of fun. Here the setting is the Wild West of the turn of the century, specifically a lost valley full of monster reptiles. So it's cowboys and iguanodons, and a roped tyrannosaur, taken to the great outside world for exhibit. And, by gum, wouldn't you know it would go and escape?

MOTHRA:

The monster rally of the 1950s came to a kind of climax of silliness with the emergence from its cocoon of a very large moth (a sort of behemoth, one might say) unimaginatively dubbed Mothra. The only threat it posed was the windstorms stirred up by its giant (though beautifully marked) wings. Stronger measures than a large supply of camphor were needed to get rid of it.

ONE MILLION YEARS B.C.:

The remake of the prime prehistoric epic of the 1930s was a winner, due to excellent effects and some fine photography. Unfortunately, so much attention was paid to Raquel Welch in skins (hers and others') that the dandy dinosaurs went almost unnoticed. Here's a particularly good one, menacing a cave moppet.

THE VALLEY OF GWANGI:

Clearly, this is not your ordinary rodeo steer-roping contest. The 1969 movie combined cowboys and dinosaurs, and succeeded in being highly diverting with the unlikely mix. It all had to do with the discovery of the familiar "lost" valley, in which the saurians had managed to survive. This geologic time capsule happened to be in the Old West, which enabled the cowhands to try their skills on some unusual livestock.

AT THE EARTH'S CORE:

Paleontologists might have a problem recognizing these beasts, but that's because they're native to Pellucidar. Pellucidar is the interior surface of the Earth, a hollow sphere (according to speculation by Edgar Rice Burroughs); this 1976 movie was made from the first book of Burroughs's series about the place, a haven for prehistoric monsters strayed from the surface.

THE LAND THAT TIME FORGOT:

One of the disadvantages of discovering a lost continent is coping with its denizens. The surviving fauna of the Antarctic land of Caprona, as invented by Edgar Rice Burroughs, presents all sorts of problems. Here a sailor just emerged from the submarine by which the outside world has penetrated Caprona is about to become an object lesson.

Although Tarzan had been a fixture on movie screens since 1917, almost none of the other works of his prolific creator, Edgar Rice Burroughs, had been filmed. Burroughs had been fond of dinosaurs (as plot elements—even Tarzan had met more than a few in his literary career), and one of his series had been devoted to Caprona, a lost continent in the Antarctic edged with formidable cliffs, warmed by interior hot springs, and inhabited by the usual leftover life forms. The movie of *The Land That Time Forgot* (1975) wastes a little too much time getting us to Caprona; there's a good deal of hanky-panky aboard a German World War I submarine captured by shipwrecked English seamen. But once the sub works its suspenseful way through an underwater passage beneath the cliffs and comes to rest in an inland sea from which a long-necked dinosaur emerges to gobble up a sailor, the action is fast and amusing.

Less successful was the movie of another of Burroughs's works about an epic lost world, Pellucidar, the interior surface of the supposedly hollow Earth. The theory was that during successive geologic eras, every sort of animal life had wandered into Pellucidar and survived. And to boot, the reptiles there had developed an intelligent (albeit cold-blooded) race called the Mahars, which dominated the interior world and its various primitive human species.

Putting Pellucidar on film had its problems. A major one was that the horizon of Pellucidar curves *up* (think about it). Another was that of depicting *intelligent* dinosaurs with their own culture. When the first book in the series, *At the Earth's Core,* was finally brought to the screen in 1976, the first problem was blithely ignored—Pellucidar was demoted to a series of huge caverns—and the second not solved very satisfactorily; the Mahars looked like lumpy rejects from *Sesame Street.* Nevertheless, there was some of the old Burroughsian excitement as hero David Innes and his eccentric inventor pal, Abner Perry, burrow through the Earth's crust in Perry's digging machine and end

up in Pellucidar battling dinosaurs and rescuing fair cavemaidens.

Another film about Burroughs's Caprona, *The People That Time Forgot* (1977), follows an expedition sent out to find two of the first movie's characters who had missed the boat (literally) at the climax and stayed on. This film reveals Caprona's real mystery: its human inhabitants progress from apelike primitivism to true humanity in the course of a lifetime. This peculiar manifestation adds a touch of variety to the now familiar dinosaurs.

Monsters of all sorts had by now become overfamiliar commodities on the screen. The coup de grace was probably given by the remake of *King Kong* in 1976. The picture was as elephantine as Kong himself, and endless debate was waged as to the aesthetics. Somehow a modern, wide-screen version in color lost a quality that the small, antique movie in black-and-white had captured. Certainly the World Trade Center had none of the impact of the Empire State Building (perhaps the difference is explained in the *bon mot* that a World Trade Center tower looks like the box in which the Empire State Building came). One improvement was noted by an astute few: the heroine in the new

KING KONG (1976):

The giant remake of the great little movie from 1933 proved that a small film about a big ape was better than a big film about a big ape. Nevertheless, some of the effects were stunning. The arches beyond the body of the dying Kong in this photograph are those of the World Trade Center, which just did not have the pizzazz of the Empire State Building for the climactic scene.

version was not just a pretty blonde with good lungs. This one showed a remarkable presence and a good deal of personality; she was, in 1976, a newcomer named Jessica Lange.

It seems that today monsters themselves have faded away like the legendary old soldiers. Recent attempts to revive interest in them, ranging from cuddly baby dinosaurs to a Godzilla *redux,* have been greeted with nothing but yawns. Perhaps a clue lies in the fact that in the movie of *Dune* we are presented with a horrific giant creature in a tank. Until recently it would have certainly been a menace, destined to escape and terrorize the humans. In this case, however, it is just another character, engaging in the future equivalent of labor relations. Monsters just aren't what they used to be.

ALIENS AMONG US

am a man, and reckon nothing human alien to me," said Terence. The early days of science fiction xenophobically reversed that view by regarding nothing alien as human. H. G. Wells's view of Martian invaders settled into the public conciousness the image of the inimical being from another world, and it was a major step for science fiction to create aliens that were sympathetic, particularly if they were nonhumanoid in appearance. Most science fiction films have gone along with the alien-as-menace viewpoint, but there have been a surprising number of exceptions.

One of the earliest alien-invasion films stuck to the idea of the fearsome intruder. Out of the adventurous German cinema of the silent years came *Algol* (1920). All prints of this film have been lost, and accounts vary as to its content, but it is acknowledged to concern a visitor from the star Algol who arrives with a machine that can give its wielder untold power. Calamity, of course, is the result. Extant still photographs give us an idea of the extraordinary sets by Paul Sheerbart, a noted poet and architect, and Walther Reimann.

Few visitors from other worlds arrived on the screen for many years after that.

The ethnocentric public view of the universe seemed to accept Flash Gordon visiting other planets, but somehow found it not quite proper that aliens should visit us. However, Hollywood began to explore various aspects of science fiction in the wave that followed *Destination Moon,* and came upon a story ("The Return of the Master" by Harry Bates) that seemed promising (partially because minimal effects were needed). The result was *The Day the Earth Stood Still* (1951), one of the most respected science fiction films of all time. Atypically for what was to come, the visiting alien (who arrives, true to the times, in a saucer-like spaceship) is not only powerful, but beneficent. He has come to establish relations with humanity (he himself looks thoroughly human, in the person of the aristocratic Michael Rennie), but true to form, humanity first shoots, then imprisons, then kills him. His companion, a giant robot, rescues the body, revives it with alien supermedicine, and then stays on Earth to guard against the proliferation of atomic weaponry.

Philosophically, there can be some argument with the film (who are these interstellar meddlers to threaten us with destruction unless we behave?); it can be viewed as early wish fulfillment for a big

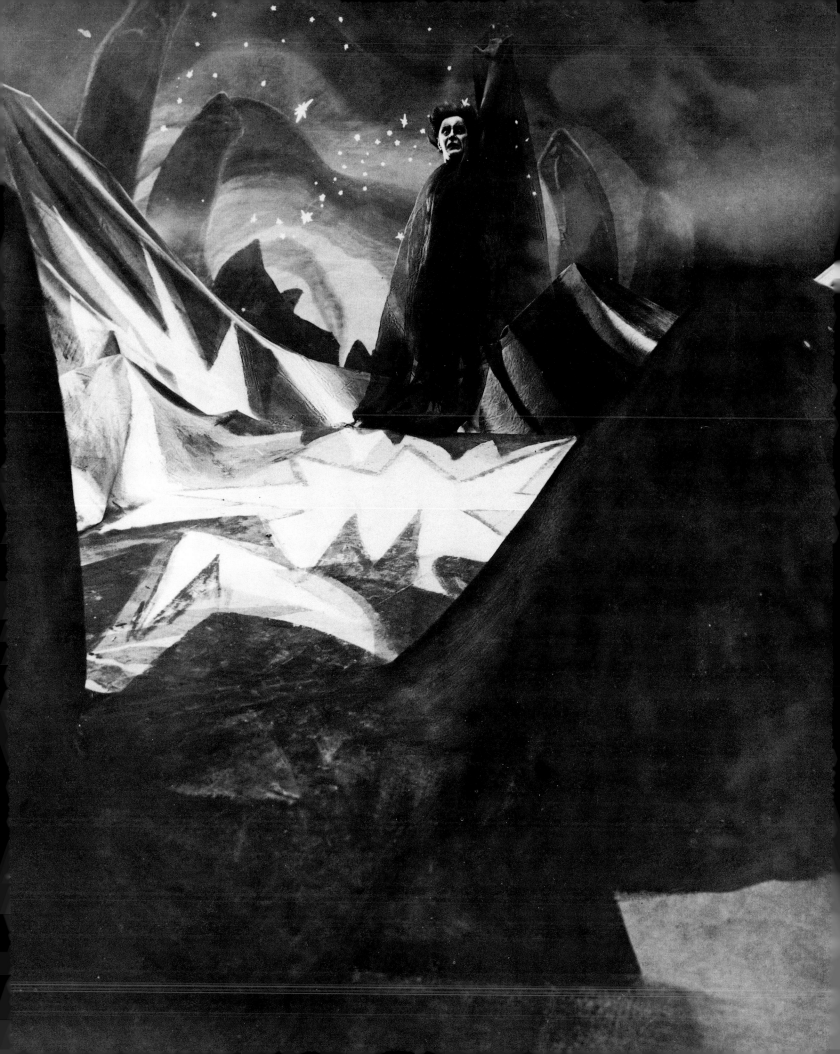

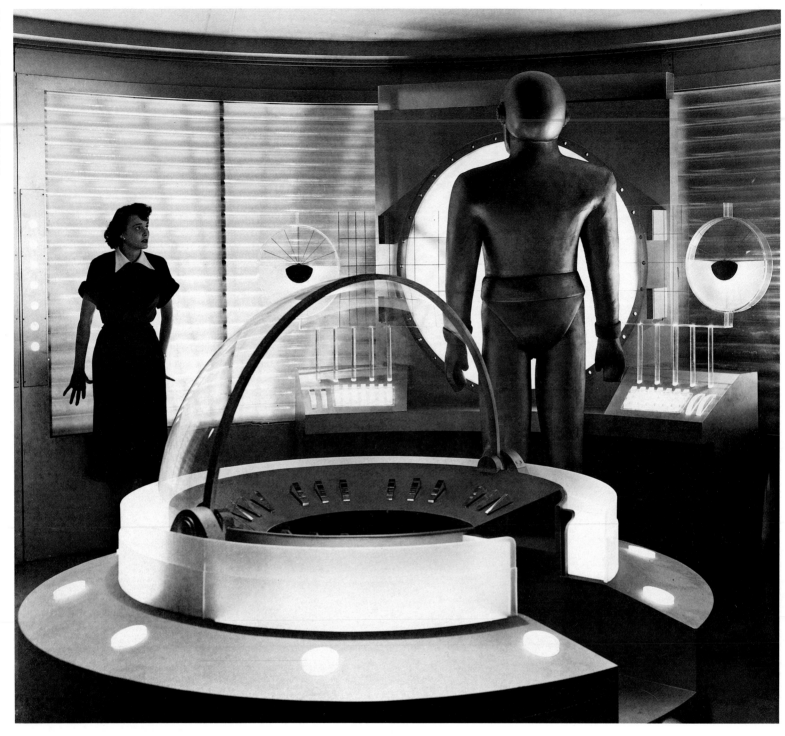

THE DAY THE EARTH STOOD STILL:

The first real classic of the midcentury wave of science fiction films, this didn't start the trend toward thoughtfulness it might have because monsters from outer space took over the genre. Patricia Neal was hardly the usual screaming blonde heroine, even when confronted by the awesome giant robot, Gort.

THE THING:

The pleased expressions on the faces of the members of an Arctic expedition are not going to last, because the block of ice is going to melt, and the specimen inside, which they have retrieved from the remains of a flying saucer, is going to come back to life and present a few problems. Howard Hawks's superb little science fiction horror show has seldom been equaled, mainly because of its crisp ultrarealistic direction; a remake didn't come close.

daddy from the sky to save us from ourselves, a forerunner of the third kind of close encounter. But the comparatively low-key handling of the plot and the better-than-usual acting (Patricia Neal is the human who befriends the alien) maintain the movie as an above-average example of its kind.

Curiously enough, in the same year another alien landed (in an equally circular vessel) who could not have been more different. This one, in fact, reenforced the image of the Awful from Outer Space to a degree that would influence movies for decades. The film was *The Thing (From Another World)*, and it also was low key and well acted. The alien, however, was anything but beneficent. Crash-landed in the Arctic, it is frozen solid; carved out by a scientific expedition, it thaws, lives, and proceeds to wreak havoc in the expedition's camp, which is isolated from the outside world by weather conditions. Not only does the thing seem invulnerable, it's determined to reproduce.

The movie is a terrifically successful thriller. Here the switch is definitively made from the supernatural supermenace to the scientific, which, as the second half of the twentieth century started, was that much more believable. Adding to the *verismo* are Howard Hawks's (uncredited) direction and the realistic, overlapping dialogue that gave a near-documentary feel to much of the action. These factors, plus the claustrophobic device of the isolated circumstances, make for a truly scary film. The sequence in which the lone watchman sits with the dripping, thawing alien is one of the more memorable in screen history.

H. G. Wells's Martians invaded movie theaters in 1953, having already, as noted, made their impression in print and in that most famous of all radio broadcasts by Orson Welles. *The War of the Worlds* set the action in contemporary California, and most of the fun of the film is in seeing the sleek and beautiful flying machines of the Martians pulverize Earth's cities. The crafts are accompanied by one of those singularly unnerv-ing sound effects, and their cobra-like periscopes add menace at close quarters. They are finally defeated, not by any invention of humankind (even atomic bombs fail to stop them), but by Earthly diseases against which they have no immunity.

This Island Earth (1954) begins with aliens among us, then throws in space travel, interplanetary warfare, monsters, and a kitchen sink or two. Two nuclear scientists (Rex Reason of the unlikely name, and Faith Domergue of the unlikely physiognomy — for a scientist) join a mysterious research project run by a "man" named Exeter, whose physiognomy is unlikely for *any*body. The facts that his forehead is about twice the height of anyone else's (except his assistant's) and that he communicates on a sort of videophone with others of his sort raise the suspicions of the two humans. Indeed, Exeter is from another planetary system, desperately seeking aid and resources for the defense of his world, Metaluna, against another that is waging war on it.

Exeter kidnaps the two scientists in his space vessel (which is, of course, of circular design) and takes them to Metaluna, where they are menaced not only by the interplanetary war that has brought Metalunan civilization to near collapse, but by the Metalunan domestics, which are "mutants," half-human, half-bug. Escaping the dying planet in Exeter's ship, the earthlings must do battle with a mutant that boarded the craft, but they make it safely back to Earth eventually.

Pure pulp fiction, *This Island Earth* attempted a big production in the class of *Forbidden Planet* a year later but failed to match that film in intelligence of script or slickness of production. Nevertheless, it's good, eye-filling fun.

Beware *The Blob* (1958), as the ads would have it, since it epitomizes the low-budget, high-grossing film that combined adolescents and aliens and singlehandedly convinced producers that there was no need to pour money into big productions when the same public would turn out for cheaper ones. In *The Blob,* a tiny meteorite lands near a small American

THIS ISLAND EARTH:

Monsters were *de rigueur* in science fiction films until recently; even in such a comparatively sensible film as this one, concerning a planet inhabited by wise humanoids that is being bombarded by enemies from space, some terrifying thing had to be introduced to menace the heroine. In this case, it's one of the mutant servants of the aliens. The war-torn landscape of Metaluna can be seen through the window.

WAR OF THE WORLDS:

First came the Wells novel, then the Welles broadcast, finally the movie. It very cleverly never gave a clear view of the Martians themselves but used their frightening machines for menace. Only at the very end, when the flying machines begin to crash, do we get a glimpse of the limb of a dying Martian as a hatch opens. Nothing that humankind could bring against them won the day; it was the lowly germs of Earth.

THE BLOB:

Olin Howlin is trying to find out what in tarnation just fell out of the sky and blasted a crater in his field. That little meteorite has in it a blob of pink gelatin that is going to try and swallow the county just as soon as it's broken out and, incidentally, become the best-loved of all the shapeless movie monsters.

town and disgorges a blob of what appears to be raspberry preserves, which absorbs anyone who comes in contact with it. Feeding on the local populace causes it to grow larger; it invades the town, oozes into the projection booth of the local cinema, swallows the projectionist, and then slides down into the auditorium. The screaming crowd that emerges into the street convinces the local police that the teenagers who first saw the thing and had been trying to convince anyone of its reality are indeed telling the truth. But in the meantime it has grown as big as a house and engulfed the town diner in which the unfortunate adolescents (including a twenty-eight-year-old Steve McQueen) have taken refuge. Over the years, *The Blob* has become a camp classic, if only because it so perfectly represents a period genre of science fiction film.

The Blob was the top feature (believe it or not) of a double bill; the second half was the unfortunately titled *I Married a Monster from Outer Space* (1958). This does not have the reputation it should have as a good little thriller, possibly because everyone is too embarrassed to cite a film of such a title. To make matters worse, the title is reasonably accurate; the poor heroine does indeed marry an alien being who has taken on the semblance of her fiancé. In fact, quite a few of the local men have been simulated by the extraterrestrials; the real humans are kept in a kind of suspended animation in the alien spacecraft. The audience is in on the secret; we see the true monster momentarily. The girl suspects it, but no one believes her. It's a truly suspenseful situation, and also reflects the classic dilemma of female psychology ("Have I married a monster?") that goes back at least as far as "Beauty and the Beast."

At long last the filmmakers turned to a contemporary science fiction novel for a sophisticated view of encroaching aliens. John Wyndham's diabolically clever *The Midwich Cuckoos* became the classic film *Village of the Damned* (1960). In it, the aliens are unseen and unexplained. In

I MARRIED A MONSTER FROM OUTER SPACE:

The bridegroom cometh, and despite the title and some unsubtle makeup for the monster, there were authentic chills and suspense in this B movie.

fact, the only evidence of their existence is the fact that the small English village of Midwich is suddenly cut off from all communication with the outside world for a day and the inhabitants rendered insensible for that period. This curious phenomenon is dismissed as some sort of freak event until it is evident several months later that every female of childbearing potential in the village is pregnant. The twelve children that result are immediately identifiable as "something different" by their extraordinary eyes. As the children grow up, it becomes obvious that they share nonhuman mental abilities: what one knows, they all know, and they can also read others' minds. This is not strictly a case of aliens among us; these are half-aliens.

Their development, physical and mental, is astonishingly rapid; in a few years, they are preternaturally mature. Regarded as devil's children by the villagers, they meet the violence of the humans with a mental violence of their own—and kill to protect themselves. A Midwich scientist whose wife has borne one of the children first tries to protect them but then realizes that they pose a threat to humanity. But the children are almost unkillable, since they can read malefic intent immediately (a Russian village, apparently afflicted with the same sort of "colony," resorted to dropping a nuclear bomb). The climax of the film is the scientist's desperate scheme to finish the half-aliens off.

Village of the Damned baffled many reviewers, who felt the lack of clear explanation for the events of the film implied some murky supernatural agency. To the knowledgeable, the wonderfully ambiguous questions of *from where* and *why* the children only added to the scariness; this was an invasion from space like no other.

VILLAGE OF THE DAMNED:

Not your average grammar school class, this deadly group of moppets has extremely strong psychic powers: what one knows they all know, they can read minds, and they can impose their wills on any mere human. Their fathers were extraterrestrials (the original novel by John Wyndham was fiendishly titled *The Midwich Cuckoos,* since they were all born in the town of Midwich). The problem the film poses is—how do you get rid of them?

THE ANDROMEDA STRAIN:

Despite appearances, this is not a spacegoing Holy Family. The baby is one of only two survivors of a village struck by a deadly disease from space; medico James Olson (holding baby) is part of a team frantically trying to learn the secret of the alien virus. The "space suit" is armor against infection.

Anglo-American science fiction films in the 1960s had become limited to low-budget productions; only the Japanese film industry tried for anything ambitious. The results were often ludicrous but sometimes diverting. *The Green Slime* (1968) is really just a *Blob* of another color. It is green, comes from space, and attaches itself tenaciously to human beings and other digestibles. However, its life cycle is more complex than the Blob's; after a certain amount of ingestion, it develops into tentacled monstrosities that are, to say the least, unfriendly. Slime and offspring manifest themselves on an inhabited space station. The enclosed environment again provides the excitement, since the beleaguered inhabitants cannot evacuate without contaminating Earth with the omnipresent slime. There's some attempt to present a future society (dancing in the space station recreation area is an amusing example), and the monsters, despite their antisocial attitude, are rather endearing, flailing their tentacles and emitting high-pitched beeps like preliminary sketches for R2D2.

Considering the number of memorable mad scientists to appear on the science fiction screen, it's interesting to note how few sane scientists have been presented as heroes. Sometimes it's a scientist who saves the day in a monster film, but these few are generally lacking in personality, and their supposed scientific achievements are always downplayed, probably for fear the audience would regard them as oddballs. One exception to this rule is the British rocketry expert Professor Quatermass, whose adventures with curious phenomena from space were chronicled in several BBC serials, all of which were later made into films. By far the best of the lot was *Five Million Years to Earth* (1968—aka *Quatermass and the Pit*). A London subway excavation uncovers some curious objects, a metal cylinder and some skeletons. The area in which the find was made had always been considered "haunted" due to inexplicable sightings of curious beings. The cylinder is first thought to be an unexploded Ger-

THE MAN WHO FELL TO EARTH:

An alien family on an unspecified planet, the father of which will come to Earth and become corrupted by human ways. A little too much of Nicolas Roeg's film was unspecific for science fiction aficionados, but cinema enthusiasts fell on it with joy.

man bomb, but when Quatermass is called in, he and the anthropologists working on the matter discover that the artifacts date back millions of years and that the skeletons are those of the most primitive species of man. What's more, the preserved body of an alien insectoid creature is found inside the cylinder, as well as evidence leading to a startling conclusion. The insect creatures are Martians who five million years ago genetically altered the anthropoid inhabitants of Earth in order that they might inherit the Martian intelligence; in other words, they staged a proxy invasion ("We *are* the Martians," says Quatermass). Additional excitement is provided by the fact that the cylinder is still active and is programmed to interfere with Earth intelligences, which it does to chaotic result.

Five Million Years to Earth is rare in the field of science fiction films in that its script is so intelligent that the production seems unworthy of it. The concepts are realized on screen as well as could be expected for a minimal budget, but the results are at least adequate. It is interesting to note, however, that a film that opened soon afterward used one of the same themes (that of alien interference in our development), with a production that was worthy; it was, of course, *2001: A Space Odyssey.*

An alien as invisible as the fathers of *Village of the Damned* and even more frightening was *The Andromeda Strain* (1971). This alien arrives on Earth on a returning, unmanned space probe. A deadly virus, it kills almost all animal life with which it comes in contact. Two people who have resisted it, strains of the virus, and four scientists are enclosed in a unique government laboratory especially prepared for this kind of emergency. The lab includes even an atomic bomb set to destroy the installation if the virus should get loose within it. The main part of the picture is devoted to the four scientists' painstaking research into the deadly puzzle presented by the invisible killer; interest is sustained not only by the scientific detective story being played before

FIVE MILLION YEARS TO EARTH:

This was the third film to feature the exploits of the scientist-detective, Professor Quatermass, and the most complex and interesting of all of them. Investigating the report of what seems to be ghostly manifestations in a London excavation, Quatermass and Colonel Breen of the British Army (Andrew Keir and Julian Glover) discover the remains of an expedition to Earth from Mars from five million years ago.

THE GREEN SLIME:

The inhabitants of Space Station Gamma III didn't wipe their shoes properly when coming through the air lock, thereby tracking in some green slime that grew into these tentacled creatures. The resulting battle for control of the station is good space operatic fun. That's Richard Jaeckel holding the door.

us, but the amazingly detailed sets of the many-leveled laboratory, a technological miracle. The production is a visual tour de force, probably the most stunning depiction of believable superscience movie audiences have ever seen. Naturally things go awry, and the film ends with a heart-stopping chase to prevent the bomb from exploding and scattering the deadly virus all over the landscape.

Phase IV (1973) proved that aliens need not come from space. The menace here is ants—ordinary, normal-sized ants. However, these ants are even more of a danger than the giant *Them!*, because they have a kind of intelligence utterly alien to humankind, and not just because it is a "hive" intelligence consisting of many individuals who alone are valueless. After they have overrun farms in the desolate area where they have developed, an experimental station is set up to study them. The ants succeed in outwitting every form of destruction aimed at them; they fight back by cutting off communication to the station and by erecting huge towers with reflective material at the tops to focus sunlight on the station house and raise the temperature to unbearable levels. The chief scientist learns how to communicate with the ants; they demand hostages. Met with refusal, they infiltrate the building. The scientist is killed; two young people are taken and, in a quasi-mystical ending, are shown to be changed by the ants into something "beyond the human."

Phase IV is often infuriatingly ambiguous, particularly in its ending; however, the suspense is beautifully sustained as new measures are waged against—and resisted by—the ants. And the microphotography is extraordinary: the ants, for instance, generationally change colors as they adapt to various chemicals (this may be the first use of ant makeup), and an egg-laying sequence showing the (relatively) huge body of the queen turning out offspring is stunning.

Ambiguity was also a pervasive quality of *The Man Who Fell to Earth* (1976). An alien comes to Earth, in essence to trade his superior technological skills for water for his drought-stricken, dying planet. Such matters as from what planet he came and how he got here are barely touched on, which is the kind of cavalier treatment of detail that tends to infuriate science fiction aficionados. Filmmaker Nicolas Roeg also seemed determined to use every cinematic trick in the book, which did not help to clarify matters. What does emerge from the chaos is that the alien succeeds in making a good deal of money from things such as a revolutionary type of self-developing film, but he is cheated out of it and must remain here, unable to save his planet. Basically, *The Man Who Fell to Earth* is a moralizing fable rather than true science fiction, but some of the details (such as the peculiar ones of the alien's bodily structure—no nipples, among other lacks) are fascinat-

PHASE IV:

Ants, again, but this time gigantic intellectually rather than physically. The ant colonies here have developed a weird intelligence with which they successfully combat human beings in an isolated location. The script was intelligent, if a trifle opaque at the end, and the microphotography of the ants was a technical tour de force.

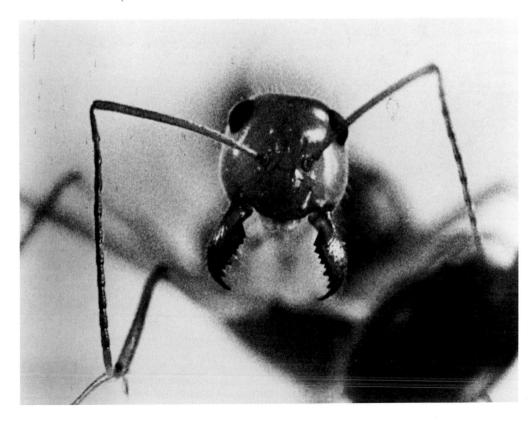

ing, and rock musician David Bowie is quite literally unearthly in the central role.

The mythos of the flying saucer cult has always been a source of embarrassment to the science fiction field. And in its way, so was *Close Encounters of the Third Kind* (1977), an endless film about some hopeless humans from the pages of the *National Enquirer* who see, sense, chase, and/or are kidnapped by UFOs. However, the final half-hour of the movie,

in which the "mother ship" (from which come the smaller saucers) lands on Devil's Tower in Wyoming, almost makes the whole thing worthwhile. It is the alien landing as Epiphany, the coming of gods rather than extraterrestrials, and all the stops are pulled out in the way of special effects. The gentle, childlike aliens refuse the "astronauts" that are offered them as emissaries and take only the protagonist of the movie, for no obvious reason ex-

cept that he has been so obsessed with their Coming that he's been sculpting the Devil's Tower in mashed potatoes and shaving cream. Critics vied with each other in describing the mother ship ("Las Vegas torn up by the roots"; "a flying banquet table with all the candelabra lit"), but there was no denying that the landing sequence was a knockout—if you weren't rendered slightly queasy by the daffy religious implications.

CLOSE ENCOUNTERS OF THE THIRD KIND:

The docking of the "mother ship" is, in visual terms, closer to a visitation from the kingdom of heaven. A mixture of flying saucer lore and science fiction (not necessarily the same thing at all), this amazingly popular movie made many viewers uneasy with its religious overtones, equating extraterrestrial beings with supernatural beneficence.

INVASION OF THE BODY SNATCHERS (1978):

This remake of the 1956 classic changed the setting from a small town to a city, but the pod people were still taking over. Here Donald Sutherland sleeps as a pod person forms.

The 1978 color remake of *Invasion of the Body Snatchers* carried through with all the intriguing aspects of the original cult classic, made in 1956, and, alas, its flaws also. It sets up a dilly of a premise; an alien *something* grows pods that reproduce specific people, and eventually the reproductions take over and carry on the humans' daily lives, while placing more pods to do the same. The hero discovers that what seems to be half of San Francisco has been taken over by the simulacra; whom can he trust? Unfortunately, after setting up the rules of the game (primarily that the pods must be placed near their doubles while they form), it breaks them toward the end for a cheap surprise (the heroine has been taken over). Knowledgeable audiences had a good time when the protagonist of the first version, who is left trying to stop traffic to warn of the "invasion," turns up doing exactly the same thing for a brief moment in the remake.

Probably the most famous of all aliens among us had been around for several decades before he got his cinematic dues. Superman is, as everyone knows, from the planet Krypton, rocketed off as an infant just before it explodes. Landing on Earth, the foundling is raised by a kindly human couple; as an adult, he uses his super, Kryptonic powers to leap tall buildings . . . etc. His earlier film career came in the days when comics were considered only a basis for Saturday matinee fare. The superproduction of *Superman* in 1978 was a festival of special effects, not the least of which was the blowing up of the planet Krypton. Perhaps the greatest miracle of all was that Christopher Reeve managed to make Superman a superappealing hero.

Humanity need not be on Earth to have alien trouble in its midst, as we were shown in *Alien* (1979). Here again we return to science fiction with the conventions of a horror film: a group of people in a closed environment with an unseen killer among them. The enclosed environment is a spaceship, a freighter. The killer is a rapidly developing alien acquired

SUPERMAN:

A contemplative moment for the legendary man of steel (Christopher Reeve) in one of the knock-out sets of the 1978 movie, a far cry from the low-budgeted earlier incarnations on film and television.

ALIEN:

A return to the old-fashioned mix of horror and science fiction, it gave us a spaceship instead of a haunted castle and a nasty extraterrestrial with lethal ways instead of a shambling creature. The atmosphere was established early on when the humans discover the wreckage of the alien ship. Its organic design was by H. R. Giger, and remarkably unpleasant it was, too, as evidenced by this sample of the remains.

while the crew set down to investigate a huge craft that had crash-landed on an uninhabited planet; the grotesque extraterrestrial crew members are dead, but their eggs are still viable. One of them hatches while a human is near it; it attaches itself to him and is taken aboard the freighter. From then on, it is unstoppable. The suspense is terrific; there are a lot of dark corners in a space freighter. Particularly notable is the startling design of the alien craft and its interior by the artist H. R. Giger. Here is a return to the influential beginnings of German cinema—an artist of the bizarre designing the unearthly. It worked brilliantly.

In the early days of movies, the waif was surefire material, whether it be puppy, kitten, fawn, or Jackie Coogan. However, as times became more cynical and heartstrings harder to tug, the homeless youngster became overdone and was dropped from the screen. But the theme merely needed a new kind of waif, which was provided by *E.T., The Extra-Terrestrial* (1982). Here a baby alien is left behind by its mother ship, and is given help and refuge by three Earth children. The small rubbery thing at first seems repugnant, but the huge Disneyesque eyes clue us that it is really a little dear, and heartstrings were tugged by the millions as the creature and the three children evade the more stringent aspects of Earth society. The young Henry Thomas gave an extraordinary performance as Elliott, the principal earthling, and even the most cynical melted as E.T., his ship returned for him, says, "Come," and Elliott replies, "Stay."

The other end of the age spectrum became involved with otherworldly visitors in *Cocoon* (1985), specifically a group of oldsters who live in a sunset community in Florida. The men habitually sneak into the derelict mansion next door to swim in its pool and don't stop when a mysterious group of people preoccupied with finding strange rocklike objects on the ocean floor store these objects in the swimming pool. The old men discover that the pool has turned into a fountain of youth enabling them to do things (on the dance floor

E.T., THE EXTRA-TERRESTRIAL:

One of the great film hits of all time, *E.T.* cunningly manipulated its audience with the lost innocent theme, long abandoned by the movies as passé. The gimmick here was to make the waif initially repugnant to the eyes of the audience, as is obvious in this still. Henry Thomas, as E.T.'s human friend, was superb.

COCOON:

Brian Dennehy and two of his confederates, all aliens disguised as humans, inspect one of the cocoons they have come to Earth to rescue. If the shirtless gentleman reminds you of Tyrone Power, it's because it's his son, Tyrone Power, Jr.

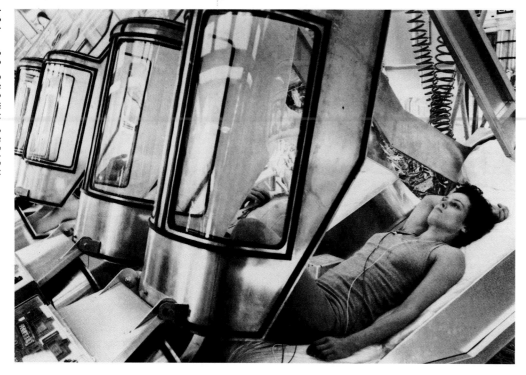

ALIENS:

The way to travel in the future—Sigourney Weaver comes out of the suspended animation necessary for star traveling.

and in the bedroom) they hadn't been capable of for years.

The mysterious strangers are, in fact, visitors from another star system, here to rescue others of their kind left behind in the sinking of Atlantis—the rocklike objects are their fellows, in a sort of suspended animation. The rejuvenation effect of the pool is part of the revivification process, and the old folks have used it all up. Everyone is frightfully nice about it, and it all ends with the entire community of elders being taken up, up, and away in yet another mother ship (or in this case, a grandmother ship?). It's utter balderdash, but saved by a cast of golden oldies (Don Ameche in an Academy Award–winning performance, Gwen Verdon, Hume Cronyn, Jessica Tandy, Maureen Stapleton) who show what real movie-acting is like.

But you can't keep the nasties down, and the nastiest of all was revived in *Aliens* (1986). In this sequel to *Alien,* Sigourney Weaver, the sole survivor of the doomed freighter that has inadver-

tently taken aboard the killer extraterrestrial, is back home and having nightmares (understandably). Word comes through that a far-distant colony is having trouble (to put it mildly), and it's suspected that the cause is a hive of aliens of the sort that wiped out Weaver's shipmates. Will she kindly step back into her nightmares and accompany an armed force to the colony? She inexplicably does, and from there it's *us* against *them* on a fog-shrouded world in a deserted settlement of warehouses and laboratories, again filled with dark corners out of which things can jump.

As with the first film, there is an attention to detail, the *verismo* of which enhances the fright index. Particularly well done are the ramshackle colony and the squad of soldiery—future warriors who are literally fighting machines, physically and psychologically—and their advanced weaponry.

Aliens notwithstanding, in this area the view of the outside universe has altered over the years, and friendly nonhumans seem as probable as the nasties—at least in the movies. If there *are* aliens among us, in hiding in Earth society (a scenario no less likely than many of the above), they must be relieved at the change.

ALIENS:

That's Sigourney Weaver's face peering out of the Power Loader, a machine that electronically and mechanically enhances the "wearer's" physical strength.

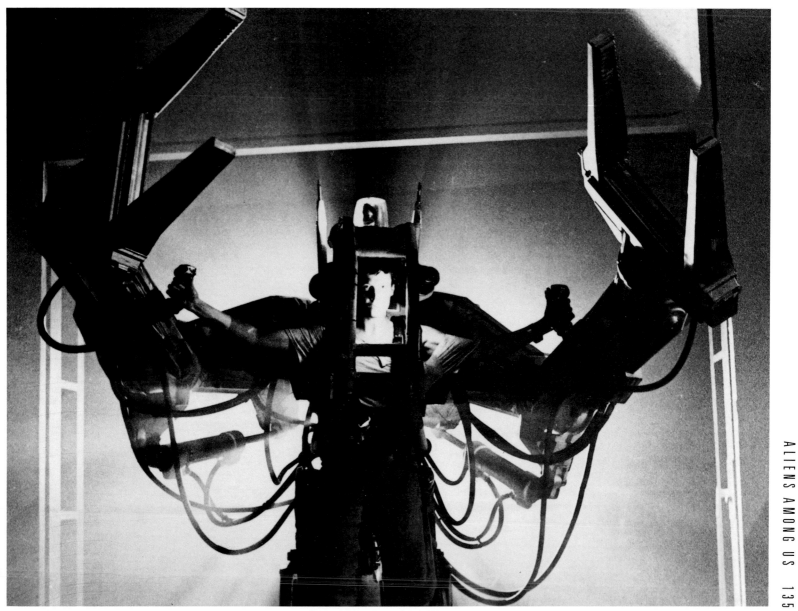

LIGHT FANTASY

The object of fantasy is to enthrall, frighten, or amuse. In an age of science, old fantasy—that of fairy tales and myths and nighttime things that go bump—has primarily amused, since the "rational" adult is not supposed to take such things seriously.

Science fiction is the new fantasy. Marvelous people, places, and things are given some sort of scientific rationale, and it is the duty of the storyteller (in print and on film) to convince us of these marvels, to make us at least temporarily suspend our disbelief. But it has not replaced the magical beings—the witches and leprechauns and angels—of old fantasy.

During much of the movies' history, such beings were used for humor or relegated to children's fare, for which adults could always use the great excuse that "the kids want to see it." If a fantasy film was aimed at adults, it was treated as whimsy; songs were often added to make it even more fanciful. One of Hollywood's avowed aims was to "make you feel like a kid again."

And sometimes it did. Scriptwriters' imaginations and movie magic and a dash of wit provided some glorious moments on screen.

For complex reasons, the silent film had little to do with light fantasy. Comedy was king, but the kingdom was slapstick, and dialogue in excess of the silent screen's ability was needed to get across the comedic potential of visiting Greek gods or witches in contemporary dress rather than pointy hats. The transition was evident in the talkie *Million Dollar Legs* (1932—not to be confused with the later Betty Grable opus of the same title), which combined slapstick, snappy dialogue replete with puns, and the unclassifiable nonsense of W. C. Fields cast as the king of the mythical country of Klopstockia (presumably somewhere close to the Marx Brothers' Fredonia). Reporter Jack Oakie discovers that the inhabitants of Klopstockia are all superb athletes (the king's daughter reveals this by removing her clothes and diving from a two-hundred-foot-high bridge) and the attempt to put together an Olympic team provides what passes for a plot. The country also harbors such inhabitants as Mata Macree, a spying vamp played by one of the dizzier of filmdom's blondes, Lida Roberti.

Presold literary classics were always a sure thing in the 1930s, so why not *Alice*

ALICE IN WONDERLAND:

Charlotte Henry as Alice didn't go on to lasting stardom, but the actor in the Mock Turtle suit certainly did. It wasn't from this role, however, that Cary Grant won his reputation for suavity.

MILLION DOLLAR LEGS:

The mythical kingdom of Klopstockia contained some unlikely inhabitants. Here are three of them — the one on the right being the kingdom's even unlikelier ruler, W. C. Fields. Its inhabitants are notable for their extraordinary athletic prowess; even the rotund monarch is a weight lifter.

in Wonderland, which might be considered the original whacko fantasy? The film version made in 1933 was a massive failure, like the many others that would be made over the years; the Reverend Dodgeson's verbal whimsy simply does not lend itself to dramatic treatment (as one English critic has noted, the rhythm of Carroll's prose is unphotographable and Tenniel's illustrations are unactable). However, the all-star cast assembled for this production included some breathtaking triumphs of typecasting: tall, laconic Gary Cooper anticipated his horseback future as the White Knight; the omnipresent W. C. Fields was acerbic as ever as Humpty Dumpty; Edward Everett Horton dithered at genius level as the Mad Hatter; and the terrifyingly hatchet-faced Edna Mae Oliver was born to play the Red Queen.

The true path of screen fantasy was set when Hollywood discovered the works of the best-selling author Thorne Smith. Smith took the British tradition of mixing the supernatural with ordinary folk to chaotic and hilarious effect and applied it to contemporary American suburbia. This dovetailed neatly with that art form of the thirties, the screwball comedy; the results were several of the funniest movies ever made. The fact that Smith's books were considered "ribald" did not hurt the box office one bit, though by current standards the film scripts were snowy pure. A somewhat tentative start was made with *Night Life of the Gods* (1935), in which a hapless modern man discovers a magic ring that turns people into statues and, contrariwise, brings statues to life. When this is worked on a gallery full of Greek statuary, contemporary New York is confronted by Neptune, Hebe, Venus, Apollo, Bacchus, Perseus, and Diana, with utter confusion on both sides.

Full stride was hit with *Topper* (1937), in which Cosmo Topper (one of the inspired names of all time), a dignified, totally respectable, middle-aged suburbanite, acquires a sporty car and, unwittingly, the car's former owners, a madcap couple who are now ghosts. The running gag is that only Topper can see the ectoplasmic Kirbys, but the true humor comes from the clash of life-styles as the sportive, high-living (as it were) ghosts dedicate themselves to spicing up his life. Part of the film's success is due to that rarity, a

THE GHOST GOES WEST:

Murdoch Glourie (Robert Donat) is going to spend eternity popping out of walls instead of bushes, if his father's curse maintains its hold on him after death. It does, even when his ancestral castle is exported to the United States and he, perforce, goes with it. A funny idea, a smart script, and René Clair's direction made one long for an actor slightly less insipid than Donat.

THE NIGHT LIFE OF THE GODS:

When a gaggle of Greek gods comes to life in this century, culture shock reigns and chaos results. Here Hermes, Poseidon, Apollo, Hebe, and various other deities watch an impromptu beauty contest between a modern young lady (Florine McKinney) and Venus (Marda Deering), who is doing her best to look like that statue in the Louvre. (She really does have arms.) Alan Mowbray is the bemused gent in modern dress responsible for the mess.

TOPPER:

Poor, ghost-ridden Cosmo Topper is being told to shake a leg by his resident haunts, George and Marion Kirby. Two television remakes of Thorne Smith's comic novel of the thirties did nothing to erase the memory of Constance Bennett and Cary Grant as the sophisticated, boozing ghosts and Roland Young as the henpecked mortal who learns to live through his association with the dead.

perfect cast: Cary Grant and Constance Bennett as the ghosts, Roland Young the epitome of befuddlement as Topper, and Billie Burke as Mrs. Topper, eventually reduced to gibbering in the most ladylike fashion by the supernatural goings-on.

The English, of course, have a tradition of mortals mingling with the supernatural that goes back to *A Midsummer Night's Dream.* Their films of light fantasy were in a slightly different key, gentler and more romantic (romantic in the sense of sentimentality, as well as in the undercurrent of the darker aspects that were so promi-

nent in nineteenth-century romantic fantasy). For instance, *The Ghost Goes West* (1936) explored the humor of a Scottish castle bought by a rich American and transported lock, stock, and ghost to Florida. The ghost, condemned to walk by a father's curse for cowardice, is a nice enough fellow and certainly more or less taken for granted by the modern denizens of the castle, but the humor of the situation is balanced by the fierceness of the curse and an awareness, underplayed but there, of the weariness and horror of the ghost's plight.

THE WIZARD OF OZ:

The set designers made darned sure that Dorothy (Judy Garland) and the audience were certain that they weren't in Kansas anymore.

THE WIZARD OF OZ:

Dorothy Gale and the Scarecrow (Ray Bolger) are seen here in one of several encounters with the Wicked Witch of the West, played by the indefatigable Margaret Hamilton. Of the many fine character actors in the movie, Hamilton most enduringly caught the audience's fancy and became a legend in her own time.

The darker aspects of the American light fantastic were not so subtle; what could be less subtle than Margaret Hamilton on a broomstick wearing a pointy hat? Oz may not have been the first magical kingdom, but it is certainly the most famous and was an all-American creation; L. Frank Baum's Oz books could almost be called frontier fantasy, with feisty American children (Dorothy was only the first) coping with myriad magical creatures, usually with the direct approach of clobbering them with everything from a bucket of water to an entire house. *The Wizard of Oz* (1939) was a lavish production indeed, and while true Ozophiles winced at the liberties taken with the geography and history of Oz (well codified by that time in over thirty books) and the only-a-dream ending, an extraordinary cast headed by the precocious Judy Garland and the expensive, imaginative sets and costumes have captured the hearts of America for nearly five decades. And there *were* magic moments in the film, such as the first glimpse of the Emerald City, a triumph of Art Deco, and the flight of the winged monkeys.

Movies made from the works of Thorne Smith continued to provide more adult fare. *Turnabout* (1940) was an exercise in early sexual revolutionary polemics, with the personalities and bodies of a bored suburban couple switched by a mischievous Oriental idol. Carole Landis and John Hubbard couldn't quite carry off the difficult sexual innuendos of the situation, and they weren't helped by having their dialogue dubbed in the other's voice.

Much more successful was *I Married a Witch* (1942). A New England witch and her warlock father return to the modern world to revenge themselves on the descendant of the witch-hunter who brought about their deaths. This hapless gentleman (Fredric March) is an upright citizen about to be married, and the entrance into his life of the lovely witch, her pranksome father, and their combined magic powers confuses his life mightily. The witch, setting out to seduce him, instead falls in love herself and must de-

I MARRIED A WITCH:

One of the more hilarious scenes in a generally hilarious movie was that in which Fredric March's car, which happened to be carrying the witch returned to life played by Veronica Lake, suddenly became airborne.

THE CANTERVILLE GHOST:

That's Charles Laughton, head in hand, as Sir Simon de Canterville, fated to walk the halls of Canterville Castle for his highly improper behavior of several centuries ago. His successful spook act, however, is not being bought by the company of American soldiers billeted in the castle during World War II, who regard his ectoplasmic tricks as out of date. Laughton's performance, hilarious and touching, was a tour de force.

BLITHE SPIRIT:

It has been established that the current Mrs. Condomine (Constance Cummings, brunette) cannot see the first Mrs. Condomine (Kay Hammond, blonde), who is a ghost. Mr. Condomine (Rex Harrison), however, can, and finds himself in a state of "astral bigamy." Here he is attempting to prevent the volatile first wife from braining the second; all that she sees is a chair seemingly floating in air.

feat her unforgiving father for her lover's life. (Smith, too, sometimes hinted at a darker undercurrent.) The tiny, sultry Veronica Lake, showing unexpected comedic talent, was quite literally enchanting as the magic-making heroine.

The Canterville Ghost (1944) was from a story by Oscar Wilde so freely adapted that even Wilde could well have had trouble recognizing it. It was probably the prototype of all those stories about the ancient ghost confronting the modern world (and vice versa), with a nobleman cursed to walk the corridors of the family castle, which is rented by an American family. In the movie, the American family becomes an entire troupe of Yankee GIs; it was filmed during the middle of World War II, and this was just one of several movies aimed at promoting Anglo-American understanding (in the lightest possible way, of course).

The ongoing joke is of British tradition, represented by the ghost and the current representative of the family, Lady Jessica, running head-on into American high spirits and hardheaded rationality. What might have been an exercise in sentimen-

tality was promoted to high comedy by the brilliant performance of Charles Laughton as Sir Simon, the ghost, hilarious in his frustrated attempts to frighten the irrepressible Yanks and touching in his recounting of the lonely centuries he's endured in Canterville Castle. He was ably abetted by the seven-year-old Margaret O'Brien as Lady Jessica; she showed audiences that a child actor could transcend the cute and still be endearing.

A very different look at British ectoplasm was provided by the filming of Noel Coward's *Blithe Spirit* (1945). The result was about as sophisticated as the screen could get in those days. The blithe spirit hailed in the title is that of Elvira, first wife of Charles Condomine. Raised by a seance held as a joke, she stays. Understandably, the *second* Mrs. Condomine is not at all pleased by this situation of bi-worldly bigamy, particularly since she can neither see nor hear Elvira, who is disposed toward catty, Cowardly remarks. Margaret Rutherford neatly stole the picture from this engrossing situation as Madame Arcati, the inept spiritualist who summoned Elvira but is totally unable to banish her. Rutherford was the essence of every dotty little lady devoted to spiritualism. No viewer will ever forget her determined progress to and from the haunted Condomine household via bicycle, or her games-mistress enthusiasm as she begins the seance ("Let's make it a real rouser!").

Postwar films gave us a multitude of mythical beings appearing in the modern world and causing confusion of one kind or another. Angels were particularly popular in America. Members of the heavenly host had appeared in films as early as *Intolerance* (1916), but the whimsical use of a muddled messenger from above was a 1940s creation, and it was presented in many variations.

Among the first was one in the unlikely person of Jack Benny as Athaniel in *The Horn Blows at Midnight* (1945). Apparently the two-thousandth trumpet in a heavenly orchestra consisting of what seems to be several million players, he is sent to Planet 339001 (Earth) by the Department of Small Planet Management to blow the trump of doom for its inhabitants' misdeeds. Needless to say, he runs into all sorts of problems in fulfilling his

THE HORN BLOWS AT MIDNIGHT:
On view is only one small section of the heavenly orchestra of thousands of "angels" in the slyly conceived celestial sphere of this Jack Benny comedy. Benny, of course, was a member of the violin section. The movie became a running gag on Benny's radio show as a failure, but it had its moments of high comedy and imaginative production.

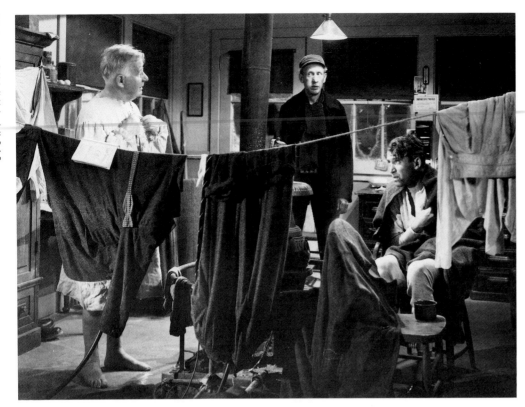

IT'S A WONDERFUL LIFE:

An expertly made piece of propaganda singing the praises of the life of the common man, this became a cult classic after several generations of television exposure and began showing up on cinema "best" lists. An angel (in the peculiar form of eternally dear old Henry Hathaway, left) gives would-be suicide James Stewart (right) a vision of what the world would have been if he hadn't existed.

assignment, among which are two fallen angels determined to undermine the mission. Some of the more inspired comic moments of the film deal with the descent from above of Athaniel (and eventually, several others), accomplished by means of an elevator in a luxury hotel. The periodic disappearance of the elevator is a running joke throughout.

Heavenly messengers continued to haunt the screen in the postwar years. An inept would-be angel attempting to "earn his wings" plays a major part in *It's a Wonderful Life* (1946) by showing a suicidal young businessman what the world would have been like without him. Frank Capra's hymn to the ordinary values of small-town America didn't sit that well with the exuberant mood pervasive after the war, but the film achieved a wide cult following after a quarter of a century of television exposure and is now considered a Christmas classic.

A bumbling angel starts the proceedings in *A Matter of Life and Death* (aka *Stairway To Heaven;* 1946) by failing to collect the soul of an English aviator downed over the Channel during World War II, but matters soon extend far beyond this initial situation. It seems that in the extra few days of life granted by this error, the airman falls in love (with an American WAC) and soon all heaven is trembling with the case. Should he, as he firmly maintains, be allowed to live because of the mitigating circumstance of love?

The case is brought to trial in a heavenly court, and soon becomes a contest between American and English sensibilities, represented by the dead—plain or prominent—of both countries. The Englishman, in the meantime, is recuperating under the care of his lover and a psychiatrist, both of whom view all the supernatural brouhaha as mental aberration. When the psychiatrist is killed in a cycling accident, he becomes the chief

A MATTER OF LIFE AND DEATH:

No, it's not a torture scene involving Kim Stanley and Roger Livesey. They are hanging on the ropes of a device called a camera obscura while discussing a matter of life and death—the delusion of Stanley's lover that he has been dealing with heavenly messengers who say his death is overdue. The American title of the film is *Stairway to Heaven.*

witness for the defense. The judgment is handed down as the hero undergoes life-or-death surgery, and in the finale the angelic court extends downward to the operating theater in a giant stairway of cinematic splendor, which may or may not convey him to the afterlife.

The taste, beauty, and intelligence of *A Matter of Life and Death* go beyond whimsy. Produced by the British team of Michael Powell and Emeric Pressburger (who went on to make *The Red Shoes* and *Tales of Hoffmann*), the visual aspects of the heavenly sequences are quite literally out of this world. They are shot in a luminous, silvery monochrome (as opposed to the Earthly scenes in color), and heaven is conceived as a vast and efficient (though warm) terminal run by smartly uniformed angels. In one memorable moment, the camera pulls farther and farther back from the vast amphitheater of the courtroom as the scene slowly dissolves into a distant view of a spiral nebula. David Niven

was at his most charming as the Englishman with the dubious lease on life; Kim Stanley as the WAC represented America with equal charm; Raymond Massey spoke fiercely against England as a frontiersman from the Revolutionary period; and Marius Goring added a dash of Gallic wit as the butterfingered angel, formerly a French aristocrat who lost his head in another famous revolution.

Night in Paradise (1946) was a maverick for the postwar period; something of an anachronism, it harked back to the romantic fantasies laid in exotic locales of the time of the making of *The Thief of Bagdad*. Its setting was the classical Greek period, specifically the court of the rich King Croesus of Lydia. The philosopher/fabulist Aesop comes as an emissary from Samos to request alliance rather than pay tribute. The impertinent suggestion nearly costs him his head, but the newly arrived Princess Delaria of Persia, Croesus's fiancée, saves the life of the

NIGHT IN PARADISE:

The court of Lydia's King Croesus (Thomas Gomez, reclining), who is rich enough to afford all this folderol. The luscious Merle Oberon (left) is a Persian princess in this witty piece of mythological fluff.

ancient storyteller. In the meantime, the sorceress-queen Atossa uses her witchcraft to confound Croesus and supplant Delaria. When the proud Delaria discovers that Aesop is in reality a young and handsome man (masquerading as an elderly one since youth is not respected), things get really complicated. *Night in Paradise* is a multicolored soap bubble with some stunning sets and costumes, the exquisite Merle Oberon as Delaria, and amusing anachronisms ("Would you put that into plain Lydian?" asks Delaria of Aesop).

David Niven again became involved with an angel in the American *The Bishop's Wife* (1947), but with a good deal less spectacle than in *Stairway to Heaven.* Never before had there been as

THE GHOST AND MRS. MUIR:

In the gentle fantasies of the 1940s, almost all supernatural beings were benevolent, even ghosts that haunted houses. The house in this case was a sea captain's cottage and the ghost that of the captain himself. Being Rex Harrison, his surface manner was less benevolent than crusty, but it was obvious that he was a gentle soul underneath. The hauntee is Gene Tierney.

suave a guardian spirit as Cary Grant, who descends to teach a bishop the error of his ways (basically paying more attention to the cathedral building fund than to his parishioners and wife—the bishop is Anglican, of course). The skill of the leading players (Loretta Young rounded out the odd triangle) pulled the script from dangerously sticky ground.

The gentleman ghost reappeared in the form of Rex Harrison, the ghost in *The Ghost and Mrs. Muir* (1947). Perhaps gentleman is not quite the right word for the salty sea captain whose spirit haunts the cottage rented by the widowed Mrs. Muir, but we know, and she soon finds out, that he is really a seagoing pussycat. The loving relationship that develops between the two mismatched souls has a true poignancy that gives the film an authentic sweetness.

The supernatural being in *Miracle on 34th Street* (1947) is Santa Claus—or is he? A modern, cynical (in 1947 terms) department-store publicist hires a jovial, bearded layabout to act as Santa Claus, and, by golly, he turns out to *be* Santa Claus. Or at least that's the conclusion reached in the unlikely court case that develops from the gentleman's insistence

THE BISHOP'S WIFE:

The "naughty" title of this forties hit was meant to titillate, but the bishop (David Niven) is, of course, Anglican. However, his endlessly patient wife, played by Loretta Young, does start to have an uneasy attraction to a stranger, not knowing that he is an angel sent to help with the cathedral building fund. A meddlesome angel named Dudley sounds like a deadly proposition, but when played by Cary Grant, Dudley indeed proved heaven-sent.

on his identity. In the process the publicist's little daughter, a product of modern education, learns the validity of fantasy and fairy tales. Despite the treacle, the movie was a huge hit, and remains so, having become a television ritual of the Christmas season, and Edmund Gwenn as Santa achieved the stardom so rarely visited on a character actor.

Mythologies meshed in *Down To Earth* (1947), as did genres — this was a musical light fantasy. From a curiously pantheistic heaven speeds the demi-goddess Terpsichore (Rita Hayworth), who is angered by a Broadway show currently using her name in vain. Taking it over, she creates a monumental flop of great artistic merit and finds contentment only when, at the end, she learns to "swing it," as current usage put it.

DOWN TO EARTH:

Terpsichore comes to Earth to prevent desecration of her art and her image on Broadway, but ends up getting hep and lending her talents to this jazzy ballet. The male dancer is Marc Platt, who danced with the Ballets Russes as Marc Platoff.

MIRACLE ON 34TH STREET:

Natalie Wood, as good a performer as a child as she would be as an adult, is imitating a monkey for John Payne and the "miracle" himself, Edmund Gwenn. There may be a few people left in the world who don't know that Gwenn's role in the film is that of the real Santa Claus, whose authenticity becomes the subject of a lawsuit. Here he is seen out of uniform.

ONE TOUCH OF VENUS:

The young Ava Gardner was about as close to the Goddess of Love as the 1940s cinema could get, so it was lucky that she had just appeared on the scene when this Broadway hit by Kurt Weill came to the screen. Robert Walker was the department store employee who falls in love with a statue of the goddess, only to have it come to life.

THE LUCK OF THE IRISH:

Hollywood aimed many movies at the sizable Irish-American population of the United States, so it was inevitable that the light fantasy film featuring mythical, whimsical creatures would eventually get around to the leprechaun. Tyrone Power, as an American journalist, has by accident obtained the leprechaun's pot of gold. The "wee" creature was played by Cecil Kellaway at his most fey; it earned him an Academy Award nomination.

Certainly no one in Hollywood could look more goddess-like than Rita Hayworth at that point, though the next year there was a strong contender in the person of the young and strikingly beautiful Ava Gardner. She was the Venus of *One Touch of Venus* (1948), which was also a musical. This one has the enormous advantage of a score by Kurt Weill; it and Ms. Gardner bolstered the fairly vapid story of a department-store clerk who falls in love with a statue of the Goddess of Love, which comes to life with any number of unforeseen consequences.

The leprechauns had their chance in *The Luck of the Irish* (1948), in which Cecil Kellaway, trying to out-twee Edmund Gwenn, is one of the Irish Little People come across the sea to look after a modern Irish-American reporter in New York. His misadventures in the big city achieved a certain amount of humor (he steals all the milk delivered to the apartment doors in the building), though matters were not helped by tinting the screen a bilious green monochrome in the introductory section that takes place in Ireland.

The enormous popularity of the light fantasy in the late 1940s almost exhausted the pantheon of mythological creatures that could be introduced into the modern world, or at least those well known to the general public. At least one remained, however—the mermaid—and it (if one can be so boorish as to refer to the epitome of romantic femininity as "it") was featured in films produced almost simultaneously in Britain and the United States. The American entry was *Mr. Peabody and the Mermaid* (1948); Mr. Peabody is a middle-aged American businessman on vacation in the Caribbean who catches a mermaid. The results are predictable, to say the least, but William Powell did his urbane best to enliven the proceedings, particularly in a boutique scene in which he attempts to buy only the top of a woman's two-piece bathing suit. Ann Blythe was the scaled and tailed lady, and there was magic in the underwater shots of her shooting through the sea, blonde hair streaming.

England's *Miranda* (1948) was an entirely different kettle of fish. She does the catching, in this case, and brings the hapless fisherman to her sea grotto. Totally enchanted, he takes the mermaid home with him, ingeniously disguising her as an invalid in a wheelchair. The British way

MIRANDA:

Glynis Johns brought not only obvious visual advantages to the role of the mermaid Miranda, but one of the most provocative voices ever to be heard on a sound track—a combination of purr and chirp. The British idea of a mermaid was an interesting contrast to the American Mr. Peabody's; the arc and length of the tail give Miranda a much more inhuman quality, which Johns reinforced with voice and acting.

MR. PEABODY AND THE MERMAID:

The fantasies of the forties were often concerned with the classic situation of the mortal (inevitably male) enamored of a mythical female being. The luckless Mister in this case was William Powell; the Myth was Ann Blyth, as an innocently seductive mermaid. The legendary question asked in such a case by the apocryphal Indian chief ("How?") was avoided; the major problem was the embarrassment of buying only the top half of a swimsuit.

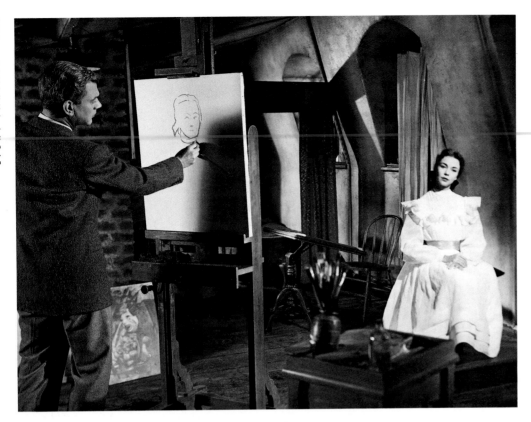

PORTRAIT OF JENNIE:
Whimsy transcended itself into sheer romanticism in this lushly photographed Robert Nathan story of a ghostly girl who returns periodically to a struggling artist, who uses her as the model for his masterpiece and falls in love with her in the process. Joseph Cotten was the artist; Jennifer Jones was suitably haunting as Jennie.

with fantasy again proves itself; *this* mermaid has a pagan, dark quality, and one can imagine her luring sailors to their deaths. Even her tail has a sinuous, wet quality to it which is just the least repellently ahuman. The upper half was the husky-voiced Glynis Johns; she was the definitive mermaid.

The sumptuous *Portrait of Jennie* (1948) was entirely peopled by humans, for a change. A young New York artist encounters a little girl in snowy Central Park and is struck by her odd quality, not to mention her curious habit of referring to things in the past as if they were current. He meets her again, and again in Central Park, skating on the lake; she seems older, well into adolescence. He persuades her to sit for her portrait; when she does, she is close to maturity. "Wait for me," she says, "I'm hurrying." The artist Eben begins to search for evidence of Jennie; there was such a girl, years ago. He meets people who remember her, and finally learns that she met her death in a great hurricane in New England. Can he somehow prevent it from happening "again" to the girl he has learned to love?

Every effort was made in this David O. Selznick production to convey an atmosphere of impressionistic enchantment (including Debussy on the sound track), and for the most part, it was successful. New York and Central Park became magical places, tinted and textured through Joseph August's camera lens. Jennie's second entrance, skating out of the sun's glare, is a memorable moment, and the often problematic Jennifer Jones delicately conveyed a character who is not quite a ghost, not quite flesh and blood. The fragile ambiguity of the entire film for once added to the magic rather than simply reducing it to confusion.

With the growth of television after 1950, light fantasy found a perfect home, and the small screen has been overrun with angels, genii, talking horses, talking cars, witches, and ghosts ever since. On the movie screen, it has been confined, for the most part, to indifferent children's films, often perpetrated by the Disney Studios. But even in the subsequent lean years, certain movies in the genre have stood out as noteworthy.

Certainly one from way out in left field was the puppet version of *The Emperor's*

CAROUSEL:
In the eccentric heaven envisioned by Rodgers and Hammerstein (out of Molnar's "Liliom"), Gordon Macrae as Billy Bigelow has been put to work hanging stars at the direction of one of the more commonly dressed angels the screen has provided. Tiring of the task (and who can blame him?), he asks to return to Earth to see how his family is getting on.

Nightingale (1947, released in the United States in 1950) from Czechoslovakia. "Animated" puppet films were nothing new to the West, but had been mostly confined to short and heavy-handed cartoon releases. Jiří Trnka's retelling of the Hans Christian Andersen fairy tale was a revelation for the medium in its exquisitely wrought puppets and even more exquisite backgrounds. (Czechoslovakia, of course, has been noted through the ages for its decorative work in wood.) Typical was the moment when the nightingale is brought to the emperor through the halls of the palace, whose intricate walls are miracles of wooden lacework; in each opening sits a tiny, nodding, smiling member of the court. A final sequence is close to genius: Death, a skeletal figure with a large black umbrella, is driven from the emperor's side by the nightingale, and retires to his "garden," a vast, peaceful cemetery, strewn with the ornate headstones of Middle Europe.

Also from Middle Europe, by a circuitous route, came *Carousel* (1956), which was based on the play *Liliom* by the Hungarian Ferenc Molnar. In this American musical version, the action was transferred to nineteenth-century New England. The central character, a no-good carnival barker married to a decent working girl, is killed while committing a robbery. In a rather peculiar heaven where the angels spend time hanging stars on strings from the ceiling, he is allowed to return to Earth to see his daughter, unborn at the time of his death, now in early adolescence. The first half of the film was styled in the new "realism" that Rodgers and Hammerstein had introduced into musical theater (realistic only by comparison with older musical comedy—now men actually hit their wives and characters died). The last part, however, achieved a true sense of fantasy, mainly due to Agnes de Mille's ballet sequence in which the daughter, Louise, watched by her ghostly father, encounters a carnival troupe and feels the pull of his free spirit (this to the famed "Carousel Waltz"). This scene nearly justifies the infliction on the viewer of some of the most treacly songs ever written (an ongo-

ing peril of musical fantasies) and accents of an excruciating phoniness (they bear a strong resemblance to those used by the same cast in *Oklahoma!*).

A supernatural being curiously neglected in the spate of light fantasies of the postwar years was the witch, who'd made no major appearance on screen since Veronica Lake's charming sorceress in *I Married a Witch*. A Broadway play provided a suitable spellbinder: John Van Druten's *Bell, Book, and Candle* gave us no reincarnated witch but played with the intriguing premise that witchcraft remained operable through modern times and had a distinct subculture with its own social life and gathering places.

The cast for the film version (1958) was a stunning one, a gaggle of comic characters centering around Gillian, the present-day enchantress, played by the beautiful Kim Novak, whose odd combination of lethargic sensuousness and alert intelligence was perfect for a modern practitioner of the black arts. Other witches were played by the maniacally overwhelming Hermione Gingold, as the matriarch of the magical society, and Elsa Lanchester, dithering divinely as Gillian's aunt. The male side was carried by Jack

Lemon, Gillian's warlock brother, and Ernie Kovaks as a witch-hunter, a psychic investigator determined to track down the evil in our midst. James Stewart is the mere mortal involved in the sorcerous goings-on, for whom, despite her best instincts, Gillian eventually renounces her craft. To its credit, the film was minimally whimsical, making its points of comedy and fantasy with true intelligence.

Mary Poppins might be thought of as a witch, but the readers of P. L. Travers's stories about that lady knew she was simply a family nursemaid of formidable mien who put up with No Nonsense and who had some exceedingly odd friends and relations, not to mention a few peculiar belongings. There was the black umbrella, for instance, by which she arrived (and departed, often at the most inconvenient times as far as the mother of the family was concerned). The stories were unabashed whimsy but tinged with implications, some poetic, some dark, that rose above mere cuteness. When the news broke that Mary Poppins was to become, as they say, a major motion picture from the Disney Studios, the consensus was that the only person thinkable for the role was Katharine Hepburn.

BELL, BOOK AND CANDLE:
James Stewart, though loath to believe it, has fallen in with a coven of witches due to his attraction for a beautiful neighbor. This is the head witch of the lot, played with her usual panache by the inimitable comedienne, Hermione Gingold. She has just prepared a classic witches' brew about which Stewart is understandably reluctant.

MARY POPPINS:

Mary Poppins, dressed a little less severely than usual for her afternoon out, and her gentleman friend, Bert the pavement artist, take a stroll in one of Bert's works of art. One look at its inhabitants should make it obvious that the picture was a Walt Disney production. Despite this, Julie Andrews managed a certain tartness that was true to the classic children's book character. Dick Van Dyke supported ably as Bert.

Therefore it was something of a shock when it was announced that the determinedly girlish (albeit highly talented) Julie Andrews had been given the role. A major factor in the casting decision was that the film was to have songs; there was the unshakable conviction in Hollywood at this point that fantasy must be musical, particularly if aimed at children, though no one, to anyone's knowledge, had ever asked children whether they preferred musical or nonmusical drama. As it turned out, the songs were exactly the kind of Nonsense up with which Mary Poppins would not have put.

Otherwise, the movie (released in 1964) turned out to be an entertaining exercise in light fantasy, though it inevitably concentrated on the more whimsical adventures that the Banks family experienced with Ms. Poppins. Two sequences were most true to the Travers stories. One was the episode involving Mary's Uncle Albert, who tends to float when laughing (due to attacks of laughing gas). The other was the brief encounter on the steps of Saint Paul's Cathedral with the Bird Woman who sells food for the pigeons ("Feed the birds! Tuppence a bag.") and under whose skirts all the birds of London shelter during the night. Here the movie, for a moment, touched the ephemeral poetry of the books. And Miss Andrews, keeping her girlishness well under control, scored a well-deserved personal triumph.

SEVEN FACES OF DR. LAO:
Tony Randall plays almost every exhibit in the circus of Dr. Lao (including Dr. Lao himself). The most pathetic is an old and tired Pan who has seen all of human lust and is bored by it. The unimaginative inhabitants of the small town in which the circus plays have absolutely no understanding of the exotic creatures they are being shown.

From a magical nanny to a magical Chinaman was not that great a step. George Pal, who might be thought of as the poor man's Walt Disney, brought Charles Finney's strange and wonderful novel *The Circus of Dr. Lao* to the screen in the same year. *The Circus of Dr. Lao* had been something of a cult work since its publication in 1935. Totally unclassifiable, it tells of Dr. Lao's small circus, which visits a jerkwater town in Arizona. The circus features real wonders (a faun, a gorgon, a sea serpent), and the substance of the novel is the reaction of the cloddish inhabitants to the ancient and sophisticated beings displayed for dimes. The novel is definitely not for children; the movie, entitled *The Seven Faces of Dr. Lao,* was. But curiously enough, it became something of a charming entity of its own, despite the injection of a plot and a dear little boy.

Tony Randall pulled off a tour de force by playing Dr. Lao and most of the exhibits (Merlin, the abominable snowman, Medusa, Apollonius, and Pan. Despite the juvenile frame, certain moments of Finney's satirical magic surfaced in the film, particularly when the repressed schoolteacher (here a beautiful widow) enters

the tent of the faun and is totally undone by the steaming atmosphere of sensuality projected by the goat-footed creature who pipes and dances for her.

In the 1970s, light fantasy practically vanished from the movie screen, but the popularity of the supernatural horror movie eventually brought forth spin-offs and send-ups and rather peculiar hybrids, such as *Poltergeist* (1982), which suffered from not being able to make up its mind as to whether it wanted to be scary or funny. Inevitably, the humor undermined the horror, and the film became a study in what happens when a suburban family straight out of a detergent commercial finds that its split-level home is haunted by a poltergeist (a form of ghost that might be defined as the original bump in the night).

And, in a curious mutation, light fantasy worked its way from the television screen to the movie screen in *Twilight Zone— The Movie* (1983). The "Twilight Zone" series had been the epitome of television light fantasy—brief tales of the most ephemeral sort, which had nonetheless introduced several generations of children (the later ones through reruns) to fantasy. After the cult had persisted and grown

TWILIGHT ZONE—THE MOVIE:
In the usual run of things, successful movies become television series. In fantasy and science fiction, successful television series become movies. The film drawn from the perennial fantasy series *The Twilight Zone* reworked four episodes. The best of the lot had John Lithgow as a terrified airplane passenger, and something really nasty just visible on the wing of the plane.

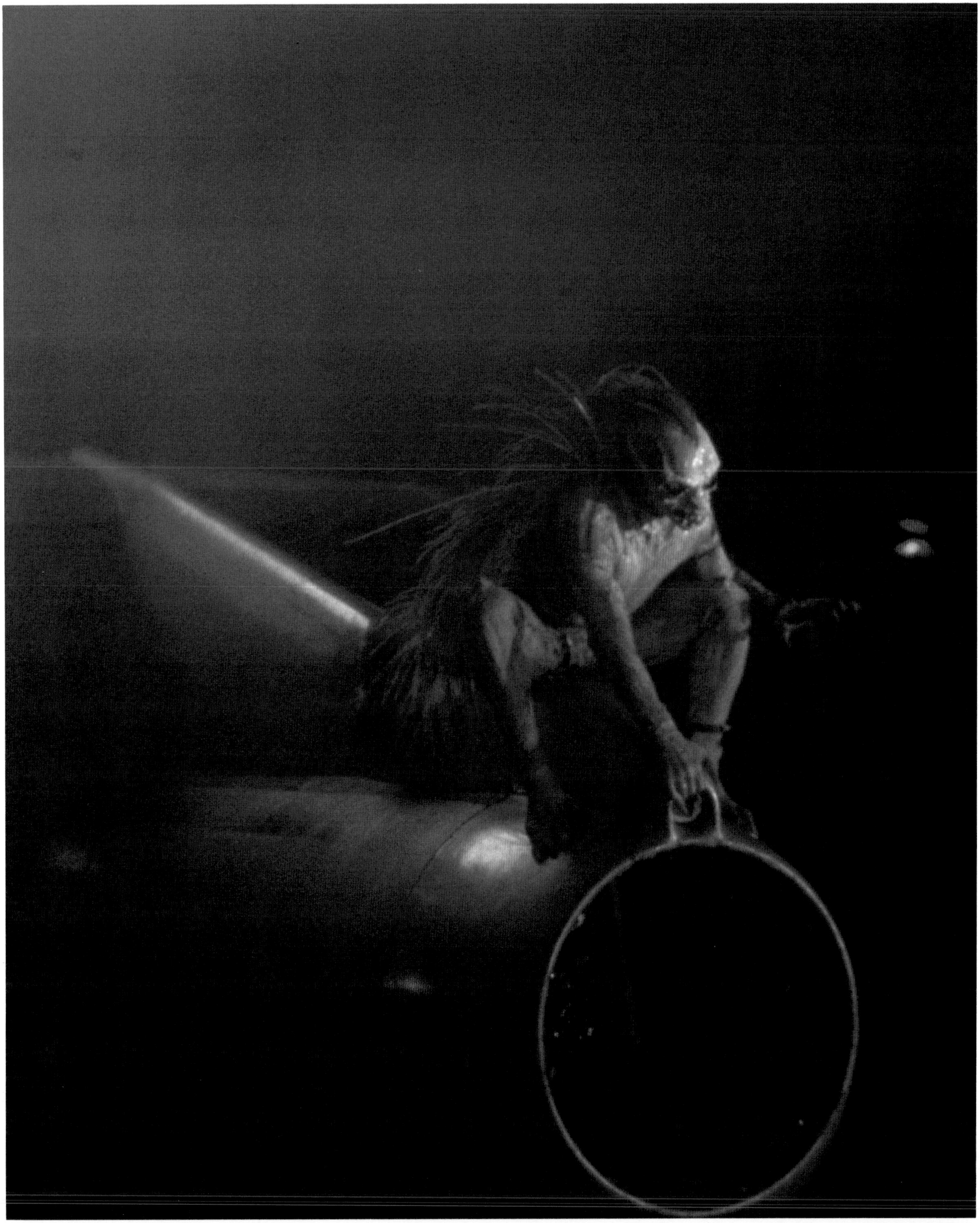

POLTERGEIST:

Heather O'Rourke is hanging onto the wicker-work for dear life because the malevolent forces at work in her nice suburban home are determined to blow her and her nice suburban family away. This schizophrenic film couldn't make up its mind whether to be a comedy about a sitcom family confronted with spooks or a horror movie about the dead returning. In any case, the title is technically incorrect according to spirit lore.

stronger over a score of years, four of the most famous episodes were reworked and produced for the big screen. As so often happens, this transfer worked against the material. Whimsical notions such as the inhabitants of an old folks' home who become children again, or a little boy with super mental powers who transforms his household into an animated nightmare, just didn't hold up. However, the final episode, in which an airplane passenger, terrified of flying to begin with, sees a gremlin — not the humorous gremlin of World War II flying mythology, but a demonic creature obviously bent on evil mischief — on the plane's wing, worked brilliantly. In it, John Lithgow turned in a performance of harrowing truth to anyone who has ever felt the slightest twinge of fear on board an aircraft.

The Purple Rose of Cairo (1985) took a giant step in sophistication for light fantasy; it could be called the first modern example of the genre, because the being that emerges into the real world to cause confusion here is not a creature from ancient mythology or folklore but a character from a not-very-major motion picture of the Depression years who suddenly addresses a remark to a member of the audience from the screen. This happens to be a bedraggled housewife who es-

capes her dreary life by seeing movies — the same movies — over and over again. The movie character, a sort of second lead glamour boy whose major function is to give the leading lady someone to flirt with, is dressed in puttees and a pith helmet (he's an explorer; the movie is called *The Purple Rose of Cairo*) and is enchanted by how often the housewife has been in the audience for *his* movie. So he steps down off the screen to get to know her better.

One of the delicious things about this movie (the *real* movie, not the movie *in* the movie; this can get complicated) is that from the initial unlikely premise, everything else follows absolutely logically in a wacky sort of way. The other characters in the movie are totally thrown for a loop by this unprecedented behavior, and sit around the glamorous (albeit black-and-white) penthouse set discussing how they can continue without the absentee. In the meantime, he is having a hard time adjusting to the real world, where love-making ends in sex rather than a chaste fadeout and cars don't start the minute you put your hands on the steering wheel. When the actor who has created the character is flown in to persuade the fugitive to get back into the movie, things get even more complicated (he also takes a shine to the dreary hausfrau). And when

THE PURPLE ROSE OF CAIRO:

The setting is a posh penthouse; the cast is a crowd of sophisticates about to go out on the town. However, they're in a state of deshabille since one of the leading characters walked off the screen, and the others have been waiting days for him to return. He's just done so, bringing with him a dowdy member of the audience. It's Mia Farrow, and the film will continue with her participation, to the confusion of all concerned.

the character *does* return to the movie, he takes her with him; we see her, in her dowdy, readymade frock, interacting with the movie's plot in scenes we have seen before without her, all to chaotic effect. For once, it is the bemused human who steals the show. Mia Farrow as the downtrodden moviegoer is fragile, funny, and ultimately heartbreaking as she is dazzled and deserted by her movie dreams.

Labyrinth (1986) went all the way back to the nineteenth century for its inspiration, to those Victorian children's books in which the juvenile hero/heroine, as punishment for thinking bad thoughts about a younger sibling, must go through all sorts of fantastic (and morally educational) adventures to rescue the brat, who has been abducted by supernatural forces. In this modern version, the girl (Jennifer Connelly) must rescue her baby brother from the King of the Goblins.

To do so, she must work her way through an endless labyrinth. Since the film is by Jim Henson of Muppet fame, there are any number of bizarre and diverting creatures and events waiting in its twists and turns. David Bowie made the most of the fiercely comic goblin king role, but the one-track plot, a determinedly unmagical rock score, and an unappealing performance by Connelly worked against Henson's fertile inventiveness.

Another film that went backward for inspiration was *Mannequin* (1987), which drew on the Thorne Smith tradition of the mundane confronting the magical and evoked memories of *Night Life of the*

LABYRINTH:

David Bowie is the Demon Prince who kidnaps the heroine's baby brother. He's a bit better dressed than your usual everyday ogre, and so are the members of his court.

Gods and *One Touch of Venus* with a department-store mannequin come to life. The dummy is animated by the spirit of a rebellious young lady of ancient Egypt (whose *modus operandi* of reincarnation through the ages is none too clear).

The object of the mannequin's affection is the young sculptor who has created her, in one of many jobs he has taken on and almost instantly loses because he *will* bring aesthetic sensibilities to his work (spending hours arranging a pizza topping, for instance). By sheer luck, he gets a job at the Prince Department Store where his creation has ended up; she not only comes to life magically each night, but she inspires brilliant display windows for which he gets the credit. The plot, such as it is, has to do with the villainous minions of the bigger, glitzier store that wants to buy up Prince at a bargain price and their attempts to suborn or eliminate the hero.

Mannequin has a sweetness that is rare for an eighties movie; the villains are comical rather than vicious, and the chases and general chaos in the aisles and at the counters of the department store are a sure delight for anyone who ever wanted to run amok in such a place. (Marvelous use was made of J. Wanamaker's classic premises in Philadelphia, with its multistory interior atrium.) Andrew McCarthy radiates charm as the aesthetically minded sculptor, making the viewer root for him all the way, and Meshach Taylor does a wonderful Butterfly McQueen drag turn as a flamboyantly mad window decorator. Again, depressingly, the main problem was the female lead; Kim Cattrall as the living mannequin showed all the magic of a giant Barbie doll and was easily topped in the acting department by her plastic double.

The Purple Rose of Cairo and *Mannequin* proved that the classic light fantasy movie is alive and well in the 1980s. Every era has its mythology, which can be set loose into reality, mixing laughter and wonder—a splendid combination for any age.

MANNEQUIN:

The disheveled lady making free with Andrew McCarthy's belt is the mannequin of the title. She is in reality an ancient Egyptian whose soul is currently residing in the department-store dummy, and she becomes flesh and blood at opportune moments.

DARK FANTASY

DRACULA (1931):
The archetypal Transylvanian count will always be Bela Lugosi, despite any number of other interpreters of the role. Lugosi had a successful career on the stage in his native Hungary (sometimes in light comedy!) before going into films. Typecast by his success in the role of the vampire, his career in movies would be an endless repeat of the mannerisms brought to that part. Here he has at the eternal underdog, Renfield (Dwight Frye).

The horror movie has long been an accepted (and profitable) area of filmmaking. There are really two kinds of horror movies. In one, the terror is inspired by a breakdown of human sanity, which results in some sort of menace to the ordinary folk in the film with whom the audience is meant to identify: a perfect example is *Psycho,* that masterful movie that has inspired so many unmasterfully bloody imitations. Then there's the film that's scary because the breakdown occurs not in human mentality but in the natural laws of the universe. Weird events occur, and weird creatures proliferate; the legends that have frightened listeners from the beginning of time are brought to life, and the audience is made uneasily aware that ghoulies, ghosties, long-legged beasties, and other such unnatural things just might exist.

Early movie magic often invoked the supernatural to show its stuff, and primitive one-reelers featured stage devils in (presumably red) union suits with horned hoods and wired tails. There's a classic example in the 1902 Méliès movie, *Blue-beard,* in which Bluebeard's wife is inveigled into entering the forbidden room by a Mephisto straight from a nineteenth-century production of *Faust.*

Literary sources were plundered for material, and a different sort of devil appeared in *The Student of Prague* (1913), adapted from Edgar Allan Poe's "William Wilson" (with a nod toward *Faust*), in which a poor student makes a bargain with a sinister stranger, who pays a large amount of money for the student's reflection. The reflection assumes a life of its own; it is eventually shot by the student, who then dies.

Other creatures came to life on the screen; the scientifically created monster of Frankenstein inspired any number of magically created Golems and other lumbering pseudohumans. The supernatural creature of evil came into its own with *Nosferatu, A Symphony of Terror* (1922), a German adaptation of Bram Stoker's *Dracula.* Even today, with any number of Draculas to look back on, Max Schrenck as Orlock, the Dracula figure, is memorably nasty. The makeup, the walk, the eyes all have nothing to do with humanity. And there are other elements in the film those used to the conventions of the many later Dracula movies would find surprising, such as the self-sacrificing death of the heroine, who keeps Orlock by her side until sunrise, and the vampire-inspired plague that devastates Bremen.

NOSFERATU:

The chilling figure of the vampire portrayed by Max Schreck is a far cry from the continental smoothness of the Count Dracula later immortalized by Bela Lugosi and his successors. In this early German adaptation of the Bram Stoker novel, the undead Count Orloc is only marginally human. This approach succeeds so well because it's a silent film; one can't imagine a voice loathsome enough to go with the image.

It was, however, the 1931 *Dracula* starring Bela Lugosi—the first major talking film of supernatural horror—that set the pattern for decades to come. For the first time of many we heard the touchstone line "Listen to them—the children of the night. What music they make!" delivered in the rich Middle European accents of the Count, referring to the howling of the wolves outside his Transylvanian castle.

Lugosi's performance and the legend of Dracula made a stunning impact. Despite endless variations on the theme, some of them brilliant in their own right, Dracula will always be the urbane Lugosi. The movie itself, involving a young English couple with the sinister Continental Count and his crazed, fly-eating slave, Renfield, was a superbly cinematic condensation (via the stage play) of Stoker's novel, despite moments that now seem ludicrous. (The most obvious example is an atmospheric shot of the castle's main hall complete with a pair of wandering armadillos, on the assumption that to the movie-going public of 1931 the small, unfamiliar beasties would appear to be some particularly repellent form of rodent.) Generally, however, the scenes in the dilapidated, cobwebby castle were chillingly right on target, as were the brief appearances of the Count's three vampiric consorts, dressed in white.

Dracula was only the first of three supernatural creatures who were to become, through the cinema, major factors in the mythology of our century. As with any mythology, few could name the creators of Dracula, the Mummy, and the Wolfman, but their images (and in Dracula's case, the voice) became instantly recognizable for generations to come.

Our carelessly wrapped friend the Mummy appeared in 1932, in *The Mummy* starring Boris Karloff; the discovery of Tutankhamen's tomb some years before, and the subsequent sensationalism regarding a curse on its discoverers, had laid well the way for a movie about dire happenings to those who dared meddle with such things. Here the tomb is that of Im-ho-tep, a priest of Phar-

THE MUMMY:

The setting for this early talking film was redolent of Hollywood's idea of the mystic East, and very effective it was, too. Here the exotic Zita Johann, as a modern young woman half-English, half-Egyptian, is about to be shown the past in a magic pool by Boris Karloff. She is unaware that he is an unwrapped survivor of Pharaonic Egypt, revived and determined to find his reincarnated lady love.

aonic Egypt of three thousand years ago, who was wrapped and entombed alive for attempting to revive from the dead the princess he loved. The scroll of immortality he had stolen to accomplish this was buried with him; when the tomb is opened, the scroll is read, and Im-ho-tep lives again. Im-ho-tep escapes into modern Cairo, unwraps, and seeks the reincarnation of his princess-love. The lovely half-Egyptian girl he fixes on finds strange archaic memories stirring in her, particularly when presented with the belongings of the long-dead woman. Im-ho-tep intends for her to share his immortality, but to do so, she must first die, so Im-ho-tep lays plans for a ceremonial sacrifice in the Cairo Museum. Will the hero be able to get in after hours and rescue her?

Silliness, of course, but silliness laden with atmosphere. The limping, wrapped figure was nightmarishly frightening to audiences of the thirties, and even without packaging, Boris Karloff radiated menace and mystery. It was not this film, however, that set the iconography of the cinematic Mummy, but a follow-up (without Karloff) using the same theme, which itself had several sequels. From these later films came the mummy Kharis, the Princess Ananka, and the sacred revivifying tana leaves.

Carl Dreyer's *Vampyr* (1932) must be mentioned, but it presents the inevitable problems of the real artist (the Danish Dreyer was one of a very few directors of the day to concern himself with literally creating art) who bases his work on a theme usually confined to popular entertainment. *Vampyr* is a classic to the cinéaste, but it is highly likely to send the moviegoer in search of a good horror film into a state of either torpor or confusion, due to the many touches of surrealism

VAMPYR:

This vampire film by the noted Danish director Carl Dreyer is stylized to the point of surrealism. Deliberately shot in bleached, misty images, it concerns a young man and his involvement with two sisters, the victims of a vampire. One dies; the other goes with the young man across a river, on the shore of which had earlier appeared an old man carrying a scythe, with a tolling bell on the sound track. Make of it what you will.

THE WEREWOLF OF LONDON:

Henry Hull makes the acquaintance of a lupine fellow, obviously on the night of a full moon. Hull, who was later to play any number of venerable gentlemen in films, was not subjected to the full wolf-man makeup that would eventually make Lon Chaney, Jr.'s lycanthrope so memorable, and the rest of the film was almost equally restrained (that is, as werewolf movies go).

Dreyer used throughout the film. (Pauline Kael sums it up from the highbrow point of view by writing, "Most vampire movies are so silly that this movie by Carl Dreyer — a great vampire film — hardly belongs to the genre.")

But for those who value aesthetics above simple narrative thrills, *Vampyr* is an extraordinary experience, so far as can be judged from the poorly dubbed and badly edited prints available. Loosely based on Sheridan Le Fanu's *Carmilla* (which would be filmed many more times, mostly to exploit the erotic possibilities of the female vampire), it takes place in a bleached world where a traveler encounters, in a sinister inn, a sickly girl (daughter of the innkeeper) watched over by an old hag and a mysterious doctor. The old woman is a vampire, the doctor her helper, the girl her victim. Attempting to help her, the young hero becomes enmeshed in surrealist delusions and dreams, including one of himself in a coffin being carried to the graveyard. Indeed, *Vampyr* does stand apart from other vampire films, since its aims are entirely dif-

ferent, but it must also be acknowledged as a major influence on the genre in decor, atmosphere, and camerawork.

The Werewolf had several trial runs before catching on, the most notable of which was *Werewolf of London* (1935). It's a tangled tale of a botanist in the Himalayas (Henry Hull) who seeks out a rare flower that blooms only by moonlight. While gathering the blossoms, he is attacked by a wolflike creature; on returning to London, he discovers that he too becomes wolflike during the period of the full moon. A mysterious Oriental gentleman tells him that the Himalayan flower is the only thing that will counteract the affliction. The botanist takes refuge in the time of the full moon in a cheap rooming house in the slums of London while he waits for his specimen of the plant to bloom, but the Oriental man, actually the creature that attacked him initially, beats him to it. In the end the botanist's beautiful wife (the ever-imperiled Valerie Hobson) becomes his prey and must be saved in the usual end-of-the-last-reel dustup. Here was established a final shot that

DRACULA'S DAUGHTER:

The word vampire as applied to a woman had meant an exploiter of sexuality, such as those played by the eternal "vamp," Theda Bara, until Gloria Holden portrayed an authentic female creature of the night. In the first sequel to the very successful *Dracula*, she is Countess Marya Zaleska, the daughter of Dracula, who here presides at the cremation of her father's body.

would be seen again and again — the face of the dead wolf creature dissolving into the face of the anguished hero.

Despite one or two illogical moments, *Werewolf of London* is neat and intelligent, without any of the howlers that were to plague the genre in later versions. And buried in the body of the film are two unexpected comedic gems: Ethel Griffies and Zeffie Tilbury as the slum landlady and a tipsy crony in a pub conversation that's pure English music hall, and clinging to each other in bibulous horror at the weird noises coming from the wolfman's room.

In 1936, to Dracula comes a daughter. *Dracula's Daughter* is atypical in that it continues directly from the climax of its predecessor. The vampire-fighter Van Helsing has been arrested for the murder

of Dracula (speak of ingratitude!); in the meantime, a mysterious woman cloaked in black attempts to claim the body. She is revealed as Dracula's offspring, Marya, a female vampire who longs to rid herself of the curse of the undead and is enamored of Dr. Garth, a student of Van Helsing's (who has been freed due to the disappearance of Dracula's body — stolen, of course, by Marya). Unfortunately, her natural instincts surface. There is a wave of vampiric attacks in the neighborhood, and Garth's fiancée is kidnapped. He follows them to the Transylvanian castle of the Draculas, where there is the usual last-minute rescue, and Marya is done in by a wooden arrow through the heart.

Dracula's Daughter is almost on the level of the original. The script, decor, and camerawork all show signs of sophistication. Gloria Holden has enormous presence as Marya, with a world-weary, seductive languor quite appropriate to the daughter of Lugosi's Count. Her wardrobe ranges from the expected cowled cloaks to *haute couture* deco gowns in which she looks the stunning embodiment of the exotic adventuress.

The werewolf found his place in the sun (or moon, as it were) with *The Wolfman* (1941), which finally gave the audience a lycanthrope with whom it could identify. Henry Hull in *Werewolf of London* had been a pretty chilly fellow, but Lon Chaney, Jr., as poor Larry Talbot, a nice guy who is badly bitten in protecting a girl from a wolf, stirred audience emotions as the innocent victim of a random curse. The wolf, it seems, was really a gypsy afflicted with lycanthropy, and Talbot soon begins to feel the effects of the

tradition of "bit by a werewolf, become a werewolf." Things don't go too well for him from then on; he roves the forest, hirsute, fanged, and alive with blood-lust brought on by the full moon. The movie ends in a fog-shrouded clearing, as he attacks his lady love (who, like all lady loves in such films, *will* go wandering about at night) and is beaten to death by his own father with a silver-headed cane. The junior Chaney never had much in the way of charisma, but his air of a none-too-bright bloodhound (used brilliantly a year earlier in the film of *Of Mice and Men,* in which he played Lennie) made him a sympathetic Wolfman. He was ably supported by a superior cast, including Lugosi as the gypsy wolf, the minute but unforgettable Maria Ouspenskaya as the gypsy's knowledgeable mother, and Claude Rains as the older Talbot.

THE WOLF MAN:

The pattern for werewolves was set by Lon Chaney, Jr., and his hirsute makeup. Here, on one of the bad nights of the month, he prowls the atmospheric woodlands of his family estate. The cart in the background belongs to the gypsies who afflicted him with this curse to begin with. They are, of course, from Eastern Europe, the traditional source of lycanthropy and vampirism, two intertwined legends.

THE CAT PEOPLE:

The malevolently staring cat in the portrait behind Simone Simon is a clue to her heritage. The women of her (unspecified) middle-European country are the female equivalents of werewolves. Interestingly indicative of the period in which the film was made is the idea that a female would, of course, turn into a cat, and that the change would be brought about by interior emotion rather than an external cause such as the full moon.

Large fierce felines seemed a logical step from large fierce canines, and so came *The Cat People* in 1942. It somehow seemed unmanly for a male to turn into a cat, no matter how menacing, so the "werepanther" would have to be a woman. It also seemed un-American, so she would have to be some sort of foreigner. The petite French actress of the redundant name Simone Simon was cast in the role of Irena, whose female family members (from some unnamed but undoubtedly Central European country neighboring on Transylvania) have a tradition of turning into large cats under emotional stress. The existence of this family trait is ridiculed by Irena's American husband, but when her peculiar fancies drive him to the company of another woman, a large panther-like creature indeed begins to make its presence felt, and when Irena's psychiatrist forces his attentions on her, he is killed by fang and claw. Irena meets a tragic end in the local zoo, attempting to free a panther from its cage.

The script of *The Cat People* is forced and often illogical, but the movie has achieved classic status because it succeeded in scaring the pants off the audience with almost nothing overtly menacing visible on the screen. All the fright was accomplished by implication, either visual or aural. With this film Val Lewton—one of a very few Hollywood producers to leave his mark on his films—almost singlehandedly remade the horror genre. (A sequel, *The Curse of the Cat People,* deals with Irena's daughter, but curiously enough it is a gentle fantasy having nothing at all to do with marauding human felines.)

Another werewolf emerged in *The Undying Monster* (1942). The film simplified Jessie Kerruish's extraordinarily complex thriller of inherited lycanthropy, but the

I WALKED WITH A ZOMBIE:

This, in fact, is the walk that nurse Frances Dee (center) takes with her patient (Christine Hordon), who has been zombified—by her mother-in-law, as it turns out. On the way they meet a native who has obviously been through the same process. The folklore of Haiti was the basis for this atmospheric melodrama, the basic plot of which has a strong resemblance to *Jane Eyre*.

THE UNINVITED:

In what is probably the most perfect classic ghost story ever filmed, Ray Milland and Ruth Hussey check out what seems to be a totally innocent, sunlit studio in their new house. But the flowers the lady is carrying will wilt in seconds when left behind there. Something is definitely wrong.

basic theme remained the same — the eldest son becomes a werewolf, but only under certain circumstances. The script is an intelligent one, and there is a memorably frightening moment worthy of Val Lewton when, at a lakeside by night, the shrill chorus of frogs suddenly stops, by its absence announcing the presence of the monster.

In the thirties, the public had become entranced with the primitive exoticism of Haiti, and particularly its black-magical religion, voodoo. Any number of books were written to prove the existence of zombies, the Haitian "walking dead." Inevitably the walking dead lurched onto the movie screen as another supernatural menace. Again Val Lewton created an atmospheric something out of nothing — in this case the script of *I Walked with a Zombie* (1943), which involves a Haitian plantation quadrangle of husband, lecherous half-brother, catatonic wife, and beautiful, newly arrived resident nurse. The nurse falls for the husband; guilt and her sense of nursely duty make her doubly attentive to the insensible wife. The natives believe that the catatonic lady is a victim of voodoo magic and that only a voodoo priest can cure her. In the title sequence, the nurse leads the entranced wife through the dark countryside, rife with voodoo symbols and native zombies, to meet with the local "priest." This turns out to be the half-brothers' mother, who has taken up voodooism in an attempt to introduce modern medical practices subtly to the natives. She has mastered authentic voodoo magic and is responsible for her daughter-in-law's condition, having learned that she was planning to run away with her husband's brother.

This improbable stew ends with the brother walking into the sea bearing the body of the wife, who may or may not be undead at this point. Lewton managed to package the pulp idiocies of the script into a movie with a genuinely eerie quality, and one that is often visually beautiful.

The Uninvited (1944) was perhaps the closest Hollywood ever came to produc-

THE PICTURE OF DORIAN GRAY:

Honestly, chaps, if you looked like this, wouldn't you want to stay young forever? Hurd Hatfield's male beauty made Dorian Gray's bargain with the dark powers to age his portrait rather than himself almost believable.

ing a pure, unadulterated, classic ghost story. This modest little film was something special, since the execution was as unpretentious and effective as the premise. In it, a brother and sister from the city buy an old house on the coast of Cornwall. Stella, a young woman in the village, lived in the house as a child; when she returns to it as a visitor, odd events occur, and it appears that it is haunted by the ghost of her mother. Paradoxically, there is also a sense of menace to the girl. The climax involves a manifestation of the ghostly visitor (classically done as a wavering white presence) and a hairbreadth escape for Stella, with a surprise ending as to the exact nature of the haunting.

Tension is roused with small, chilling details. A rose brought into a certain room is seen by the camera (but not the characters) to wilt almost immediately. Perhaps the most satisfying aspect of the movie is that everyone in it acts intelligently; the city folk, initially resistant to the idea of supernatural events, accept the evidence of their senses and act accordingly.

Equally successful in an entirely different way was the filming of Oscar Wilde's *The Picture of Dorian Gray* (1945). Here was a product of the extraordinary expertise that the studios of Hollywood had developed in many areas over four decades: high-keyed, menacing photography; beautiful, lavish, and more or less accurate decor and costumes; a script that caught the spirit of the Wilde novel if not the letter; and actors who were at worst competent, and in several cases exactly right, in both looks and performance, for their roles.

Portrait painting was not exactly an art in demand for films, but the very essence of the story is the titular portrait and the studios came up with perfection. (This is perhaps why the film worked so well; Wilde's concept revolved around a visual experience, ideally realized more successfully on screen than in print.) The beautiful, young Dorian Gray, darling of mid-Victorian society, resents the fact that his newly finished portrait will always remain young, while he himself will grow old. He wishes the reverse to be true, and some dark power (never specified, but visually centered on an ancient statue of a cat) grants the wish.

Years later, Dorian has not changed, though his friends have all aged. He is still the picture of healthy youth, although there are rumors in society of his scandalous debaucheries in parts of London not usually frequented by members of his class. In a locked room — the old schoolroom — of his exquisitely furnished house, he keeps the portrait hidden beneath a cover. Now and then he looks at it; it grows older, more hideous, more degenerate over the years. Dorian's ways become ever more destructive as time goes on: he is responsible for the death of an innocent music-hall singer, and he eventually murders the artist who painted the original portrait. Finally, in despair, he plunges a knife into the demonic picture; he is later found dead, an aged, debauched corpse beneath the picture of the serene, beautiful young man he once was.

The various stages of the portrait were created for the film by the Albright brothers, noted painters of the period. They are completely effective and rendered even more startling by being photographed in color, in contrast to the black-and-white of the rest of the film. The picture's subject, Dorian Gray, was an icily handsome newcomer to the screen, Hurd Hatfield. George Sanders tossed off the Wilde witticisms impeccably as Dorian's friend Lord Henry, and another comparative newcomer, Angela Lansbury, made an indelibly touching impression as the music-hall singer.

Supernatural fantasy in the movies suffered a long hiatus after World War II. Sociologists might make the case that a comparatively untroubled and optimistic society has no need for it (and also might make something of its return), but for whatever reasons, the horror fantasy degenerated into weak series and slapstick. (Abbott and Costello "met" all the legendary creatures in various low-budget features during this period.) Chills were provided instead by atom-age terrors such as the Blob.

But you can't keep a good Thing down, apparently, and the children of the night made a spectacular comeback in the sixties — but with a difference or two. The most obvious change was the almost universal switch to color. Simplistically, this

THE INNOCENTS:

Deborah Kerr gave a masterly performance as the troubled governess, Miss Giddens, in a film version of the stage hit based on Henry James's *The Turn of the Screw*. Are her young charges haunted by the ghosts of two malevolent servants? James's ambiguity is still present on screen, though the audience sees the "ghosts" even as the governess pretends not to. Peter Wyngarde is the spectral Peter Quint.

THE HAUNTING:

Based on Shirley Jackson's disturbing novel, this film took the standard situation of four varied people in a haunted house and made it into an eerie exercise of mental breakdown promoted by an actively evil environment. The design of the house was wonderfully conceived. Julie Harris, here being restrained by Richard Johnson on a highly unreliable antique stair, was the most susceptible of the four.

might account for the infinitely greater amounts of gore; the screen from then on was incarnadined. But the reasons were deeper than strictly technological. Audiences' tolerance of and desire for physical violence had grown, and all too often subtlety, craft, and the induced *frisson* gave way to hack, splatter, and nausea.

Vampire, mummy, and wolfman were revived in innumerable variations with increasing emphasis on the gruesome. Among the endless cheap thrills, however, some films still managed to chill by implication and terrify with taste. Curiously—and indicatively—most of the movies that stood out were in black-and-

white. One minor masterpiece seemed a long-delayed culmination of the old style rather than a manifestation of the new. This was *The Innocents* (1961), a movie version, via the stage, of Henry James's ambiguous ghost story *The Turn of the Screw,* coscripted by Truman Capote. It is the story of a repressed governess caring for two children in a lonely country house—which may or may not be haunted by the spirits of her dead predecessor, Miss Jessel—and that woman's evil lover, the valet, Peter Quint.

The current governess takes it upon herself to fight the insidious, unspoken-of influence of the ghosts on the children. As

BURN WITCH, BURN:

Peter Wyngarde may think that wife Janet Blair is making a salad, but the materials are those for casting spells. She is determined to advance his academic career in this story of faculty wives who carry on campus politics through witchcraft.

THE BIRDS:

It's not just the weight on the roof that Rod Taylor and his family are worried about. The gathering of gulls exudes an air of quiet menace that will soon turn murderous. The Hitchcock film is perhaps the first to use the theme of Mother Nature turning against mankind in a big way. It was based on a short story by Daphne du Maurier, better known for more conventional Gothic thrillers such as the classic *Rebecca.*

her fear grows, so does the tension of the story. The novel leaves it to the reader to decide whether there are supernatural influences at work or if everything is the product of the woman's inner turmoil. The film, by showing Miss Jessel and Quint (dimly or at a distance), confirms their existence, though some have argued that the camera is but reflecting what the governess thinks she is seeing. Whichever, the suspense is extreme, and it is all accomplished by the technique stemming from *The Cat People* and other Lewton films: almost everything fearsome is suggested but not really shown. The terror is subtly reinforced by the oblique nastiness of the visual imagery, sliding from the children at play in the sunny grounds of the house to toads and insects on the decaying statuary in the garden.

Deborah Kerr's performance as the governess was a tour de force of suppressed fright; the two children (Martin Stephens and Pamela Franklin, who became a talented adult actress) were superb. The film was directed by Jack Clayton.

Burn Witch, Burn (1962) was, confusingly enough, based on Fritz Leiber's classic novel of witchcraft, *Conjure Wife,* and not on A. Merritt's *Burn, Witch, Burn!* (which became *The Devil-Doll* on screen). It's a modest but intelligent thriller laid in that most quiet and staid of settings, the college campus (this was in the *early* sixties, mind you). A new faculty wife discovers that the wives of her husband's colleagues are manipulating university politics by witchcraft, which is treated as just as valid and coherent as any of the natural sciences, and there are some exceedingly nasty goings-on.

Carnival of Souls (1962) was an amazing little film, made independently on an absolutely minute budget. The protagonist, a young female organist, is about to take a new job away from her home, when her car runs off a bridge. Well after hope has been given up for her survival, she crawls from the river. Seemingly none the worse for her experience, she settles into her new position. But she is haunted

in a most peculiar way — she finds herself being watched by an unnervingly pale and disembodied face. The key, for a change, is in the character of the woman herself, which reveals itself to be alienated and cold, but terrifyingly stubborn. She is, of course, dead from the accident, and the creature watching her is — perhaps — Death. She is finally confronted by the creature and its minions in a deserted amusement park, built on a pier over a disturbingly still and sunlit lake.

There is stunning use of unspecific menace throughout *Carnival of Souls.* The omnipresent watcher is never overtly threatening, but its appearances are always unexpected no matter how much you anticipate them — a true sign of good scare tactics. One moment is truly memorable. The woman is driving in a deserted landscape at that special time just after sunset when everything appears not just still, but dead. Suddenly the face is staring into the side window of the moving car.

With a somber, unpleasant organ score and a peculiarly compelling performance by Candace Hilligoss (who indeed conveys a still, dead quality) in the lead, *Carnival of Souls* is the perfect example of the small-scaled, inexpensive movie made into a work of art by craft and intelligence.

More expensive films were made with craft and intelligence, too. *The Haunting* (1963), based on Shirley Jackson's novel *The Haunting of Hill House,* had two major stars of the period, those excellent actresses Julie Harris and Claire Bloom. Their characters, having shown evidence of sensitivity to psychic phenomena, are selected by a psychic investigator to help him prove that evil influences are loose in an old house with a particularly nasty history. Again the emphasis is on the characters of the people involved. The repressed spinster played by Harris, the emotional center of the film, becomes more and more unglued as the frightening phenomena of the house manifest themselves. These phenomena are particularly hair-raising because while they are insanely irrational, they are somehow tied

to her deteriorating psyche. Here the instability of madness is added to the instability of natural laws gone awry. Especially impressive is the main set, the old house, which was photographed in a manner subtly jarring to the eye; none of the angles seems quite right.

Alfred Hitchcock, who usually dealt with the aberrations of humanity, took a rare flyer into fantasy with a movie about the aberrations of the animal — or, more correctly, avian — kingdom. *The Birds* (1963), based on a short story by Daphne du Maurier, showed us a perfectly ordinary California community whose bird population suddenly, *en masse,* turns against the human: our feathered friends suddenly become our murderous enemies. The shock value of the film comes from the realization of just how much damage birds, usually considered the most harmless of nature's creatures, can do in quantity. An overwrought subplot involving the human characters was used to fill out what was essentially a one-idea script, but the birds, perched menacingly in their numbers or flying in flocks, are the stars.

During this same period the quickie producer/director Roger Corman made a series of color horror films, usually using the excellent talents of Charles Beaumont and/or Richard Matheson in the writing department and the special quality of actor Vincent Price. Many of these had something to do with the works of Edgar Allan Poe in one way or another (ranging from combining several of Poe's short stories into one film to pasting a Poe title on what was basically a story by H. P. Lovecraft). It's generally agreed that the most stylish of these was *The Masque of the Red Death* (1964), and it came about as close to being a masque as a popular horror movie could. In stately, Gothic fashion, it tells of the twelfth-century Prince Prospero, who is everything the wicked nobleman should be — he exploits the peasants economically and sexually while living a debauched and luxurious life. During an outbreak of the plague called the Red Death, Prospero holds a masked ball

THE MASQUE OF THE RED DEATH:

Vincent Price is Prince Prospero, who is giving a masked ball to distract the elite from the ravages of the plague known as the Red Death. Who is the tall cowled figure in red who enters late in the revelries? Three guesses. Taking its cue from the Poe story, the movie pulled out all the stops on its color photography.

THE FEARLESS VAMPIRE KILLERS:

The historically minded will note an odd discrepancy in costume in this ball scene. The costumers were, indeed, on the ball, since the participants are the undead of many periods, risen from their graves to dance until dawn. It was this sort of detail that made Roman Polanski's vampire movie more than just a hilarious spoof.

for his friends, little knowing that the Red Death personified (looking very much like a scarlet version of the hooded figure from *The Seventh Seal*) is waiting outside the gates (playing solitaire—a nice touch). It enters at the height of the party, gradually emerging from the costumed crowd, which is struck down person-by-person by its presence. The finale is the Red Death's pursuit of Prospero through a series of spectacular, monochromatically lit and decorated rooms. It's all pretty simplistic and even garish but nevertheless often striking, and certainly it is an attempt to bring style back to a genre in which it had been in short supply since the influence of *Caligari*'s bizarre sets had waned.

A hapless nineteenth-century apprentice encountering a mad variety of vampires, including a Jewish one on whom the cross doesn't work and a homosexual one on which his charms do (not that he wants them to), might seem more of a light fantasy than a dark one, and indeed Roman Polanski's *The Fearless Vampire Killers* (1967) had a lot of laughs. However, it didn't gain them at the expense of the genre conventions, and it was as spooky as it was spoofy. Polanski, who also starred as the young man forever gurgling in panic as both his blood and his virtue are constantly threatened, showed brilliant comedic gifts, and Jack MacGowran as the dithering vampire-hunting professor was nearly as funny.

But the vampire-ridden castle of Count Kroloc is a frightening place, and when a vampire ball is held, the spectacle of the myriad undead rising from their graves and dancing in costumes of their long-past lifetimes truly evokes a sense of horrified wonder.

A sign of the times was that a novel of the supernatural actually hit the best-seller lists in 1967. Common enough today, this was unprecedented at the time. The novel was Ira Levin's *Rosemary's Baby,* and it was transferred to the screen with all possible speed and, for a change, with all possible fidelity. The resulting Roman Polanski movie was a stunning new direction for the supernatural horror film, which would never quite be the same again. Its differences were twofold. One

ROSEMARY'S BABY:

The infant is, of course, fathered by Satan in this trendsetting movie. With material that could easily have verged on the ludicrous (as proved by many of the subsequent imitations), Roman Polanski fashioned a film that was fiercely taut, remarkably close to the novel by Ira Levin, and, above all, believable (essential to all great movies of the supernatural). Mia Farrow's performance as Rosemary was superb, a major factor in the movie's success.

was the realistic handling of the story of a young couple who move into a classic apartment house in New York City. The fragile young wife is bothered by but patient with the attentions of the kindly, eccentric old couple next door. The slow disclosure that they are devotees of a satanic cult, and that Rosemary, the young wife, has been selected to bear the child of Satan is beautifully paced and unnervingly contrasted with the ongoing daily life of the city.

The other difference was the direct usage of the darker aspects of Christian mythology. Vampires, werewolves, and the like were pagan remnants to be routed by Christian symbols signifying the good. Here the stuff of Christianity itself was used, as in medieval times, to prove the existence of evil, which, even more stunningly, was left (at least temporarily) triumphant. It was quite literally a revelation.

The works of the classic writer of horror stories, H. P. Lovecraft, have often been used as the basis for movies—but never with much success, since he was a wordsmith and his interdimensional horrors did not lend themselves to the pictorial. The most successful of the Lovecraft films was *The Dunwich Horror* (1969), which at least partially captured the quality of

THE DUNWICH HORROR:

Based on what is perhaps the best-known story of H. P. Lovecraft, this 1969 film made at least a brave attempt to capture the Lovecraftian quality, despite the introduction of a comely female (the eternal adolescent of the 1950s, Sandra Dee). Former child star Dean Stockwell was the mad Wilbur Whateley, determined to bring back the dreaded Old Ones to take over the Earth. The book is Lovecraft's famed mythical tome *The Necronomicon.*

nasty things being conjured up in the backwoods of New England by decadent, inbred descendants of colonial witches and warlocks. This one probably worked because it didn't try to show directly the monstrous thing set loose, but used suggestive special effects to convey its presence. The puritan Lovecraft, however, probably turned over in his grave at the presence of Sandra Dee as that cinematic necessity, the imperiled nubile female, particularly when his most famous literary creation, the forbidden book *The Necronomicon,* was propped in her crotch during the final ritual.

England had taken the lead in churning out the new breed of color horrors, not only by using the old themes and characters (Dracula seemed to rise at least three or four times a year for a while), but by drawing on the great wealth of the darker superstition and folklore of pagan and puritan Britain. Most of these were simply excuses for more shock tactics, but a few really evoked the fearsomeness of evil powers waiting to be set free. Such a one was *The Blood on Satan's Claw* (1970). In the seventeenth century a weird skeleton is unearthed from a field in rural England. Before it can be fully investigated it disappears, and soon the nearby village is plagued by a series of terrifying manifestations, and the inhabitants, particularly the young, are taking part in pagan rituals and satanic cults. As is so often the case with British productions, the quality of the historical period is remarkably reproduced. The film is unusual in having no particular protagonist; the narrative is concerned with all the inhabitants of the village and how the unloosed power affects them. And since that power is delib-

BLOOD ON SATAN'S CLAW:

The discovery of a demonic artifact in a village field in seventeenth-century England raises supernatural forces and revives pagan rituals among the locals, particularly the children and adolescents. That's Linda Hayden leading the revival.

THE WICKER MAN:

That's Christopher Lee heading the May Day procession, as the traditional "man-woman," and Edward Woodward hiding behind the traditional fool's mask. Woodward, as a policeman searching for a missing girl on an island off the coast of Scotland, suspects — and is about to find out for certain — that these May Day rituals are not just quaint, meaningless revivals of past customs but decidedly serious religious ceremonies.

erately unspecified, it is all the more frightening.

Another example of the small, unpretentious movie that managed to be both original and frightening was *The Man Who Haunted Himself* (1970), which updates the ancient idea of the *doppelganger*. Harold Pelham is a successful young executive who carries an umbrella and wears a small mustache, a bowler, and starched collars. He is impotent in his marriage and conservative in his business. After an automobile accident in which he is seriously injured, his heart stops on the operating table. He is resuscitated by the surgeons, and for a moment the monitoring machine shows two heartbeats simultaneously.

When he recovers, small incidents begin to plague him. An associate claims to have seen him in town when he was recuperating in Spain. A friend comes for a

drink and Pelham doesn't remember inviting him. He has been seen at the club at times when he knows he wasn't there. The incidents escalate. A beautiful young woman says that he has been sleeping with her. He finds that he is supposed to have been involved in corporate espionage.

It becomes clearer and clearer that someone has been posing as him — obviously an exact double. He comes ever closer to meeting him, just missing him at his home and his office. In every case, everyone assumes that the other person is Pelham. His wife leaves him because of their troubled domestic life, and Pelham, doubting his own sanity, checks into a sanitarium for a short period. When he comes out, the double has taken over his life and convinced all concerned — his wife, servants, and best friend — that *he* is the real Pelham. And in a sense he is. In that moment on the operating table he emerged and since then has very cleverly taken over. The film is remarkably straightforward and taut, with nothing extraneous getting in the way of the story. Roger Moore is extremely good as Pelham, particularly in the last panicky moments when he realizes that the double has won.

The Wicker Man (1972), another British film dealing with the darker aspects of Britain's legendary past, rapidly achieved

THE MAN WHO HAUNTED HIMSELF:

Roger Moore is talking to himself. This little-known film from 1970 concerned a highly respectable businessman whose life is slowly but surely taken over by a doppelgänger, a part of himself that has materialized as a separate being during a surgical crisis. Here for the first time he hears his own voice on the other end of the wire.

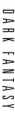

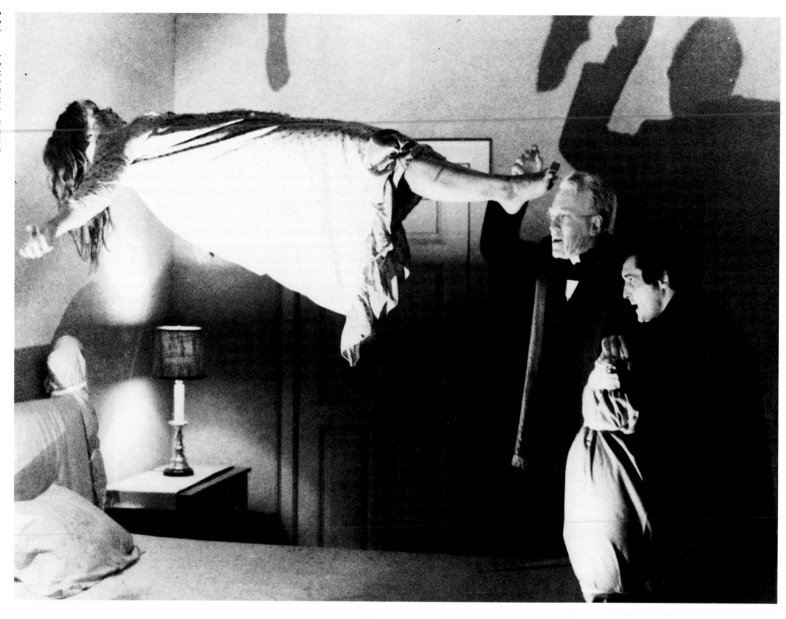

THE EXORCIST:

Though it has the look of the private performance of a vaudeville magic act, Linda Blair's levitation is one of the less harrowing manifestations of the quite unpleasant demon that has taken up residence in her body. Max Von Sydow is the titular gentleman of the cloth who is trying to get her down.

cult status despite (or perhaps because of) extremely bad distribution and a poorly done editing job on the version shown in the United States. In this film the past (or aspects thereof) still exists into modern times. A policeman goes to a small village on an island off the Scottish coast to investigate a disappearance. Everyone denies knowing the missing girl. The policeman begins to realize that the inhabitants are cultural holdouts of a pagan past, still engaged in the (sometimes nasty) rituals that we know only from such sanitized remnants as the Maypole. Afraid that the missing girl may be destined for sacrifice, he joins the May Day celebrations. But it seems that *he* is to be the sacrifice; the girl's disappearance was simply a lure. He is burnt alive in a wicker cage, in the legendary fashion of ancient Britain.

Despite the banality of the satanic-cult-meets-unsuspecting-stranger plot, which had been done badly in a hundred movies, *The Wicker Man* has surprising depth (the script is by the eminent playwright Anthony Shaffer). The policeman is no standard hero; he is a moralistic, inhibited Christian (in an excellent performance by Edward Woodward). His conflict with (and attraction to) the pagan villagers is therefore on more than a surface, action level. And the pagan rites convey the feeling of pre-Christian times; rather than the usual dreary cowled figures standing around mumbling nonsense, *these* pagans are very much concerned with fertility and everything that goes with it.

Back in the United States, *The Exorcist* (1973) was notable for being a resounding box-office hit and for letting loose a flood of demonic-possession films that has yet to stop. Otherwise, it had all the dramatic complexity of a tired doctor curing a child of whooping cough. The public, however, was captured by the unpleasant but spectacular makeup and special effects lavished on the modern girl inhabited by a demon.

The endless imitations of *The Exorcist* theme (which might be called pandemonium in the original sense of the word)

DRACULA (1979):

Any number of famous players have essayed the role of Count Dracula, including Max Schreck, Christopher Lee, Lon Chaney, Jr., John Carradine, Jack Palance, David Niven, George Hamilton, and, of course, Bela Lugosi. Perhaps the only performance to seriously rival Lugosi's was the sensuous and intelligent portrayal by Frank Langella in the 1979 remake.

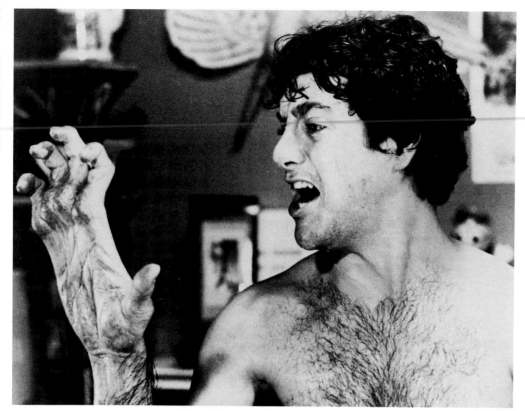

This awkwardly titled movie couldn't make up its mind whether to be a serious horror film or a teenage comedy, but there were some authentically frightening effects, such as this one when the American student played by David Naughton begins to change into a wolf for the first time. The horrendously mutable skin was a great advance on the all-too-familiar close-up of the progressively more hirsute face, overused in werewolf films.

brought the supernatural fantasy genre to another period of repetitiveness, not helped by unoriginal spin-offs of the classic night creatures, the vampire and the werewolf (often as comedies which usually weren't very funny). There were the exceptions. A new *Dracula* (1979) stuck much closer to the Stoker novel than the Lugosi version and gave us the silken Frank Langella of the beautiful voice as the vampire. *An American Werewolf in London* (1981) was uncertain as to whether it was a serious werewolf movie or an adolescent comedy, but it did have some spectacular shape-shifting scenes for the American teenager bitten by an English werewolf, using the writhing flesh effect first seen in *Altered States*. And David Bowie and the ageless Catherine Deneuve were a striking pair of modern vampires in *The Hunger* (1983), beautifully photographed if not totally believable.

There was hope in the rare attempts at something different, if not altogether new. Jack Clayton, whose way with children and the supernatural had been so aptly demonstrated in *The Innocents,* directed a film adaptation of the Ray Brad-

bury novel *Something Wicked This Way Comes* (1983). A cheap carnival comes to a small Midwestern town in the 1930s; unlike the circus of Dr. Lao, this show is purely malefic, feeding on the fantasies of the townsfolk and, in a way, gaining their souls for their fantasies fulfilled. The carnival's owner, Dr. Dark, is initially opposed by only two young boys, who realize what is going on.

Too diffuse and symbolic to match the terrifying crescendo of *The Innocents,* and at times verging perilously close to being cloying, *Something Wicked* still managed to be sometimes scary as well as often beautiful, and offered the sheer satisfaction of seeing the good and the innocent, for what seems like the first time in quite a while, win out over the forces of evil.

Fright Night (1985) is, in ways very typical of what the dark fantasy film has become in the 1980s, unable to make up its mind as to whether it's out to amuse or out to frighten. Filmmakers seem to assume that madmen dismembering as many teenagers as possible should be presented seriously, but that the horror mythology has to be self-mocking to a degree. The target audience is obviously adolescent; the "adult" movie of supernatural fantasy has become a thing of the past.

Nonetheless, *Fright Night* managed to be a cut above the usual, even with a plot and a protagonist of comic-book simplicity. Average adolescent Charley Brewster, a horror-movie addict, is instantly aware that a vampire has moved in next door, less because of natural astuteness than because the vampire is very careless about drawing the blinds during his dinner hours. Charley, in a symphony of dumb moves such as notifying the police, alerts the vampire (Chris Sarandon, looking like a young, taller James Mason) that he's onto him.

Eventually, it becomes a battle through the vampire's eerie house, with Charley and an aging actor, now reduced to being a television horror-film host, on one side and the vampire, his creature, and two of Charley's friends, now vampirized, on the other. This somehow manages to be exciting despite itself and what has gone before.

The movie is almost totally lacking in the reverberations of age-old evil that make the best of the genre memorable (the vampire next door is almost taken for granted; he could just as well be a mass murderer, drug smuggler, or Near Eastern terrorist). But William Ragsdale, as Charley, performs above and beyond the script and gives his character great charm despite his blunders. And (though it's almost lost in the works) a touching subtext is provided by Roddy McDowall as the aging actor, finally given the chance to exercise the heroics he had so often done on screen and coming close to fudging it. The funniest joke in the movie is under the credits, in which McDowall, in his character as the screen vampire-hunter in an ancient cheapo movie, lunges bravely at the monster, wooden stake held aloft, blunt end forward.

The highly original idea behind *Highlander* (1986) could have been presented in several different ways—as heroic fantasy or as science fiction, for instance. It

THE HUNGER:

The lady is obviously the great beauty Catherine Deneuve, but who is the elderly gentleman? It's David Bowie, of all people. The two brought a touch of class to this tale of two vampires, in which the female keeps her youth and looks, but the male succumbs to the rapid aging that is the bane of most such night creatures.

SOMETHING WICKED THIS WAY COMES:

Jason Robards is the father of one of two boys in a small Midwestern town who realize that the just-arrived carnival harbors malevolent forces that the town's adults do not see. Vidal I. Peterson (left) and Shawn Carson are the perceptive young 'uns.

was that in the history of the human race a few individuals have been born who are immortal and who will be called to an ultimate "gathering" in which only one would triumph. The film chose to take the direction of supernatural horror, at least in the sequences that occur in present-day New York City, where the gathering is taking place and where the immortal villain (in punk-skinhead guise) spends a good deal of time decapitating rivals with a sword, the only way in which they can be permanently eliminated.

The hero, McCloud, does his share of decapitating, too, but only when attacked. He has lived as a quiet antiques dealer in Greenwich Village for the last two hundred years (though obviously keeping up his swordsmanship). In flashback, we see his youth in sixteenth-century Scotland, his miraculous recovery from a wound received in clan battle, and his enlightenment as to his peculiar status, provided by a twenty-five-hundred-year-old Egyptian employed as swords-master to the king of Spain.

Both modern frame and flashback are rife with violence—the battles between immortals tend to demolish any edifice in which they take place (including a small castle and an underground parking garage) since their supernatural powers call down lightning bolts (and every battle is followed by a lightning-powered orgasm for the victor). The immediate impression is of a Scots-flavored kung-fu movie with supernatural overtones. But the historical scenes have a magically brutal quality of heroic fantasy, and Christopher Lambert is immensely effective as both the young Scottish warrior ignorantly bemused by his destiny and the suave modern New Yorker resigned to it. Sean Connery as the Egyptian, born ca. 1000 B.C., comes close to stealing the film, nothing new for him.

The creatures of the night, as almost every film mentioned in this chapter tells us, are immortal. And as so thoroughly proven in this century, no matter how rational the age, werewolves, vampires, mummies, and their dreadful kin will rise again—and again.

HIGHLANDER:

Despite the gray in the hair, Sean Connery doesn't look over two thousand years old. That is his age, but he is an immortal. Here he is telling the young Scots highlander Christopher Lambert that he, too, is an immortal, though he doesn't foresee that Lambert will end up as a dealer in antique weapons in the Greenwich Village of the 1980s, five hundred years hence.

igh fantasy is a term that's come into use only recently, and it can best be defined in terms of what it is *not.* It is not fantasy designed to frighten. It is not fantasy meant to be cute or funny. And it is not fantasy the wonders of which are based in scientific speculation. As to what it is, works of high fantasy almost always have links to some sort of myth, legend, or folktale, although the connection is often remote. At its best, it evokes awe and wonder; it is indeed the highest form of the genre. It is epitomized in the written literature by the works of J. R. R. Tolkien.

Movie examples of high fantasy as such have been comparatively rare until rather recently; for most of this century, anything to do with elves was for children, and mythology was to be wrapped in realistic trappings (*Mourning Becomes Electra*), music of the highest purpose (Wagner), or impenetrable symbolism (Martha Graham). Magic was for the weak-minded and the primitive, even as fictional diversion.

So screen excursions into high fantasy for most of movie history have pretended to be something else—or have been mistaken for something else. The mid-century critics insisted on regarding Cocteau's *La Belle et la Bête* as surrealism, because at the time it was in-conceivable that anyone would want to present a fantasy for its own sake. The ability of the cinema to create fantasy, however, often superseded the material; images of wonder and beauty sometimes transcended the aim of the filmmakers, and made high fantasy out of movies whose scripts, less well filmed, could have been only whimsy, or juvenilia, or feeble allegory.

The greatest of silent-screen fantasies is a good example. *The Thief of Bagdad* (1924) set out as a typical romp for the athletic high spirits of Douglas Fairbanks: a thief of the mythical, Arabian Nights Baghdad, so popular on stage and screen in the early part of the century, wins a caliph's daughter by pluck, luck, and sorcery. However, the designers and special effects creators went overboard in the opulent atmosphere of Hollywood in the twenties. The result was scene after scene of breathtaking *haute*-Islamic sets alternating with a cornucopia of cinema magic. There were valleys of dragons and vales of fire, magic flowers and "Indian" rope tricks, and, making the greatest impression on audiences, a convincing winged horse and an even more realistic flying carpet. We shall meet this thief again.

The legend of Atlantis had firmly estab-lished itself in the public mind; this com-

THE THIEF OF BAGDAD (1924):

The tiny figures toward the bottom of the picture belie the fact that this is a fragment of an Oriental carpet or some other such Eastern abstraction. The silent *Thief of Bagdad* was the most lavishly designed film of its time (or perhaps any time). The quest of its cutpurse hero through various magic milieux gave plenty of scope, as can be seen in this vision of the undersea sequence.

DEATH TAKES A HOLIDAY:

Fredric March is gazing at the exquisite Evelyn Venable like grim death, which is appropriate, since he is indeed Death. That mournful gentleman has decided to take a holiday to discover the diversions of human existence, which creates enormous problems for the world and for Death himself, since he also discovers love. A curious variation on the theme of the Persephone myth, it is an evocative and beautifully wrought film.

bined with desert exotica in *L'Atlantide* by Pierre Benois (unabashedly influenced by H. Rider Haggard, it might have been called *Elle*). It was filmed in Germany in 1932 in German-, French-, and English-language versions. The redoubtable Brigitte Helm (Maria of *Metropolis*) was Antinea, queen of the remnants of Atlantis, which lay in caverns beneath the Sahara. Her minions scour the desert sands for candidates for a brief consortship; ex-consorts are kept on display in a moribund condition. Here was the predatory, eternal-woman myth, a mainstay of the Victorians; Helm was wonderfully viperish in the role. Antinea will also reappear on the screen later in the century.

Not nearly as exotic, though equally distant from the average moviegoer's life, was the milieu of *Death Takes a Holiday* (1934), set on the Italian Riviera. The characters are of the sort who own villas that resemble small palaces and gardens that might be just a bit smaller than those of Versailles. The intelligence and strong structure of the script reflect the film's theatrical origin; it was from a hit play. It tells of Death personified, who enters one of those villas to take not one of the inhabitants but a holiday, inspired by curiosity about mankind's pleasures and pursuits. For the length of his holiday, no one in the world dies, and human suffering is prolonged. The weary Death is persuaded to return to his job by a beautiful woman with whom he falls in love, who agrees to return to . . . wherever . . . with him. Here is a peculiar, modern version of Persephone; a young, wonderfully handsome Fredric March is superb as the suave, caped Death, and Evelyn Venable brings a strange, otherworldliness to the woman he wants. The mysterious poignancy of their scenes together in the lavish garden gives the film a special air of magic.

The best known and most enduring of all high fantasies is certainly Shakespeare's tale of elves and enchantment, *A Midsummer Night's Dream*. The 1935 movie version was a strange and wonderful thing. Based on Max Reinhardt's lavish stage production, the film adaptation was directed by Reinhardt and William Dieterle. Hollywood provided an "all-star" cast, among the unlikeliest ever assembled (for any film, much less Shakespeare)—it included James Cagney, Olivia de Havilland, Joe E. Brown, Dick Powell, Mickey Rooney, Arthur Treacher, and Victor Jory.

The results, dramatically and poetically, may well have made the likes of Lawrence Olivier cringe (though Cagney's Bottom was respectable by any standards and Rooney's manic, preadolescent Puck was an extraordinary performance). But visually it was a dream—an extravagant, Hollywood, Art Deco dream, perfectly reflecting a particular period's idea of the ever-adaptable Bard. Hippolyta's armor is girdled in black serpents, while Titania

and her fairies seem to be clad in that perfect material of the thirties, cellophane. Oberon is a sinister presence; he and the mad Puck probably gave any number of children nightmares.

The centerpiece of the production is the entrance into the wood of Titania and her minions—a fairy host that seems to number in the thousands, all sweeping through the forest to the inevitable strains of Mendelssohn and choreographed by Bronislava Nijinska. A horde of grotesque creatures lurks in the underbrush. The finale of this scene is a triumph of special effects, as the fairies spiral upward around a giant oak tree and disappear into the sky. After that, the comings and goings of the human lovers are something of an anticlimax.

A MIDSUMMER NIGHT'S DREAM (1935):

Dark and light: this lavish production of Hollywoodized Shakespeare was certainly sexist in its view of the elves. Oberon (Victor Jory) and his male minions are decidedly sinister. Titania (Anita Louise) and her cellophane-wrapped ladies are the fun crowd. The exotic lad is the Indian Prince over whom they quarrel.

LOST HORIZON:

Despite the excellent efforts of a dashing Ronald Colman, who plays a newspaperman who discovers a Utopian valley in the Himalayas, and Sam Jaffe, unforgettably ancient as the High Lama of Shangri-La (as the place is called), it was the visual creation of the architecture of Shangri-La that stuck in most people's minds. This gives some idea why.

The legendary mysticism of the East combined with American anxieties in the troubled 1930s to make James Hilton's *Lost Horizon* a resounding best-seller (as well as giving Shangri-La to the English language as a new term for never-never land). The movie (1937) was an entirely successful visualization of the story of an English reporter, Robert Conway, whose plane is hijacked to a remote valley in the Himalayas, where he finds an idyllic community dominated by the lamasary of Shangri-La. Its high lama, well over a century old (as are many of the inhabitants — the pure environment retards aging), desires the young Englishman to take his place, as he knows that his belated death is near. After a great moral struggle, Conway decides to return to the outer world,

and does so in a horrendous trek through the mountains, only to realize too late what he had renounced.

The movie was exciting and intelligently done, and Shangri-La itself was a wonder of set design; it looked like something Frank Lloyd Wright might have designed for the Dalai Lama. Ronald Colman was perfect as Conway and Sam Jaffe unforgettable, in makeup and performance, as the ancient sage.

Also in 1937 appeared a movie that was to irrevocably change the course of Hollywood fantasy and set a pattern to be followed for decades. Its successors too often reeked of coyness and cuteness, but *Snow White and the Seven Dwarfs* was a great original that marked a generation with memories.

The animated film had been slowly but surely growing in sophistication since its genesis with Gertie the dinosaur. Since its visual potential was limited only by the imagination of a graphic artist, it was an ideal medium for fantasy, and the short animated films had explored all sorts of wonderful possibilities. When the leading animator of the day, Walt Disney, embarked on a full-length animated film, he chose the classic fairy tale of the princess Snow White, her murderously wicked stepmother, the seven little men who befriend her, and the handsome Prince who with a kiss saves her from death.

The bare bones of the tale were decorated with many touches of humor calculated to appeal to a modern audience, such as the characterizations of each of the seven dwarfs—simple, but effectively funny—with names to match. Essentially it was presented as a musical comedy with songs and dances. The dances, however, did not depend on choreographed dancers. Given the possibilities of animation, *anything* could be given choreography; Disney had laid the groundwork for this with his many *Silly Symphonies,* short cartoons almost always set to music.

Detractors of the project claimed that a feature-length animated movie would be a lengthy exercise in mindless tedium that no one—child or adult—would sit through. Two things saved *Snow White* from being just that. One was the seemingly infinite stream of visual invention. The other was the introduction of dark elements—the queen and her magic mirror are terrifying, and the forest in which Snow White is lost is a dark dream fantasy touching some sort of primal fear in almost everyone who sees it. (When Disney did abandon the dark elements in his later films—presumably because of the number of children who cowered beneath their seats during the scenes with the wicked witch, or had nightmares because of the death of Bambi's mother—many felt that they did indeed become exercises in mindless tedium.)

Needless to say, *Snow White and the Seven Dwarfs* was an unprecedented smash hit; people had literally never seen anything like it. Paradoxically, because of the artificiality of its process, fantasy had never seemed so real. And fantasy seemed to be needed in the troubled thirties. The major film studios took note and began producing live-action equiv-

SNOW WHITE AND THE SEVEN DWARFS:

An image that traumatized a generation and made stepmothers cringe was this one, the wicked queen offering the casket that is to hold the heart of the murdered Snow White. The extraordinary dramatic impact of the animated film had never before been realized, but the dark aspects of this film and the subsequent *Bambi* were potent proof of its power.

THE THIEF OF BAGHDAD (1940):

The remake of the famous Arabian Nights adventure was given a phenomenal production. The gorgeous sets were upstaged for the public by the special effects, however, which were remarkable for their time. Here Sabu, as the thief, is taken for an initial ride by a flying carpet.

THE BLUE BIRD:

Here, in the Kingdom of the Future, wait the souls of all children yet to be born. As their time of birth nears, they are summoned by the herald (right) to the galley of the Dawn for the trip to Earth. Maurice Maeterlinck's symbolic, fairytale stage spectacle was brought to the screen as a vehicle for Shirley Temple. The results were notably leaden, with the exception of this exquisitely set scene.

alents—lavish musical-comedy fantasies such as *The Wizard of Oz* (the fantasy elements of which, such as the witches, were a good deal less powerful than *Snow White*'s) and a big production of Maurice Maeterlinck's famous theatrical fantasy *The Blue Bird,* tailored for Shirley Temple in 1940.

The Blue Bird had been a stage spectacle of unusual magnitude. It told of two Central European peasant children's search—through fantasy kingdoms of varying degrees of allegory—for the blue bird of happiness. A sense of wonder and beauty is always present. The movie heavy-handedly cut most of the dark elements, such as the foreboding Kingdom of (personified) Night, although the opening graveyard sequence was terrifying enough to send many children fleeing. For some reason (almost by accident, one felt), the sequence in the Kingdom of the Unborn Children was retained. This was a breathtaking piece of production. Hundreds of children in Greek tunics populate a Maxfield Parrish fantasy set of white columns against a blue infinity, and the boat that bears them to Earth is a Parrish dream dhow. Even some of Maeterlinck's poignancy is retained, as the two child-lovers, fated never to meet on Earth, are torn from each other's arms.

Now seemed a good time to remake *The Thief of Bagdad,* and for once a remake was equal to the original. Since there was no actor around of Douglas Fairbanks's robust athleticism, the leading role was divided into a prince, for romantic interest, and the thief, for scapegrace comedy. The Maxfield Parrish influence was again visible in the many lavish sets. In this version, the winged horse and flying carpet, magically effective though they were, took second place to the large genie (with a Southern accent), who emerges from a tiny bottle and flies with the thief on his back to a giant temple housing an enormous idol guarded by green-tinted savages.

The choreographic element in Disney films reached a climax in *Fantasia* (1940), which was essentially seven ballets to the most serious of music (by Stravinsky, Bach, Beethoven, et al.). Plotless though it was, *Fantasia*'s imagery of fantasy has probably never been equaled on the screen. Elves, magicians, dinosaurs, gods and goddesses, centaurs, unicorns, and dancing hippopotami ran riot. Perhaps the finest sequence is that set to Mussorgsky's "Night on Bald Mountain." The bare-breasted witches were something of a shock to those who had come to see Mickey Mouse, and Satan

FANTASIA:

Fantasy is implicit in the title of this landmark Disney film, which was way ahead of its time. Among its many fantastic images, the single most powerful was perhaps that of Satan rising from the ragged mountaintop to Mussorgsky's "Night on Bald Mountain." The resulting animated "ballet" had a giant soloist and a corps of demons and witches cavorting beneath him. Here he draws back as the dawn church bells ring, leading into the "Ave Maria."

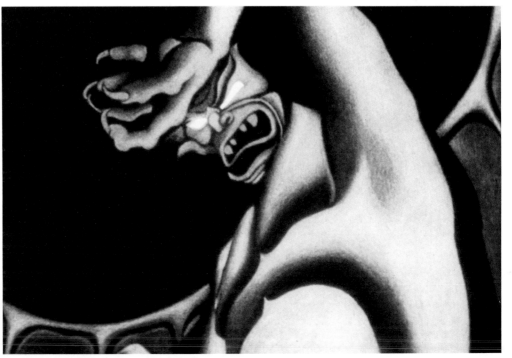

Sydney Greenstreet usually brought his ponderous villainy to bad-guy roles, but in this film he was playing, in a way, Saint Peter. A shipload of passengers embarks on a mysterious voyage that turns out to be the transition between this world and the next. Greenstreet is the "examiner" who greets them on the other side. The always trusty Edmund Gwenn (center) is the steward, fated never to leave the ship since he died a suicide.

emerged from and melted back into the mountaintop with a grace of gesture that Isadora Duncan would have envied. Humor was not lacking: Ponchielli's "Dance of the Hours" was executed by ostriches, hippos, and elephants in the most riotous of all ballet parodies (a direct and wicked takeoff of a Balanchine ballet sequence in *The Goldwyn Follies*). Deemed vulgar by many, *Fantasia* again demonstrated the power of the animated image; ahead of its time, it was not recognized as a masterpiece until three decades later.

The demands of wartime, when effort replaced escapism, brought an end to the cycle of lavish fantasies, but smaller, subtler fantasies continued to appear. *Between Two Worlds* (1944) was an all-in-the-same-boat plot, with a group of assorted passengers on a small liner, constantly hemmed in by fog. Only slowly do we (and they) realize that this is no ordinary ship; it is a link between the Earth and the afterlife, and the customs inspector (played with his usual sinister humor by Sydney Greenstreet) is the final judge.

Val Lewton's oddball sequel to *The Cat People*, called, with a certain inexorable B-movie logic, *Curse of the Cat People* (1944), though continuing with the same

characters, had almost nothing to do with its predecessor. In it, Irena, the were-panther of *The Cat People,* returns from the dead to visit the child of her former husband and his new wife. The child is an imaginative little girl, and, far from being vengeful, Irena acts as playmate and fairy godmother to her. This complicates the family's life no end, but it is played neither for humor nor for horror (though a subplot involving an eccentric and reclusive old lady and *her* disturbed daughter makes a stab in that direction). In the end, *Curse of the Cat People* is not a successful film, but it is an interesting maverick for Lewton and the period.

Since the early films of Méliès, the French had shown that they took their fantasy seriously, and with such films as *Les Visiteurs du Soir* they demonstrated a serious regard for the genre, which was about as far from the Disney-inspired cuteness of American fantasy as possible. Just after World War II, the French poet/artist/cinéaste Jean Cocteau created what many people regard as the supreme cinematic fantasy of all time. It was based on a fairy tale by Marie Leprince De Beaumont (though reportedly she derived it from British sources),

the famous "Beauty and the Beast."

The plot of *La Belle et la Bête* (1946; *Beauty and the Beast*) follows the old story faithfully. The merchant father, returning through the forest, is lost in a storm and entertained for the night at a mysterious castle, the owner of which he never sees. As he is leaving, he remembers the promise he made to his youngest daughter, who bears the descriptive name of Beauty, to bring her a rose. He plucks one from the castle's garden and is confronted by a fierce Beast, half-animal, half-human. As punishment for plucking the flower, he must send one of his daughters to the castle or return himself. Beauty selflessly volunteers to go. At the castle she is treated royally by invisible servants. At dinner, she is visited by the Beast, who is curiously gentle, and who asks her to marry him. She refuses, for the simplest of reasons: she does not love him. For weeks, she lives an existence of luxury; every night the Beast requests her hand in marriage, and every night she refuses him.

The Beast is kind to her, but she discovers his fierce nature when she sees him kill to eat at night. One day she sees in the magic mirror in her room that her father is ill and begs the Beast to allow her to return home for a visit. He finally consents, if she returns in a set number of days. She overstays, and when she finally returns to the castle she finds the Beast dying from heartache. Stricken with remorse, she realizes that she does love him, and says so. He turns back into a handsome prince, and they rise into the sky, to return to his own kingdom, where they live happily ever after.

What makes the film the magical thing it is are the many touches that Cocteau brings to the visual telling of the tale. Beauty enters the castle through a long hall in a whirl of slow motion, with her robes drifting about her. From the walls, as she progresses, arms reach out, holding candelabra that light when she reaches them. In the baroque fireplace before which she dines, the living eyes of the soot-blackened statuary watch her, and later the Beast as he paces back and forth alone.

The grounds of the Beast's castle are strewn with weathered statues of animals, and, as Beauty watches in horror from concealment, smoke rises from the Beast's hands after he kills. The riches of the Beast's treasure float and permeate the air of his treasure pavilion. And the magic is made the more real by the realism of the unmagical. The father's home is stripped by his creditors, and the country cottage to which the family retreats is alive with chickens and adrip with washing.

Jean Marais is a *nonpareil* fairy-tale prince, impossibly handsome in his final incarnation and magnificent as the Beast in black velvet and a streaked cat's head so beautiful that one wonders a bit at Beauty's long denial. (He essentially plays a triple role, since he also appears as Beauty's human suitor, the rough and ready Avenant.) Josette Day is Beauty,

LA BELLE ET LA BÊTE:

Jean Cocteau made what may be the greatest of film fantasies, a straightforward retelling of the classic fairy tale. Here Jean Marais as the Beast gazes on Beauty (Josette Day). The pure fantasy of the production so baffled midcentury critics that they had to label the movie "surrealist" to justify taking it seriously.

THE CURSE OF THE CAT PEOPLE:

The horror-show title of this movie is probably the most misleading in film history. It's the story of an introverted little girl (Ann Carter) to whom the ghost of a young woman (Simone Simon) appears. She acts as comforter and confidante, much to the distress of the girl's parents. The adult cast is continued from *The Cat People,* which was a milestone horror fantasy, but the two movies otherwise are totally different.

SIREN OF ATLANTIS:

The beautiful Dominican actress Maria Montez dominated the B movie fantasies of the 1940s with any number of films set in exotic locales and never-never situations. It was only logical that she should remake the most popular piece of exotica of the earlier cinema, *L'Atlantide*, which suggested remains of the culture of Atlantis in the present-day Sahara. With her is her future off-screen husband, Jean-Pierre Aumont.

ORPHÉE:

Beyond the mirror lies the country of Death. The modern poet, Orpheus, longs to go there, because the Princess of Death has just passed through. The retelling of the myth, in modern dress, had all the surrealism that one would expect from its maker, Jean Cocteau, but also told the story with coherence and subtlety. Jean Marais was compelling as Orpheus, torn between his love for his wife, Eurydice, and the fascinating princess.

and perhaps the only flaw in the film is that while she is indeed beautiful, she is perhaps a shade too icily so.

Because Cocteau was known as a surrealist, and because he used in *La Belle et la Bête* many of the devices he had used to surrealistic purpose in earlier films, the cinematic fourth estate labeled it a surrealist movie. But as fantasy became acceptable, a revisionist view was taken, and *La Belle et la Bête* is now accepted for the miraculously simple work of art it is.

In the meantime, American fantasy in the war and postwar years was almost entirely limited to the lightly ephemeral, animated or live. A curious subgenre, however, was the exotic adventure, for the most part inane Arabian Nights actioners, B movies palely reflecting *The Thief of Bagdad* in look and pulp adventures in plot. However, they had a pop style and imagination of their own. The undoubted queen of this category was the much-satirized Dominican actress Maria Montez, who with the "Universal stock company" (the Indian Sabu, the American Jon Hall, the Austro-Turkish Turhan Bey) made many a sand and sandal epic. These were set anywhere from

vaguely ancient Egypt (*Sudan*) to vaguely Indonesia (*Cobra Woman*) to vaguely medieval Persia (*The Arabian Nights*). The last of these was, almost inevitably, vaguely Atlantis, as Ms. Montez was cast as the cruel Antinea in a remake of *L'Atlantide,* here called *Siren of Atlantis* (1947).

Cocteau produced another masterpiece in 1950, very different from *La Belle et la Bête*. *Orphée* (*Orpheus*) could indeed be considered a surrealist film, but in reality it trod a very fine line between surrealism and fantasy. Many of the sequences set in Death's world, which lies on the other side of mirrors, are surrealist in setting and camera technique, but the film as a whole is not surrealist, since the plot is quite coherent—it is a masterly updating of the Greek myth of Orpheus.

Here Orpheus is a famous modern poet, so well known that even street vendors address him by name. Death is female, an astonishingly chic woman called the Princess who travels in a limousine with an escort of uniformed motorcyclists. They meet when a young poet is killed in a café brawl; as she takes the body, she orders Orpheus into the car

PANDORA AND THE FLYING DUTCHMAN:

The Cocteau influence was more than a little evident in this peculiar film, which one review called "divinely incoherent." Ava Gardner, indeed looking divine, was the playgirl who became involved with the immortal searover, who now sports a tuxedo and a yacht.

UGETSU:

The title means "pale, mysterious moon after the rain," which doesn't give much of a clue to the content of the strange, evocative Japanese film from short stories by the eighteenth-century writer Akinari Ueda. In it, a poor potter becomes involved with an elusive, highborn woman who turns out to be a ghost. The exquisite Machiko Kyo (right) is the phantom lady and Masayuki Mori is the potter.

also. Astonished, he obeys, and after a strange journey (the view through the car windows is in negative), they enter a deserted château. There Orpheus sees the younger poet revivified, and he, the Princess, and her attendants pass through a mirror.

In a complex series of meetings, it becomes clear that the princess is enamored of Orpheus. When his loving young wife, Eurydice, is killed by the Princess's motorcyclists, he persuades Heurtebise, the chief of her servants, to take him through the mirror in his room to her country. There he confesses his love for the princess but pleads for Eurydice's return, to which the princess agrees if he not look upon her. He eventually does, of course; Eurydice vanishes. Orpheus is attacked by a mob of young writers led by Agloanice, the owner of a woman's club where Eurydice once worked, and is shot in the scuffle.

Here Cocteau departs from the legend. It seems that the princess has exceeded her authority. Orpheus and Eurydice are reunited on Earth, forgetting all that had passed. The princess and Herteubise are arrested by her own motorcyclists in the land beyond the mirrors and led away.

Orphée is so rich that it is nearly impossible to convey its quality. Jean Marais is Orpheus, and the superb Maria Casarès is the Princess, regal, peremptory, and the image of the ultra-modish Parisienne of the new-look 1940s. George Auric's score is a triumph, with a particularly haunting major theme.

The real world of *Orphée* is that of postwar France (Agloanice, for instance, is played by the famous existentialist singer Juliette Greco). The world through the mirrors is surrealist, yes, but redolent of mystery and reverberating with nuance, an endless nocturnal wasteland of urban ruins and cramped rooms, replete with modern devices such as radios and motorcycles. Always there is the sense of vast unknown forces, manipulating the supposedly all-powerful Princess of Death as she manipulates Orpheus, Eurydice, and Herteubise. What we are told in the story is beautiful and frightening; what is implied is terrifying.

This kind of film was much too uncommercial for Hollywood, but there were sporadic attempts at lushly romantic treatments of legend. One such attempt was the Anglo-American *Pandora and the Flying Dutchman* (1950). In this contemporary version of the myth made famous by Wagner, the beautiful Ava Gardner, a modern playgirl, meets the Flying Dutchman, the ship captain fated to sail the seas forever, and sacrifices her life for his redemption. One critic has called it "divinely incoherent," the usual reaction to any attempt to do serious fantasy.

Other countries delved into their own mythologies at times, providing curious variations on legendary themes. *The White Reindeer* (*Valkoimen Peura;* 1952) retold a Finnish folktale of a sort of "were-reindeer," a woman who becomes a wild reindeer and kills hunters. The exotic locale and culture made it a fascinating experience.

And then there was an old Scottish legend of an enchanted village that appeared on the moors for one day every hundred years. Translated through Broadway and Hollywood, *Brigadoon* (1954) is one of the classic musical comedies. Despite all the conventions of the midcentury genre (uneven music and some rather forced comedy), there is still a sense of fantasy in the story of two modern Americans confronting the inhabitants of a highland village of centuries earlier and a true poignancy in the love affair that develops between one of the visitors and a girl of Brigadoon. Agnes De Mille's fierce and romantic Scottish dances helped the authenticity of the milieu, and Brigadoon's appearance from and disappearance into the mists evoked the fascination that Scotland held for the nineteenth-century Romantic movement.

From Japan came *Ugetsu* (1954), a poetic and violent film that chronicled the adventures of a peasant during the Japanese feudal wars. His life laid waste by the warfare of the aristocracy, he eventually finds refuge with a beautiful noblewoman. She and her household are ghosts, but this is not a ghost story in the Western sense of the term. Traditionally in Japan ghosts of legend are not necessarily malign, and here there is more tragedy than horror as the peasant, made aware of the joys of cultured life, eventually loses his ghostly lover.

ULYSSES:

In the filming of the classic Homeric myth, Kirk Douglas played the foxy Ithacan king who took ten years to get home from the Trojan War. A majority of the viewers and critics felt that the film was equally long, but there were sumptuous sets and a good performance by Douglas, and the most famous adventure, that with the Cyclops, was filmed with satisfyingly legendary panache.

THE SEVENTH SEAL:

Death personified has appeared in many movies and with many faces, from that of Fredric March in *Death Takes a Holiday* to the terrifying, chic Maria Casares in *Orphée*. Ingmar Bergman returned to the classic image here, a medieval Death ahumanly whimsical, who played with his victims (literally—chess, with the knightly protagonist) but led them away eventually, scythe in hand. The actor is Bengt Ekerot.

The Odyssey is one of the primal myths of Western civilization; it was brought to the screen as *Ulysses* (1955), an Italian movie that couldn't seem to decide whether it wanted to be fantasy or historical epic. This was the period of the Italian sex symbols, and Silvana Mangano was cast in the dual role of Penelope and Circe, encumbered in the latter role with green hair and an extraordinarily ugly set of draperies. However, Kirk Douglas was a jaunty, foxy Ulysses. His encounter with Polyphemus, the giant Cyclops, is just as one pictured it when reading of it as a child; the bypass of the Sirens has a suitable mystery (they are never seen quite clearly); and the court of Princess Nausicaa's father is splendidly Minoan (though the ladies' bosoms were chastely covered).

Ingmar Bergman seemed to encapsulate the full weight of Christian medieval legend in *The Seventh Seal* (1956). A Swedish knight makes his way across war-ravaged, plague-stricken Europe, returning from the Crusades. Personified Death (white-faced, black-cowled) comes to claim him; the knight delays the inevitable by challenging Death to a game of chess. He reaches his wife and castle after a journey of many horrors (the burning of a young witch being perhaps the most memorable), and, at the cost of his own life, tricks Death into letting a simple family of strolling players live. The final image, that of Death with his scythe leading a line of victims (including the knight) against the skyline, is probably the most famous in all cinematic fantasy.

The Sorceress (1956) is a French film set in Sweden; in the lowest possible key, it tells of the romance of an engineer working on a dam in a remote, backward province and a young country girl who is a witch. An outcast, she is barely tolerated by the peasants; the affair sets in motion

THE SORCERESS:

A film that has been all but forgotten, this centered on a backwoods Swedish girl with witch powers who is shunned by her own people. She becomes involved with a man from the outer world, an engineer, and the inevitable outcome is tragedy. Script and production were very low-key, but the photography and the girl, played by Marina Vlady, were ravishingly beautiful, as evidenced in this still.

THE SWORD AND THE DRAGON:

A running midcentury media gag concerned the Russians' claim to have done everything first, but in this case, they did. The three-headed dragon predated all the multiheaded monsters that would gobble up Tokyo a few years later. The movie was about the legendary Russian hero Ilya Mourometz, mostly known to the West from Gliere's programmatic symphony. It had fine effects throughout, but the beefy hero was more operatic than epic.

events that prove ultimately tragic. Only by the barest hints are we shown that the girl's powers are real. The beauty of the wonderfully photographed Swedish forests — and of Marina Vlady as the doomed girl — made *The Sorceress* a small but evocative masterpiece.

The Russians looked to their legendary past in *The Sword and the Dragon* (1956). In telling the story of the hero, Ilya Mourometz (and his lovely wife, Vilya), they anticipated the sword-and-sorcery trend by thirty years, as Ilya (a bit overfed, like so many Russian heroes) bests a wind demon, a giant, and a remarkably well-effected dragon with his enchanted sword.

In 1959 the French New Wave broke on American shores; one of the most star-

tling films it tossed up was *Black Orpheus,* which was French in its production but vividly Brazilian in its spirit. This was another retelling of the Orpheus legend, radically different from Cocteau's film of nine years earlier. The story is set against the frenetic background of Rio de Janeiro during Carnival. The handsome Orpheus is the most beloved guitarist of Rio's slums; Eurydice is a country girl visiting her cousin for the celebrations. As the neighborhood people rehearse and try on costumes for their parts in the parades, Orpheus and Eurydice meet and fall in love. But she is pursued relentlessly through the costumed crowds by a figure wearing the skeletal garb of Death, who eventually takes her. Orpheus seeks her through the mad whirl of Carnival and,

BRIGADOON:

**The gentlemen in modern dress are Gene Kelly
and Van Johnson. Their welcoming committee
consists of most of the population of the Scottish village of Brigadoon, who are clad in that
anachronistic fashion not to attract tourists, but
because their village only materializes on the
moors once in every century.**

true to legend, finds and loses her again. A brilliant adaptation, it caused a sensation because of its sensory impact; one emerged from the movie almost overloaded with the brilliant images of Carnival in Rio, not to mention the pervasive and hypnotic beat of the Brazilian music.

The Czechs approached cinematic fantasy in their own unique style with an adaptation of *A Midsummer Night's Dream* (1959) as an animated puppet feature made by Jiří Trnka, who had earlier been responsible for the whimsically poetic *The Emperor's Nightingale.* Pure Shakespeare it was not, but pure enchantment it was. The people and creatures of the "wood near Athens" were exquisitely magical, particularly the attenuated, inhu-

man elves. An example of the film's endless stream of fantastic imagery was the entrance of Titania, who is announced by the narrator (Richard Burton) to be approaching with her train. As the camera closes in, the viewer realizes that the garment is made up of hundreds of tiny beings, her fairy entourage. This was one of the rare times when an animated film achieved true artistic status.

Classical myth was again retold in *Jason and the Argonauts* (1963), a film by the master special-effects creator of the period, Ray Harryhausen. Like all his films, it was aimed at a juvenile audience, with the emphasis on action and the plot built around the special effects. *Jason* was probably the best of these, since the quest of the Argonauts for the Golden Fleece contains one thrilling encounter after another, and the special effects were miracles for the time. Especially successful are the living colossus of brass that Jason must defeat, a giant Poseidon rising from the sea to confront the *Argo,* and the skeleton warriors raised by sowing the teeth of the Hydra. The last seem startlingly real as they attack the Argonauts in a pitched battle with swords. There were also subtler moments, as

A MIDSUMMER NIGHT'S DREAM (1959):

Titania and Bottom, in her bower, in the Czech puppet version of Shakespeare's drama. They illustrate the exquisite delicacy of the puppets, which were far from the crude and broadly comic figures of American puppet animation. Titania and the other elves were, in fact, rather chillingly inhuman.

BLACK ORPHEUS:

The Angel of Death (Adhemar Da Silva) delivers a mean kick to Orpheus (Breno Mello) as they struggle for Eurydice (Marpessa Dawn) in this Brazilian-set retelling of the Orpheus myth. It takes place at Carnival time in Rio; Orpheus is the leading guitarist/singer of the *favellos,* Eurydice a country girl come to Rio for the celebrations. Mello was a well-known Brazilian soccer star.

JASON AND THE ARGONAUTS:

The large gentleman is the god Poseidon, the ship is the *Argo,* and the crew is captained by Jason of Golden Fleece fame. The god is helping Jason, who is under his protection, through the deadly clashing rocks of the Black Sea. Special-effects wizard Ray Harryhausen went overboard on this one; the result was a charming and exciting version of the ancient myth, with an abundance of magical screen moments.

when Jason encounters a traveler in the hills above Iolcus: after an oblique conversation, the stranger suddenly grows to infinite height and disappears, and Jason realizes that he has been conversing with a god.

The court of King Arthur had appeared in film more than a few times in cinema history, particularly in the various versions of *A Connecticut Yankee* and, shorn of any fantasy, as *Knights of the Round Table,* a sort of ahistorical epic centering on the Arthur/Lancelot/Guinevere triangle. The current Arthurian vogue was begun by T. H. White's *The Once and Future King,* which reached the screen in two entirely different versions, owing to the novel's curious history. It was originally

published as three separate novels, the first of which was *The Sword and the Stone.* The three were rewritten and published together as *The Once and Future King.* This became a best-seller, but the popularity of the first book continued unabated. *The Sword and the Stone* tells of the boyhood of Arthur and his apprenticeship under Merlin, who educates him in the civilized virtues by various magical experiences. It became an animated feature by Disney in 1963. There were many charming moments, but White's wonderfully anachronistic humor and sweet use of enchantment were lost by the wayside.

In the meantime, the other two sections of the novel had reached the Broadway stage as (of all things) a musical comedy called *Camelot,* which one reviewer described as "twice as long as *Parsifal* with half the laughs." It centered around the love triangle of Arthur, Guinevere, and Lancelot and the situation's tragic resolution brought about by the treachery of Arthur's bastard son, Mordred. When brought to the screen in 1967, much of the fantasy of the novel was recaptured, thanks to stunning sets, costumes, and photography, which combined to give the movie a true fairy-tale look. A strong cast helped: Richard Harris as an appealingly unsure Arthur; Franco Nero as a single-minded, simple Lancelot; the jauntily slimy Mordred of David Hemmings; and especially Vanessa Redgrave's proud but human Guinevere. Even the Lerner and Lowe score furthered the action rather than stopping it, due to some imaginative

choreography. And there was a magic moment of flashback to Merlin and his enchanted tutelage.

A very different view of Jason and the Argonauts than seen in Ray Harryhausen's film was provided by Pier Paolo Pasolini's *Medea* (1970). Vaguely based on Euripides's play, and starring the famous soprano Maria Callas as Medea (she had made a sensation in the same role in Cherubini's opera), the resulting film was odd but interesting, and it was an inspiration to use the fantastic (but real) troglodyte community (of caves carved from spires of living rock) of Turkey as Medea's hometown of Colchis.

A quarter of a century had passed since the production of Cocteau's *La Belle et la Bête* when the lively French director Jacques Demy rendered a sweet and di-

THE SWORD IN THE STONE:

In this whimsical adaptation of T. H. White's first Arthurian novel, Merlin's education of the young King Arthur (known as Wart) extends to the magical method of washing dishes. This is the same Arthur who would appear as a grown-up in the live action musical *Camelot,* also based on White's novels.

CAMELOT:

**Arthur's court in Camelot didn't do things in a
small way, as can be seen from this shot of the
Table Round. Overcrowding was taken care of by
the double rank of seats, no problem to the participants since presumably nobody was taking
notes. The lavish production was consistently
beautiful, with a real sense of fairy-tale magic.
That's Richard Harris enthroned as Arthur, with
Lancelot (Franco Nero) on his left.**

rect *hommage* to it with the charming *Donkey Skin* (*Peau d'Ane;* 1970). Taking a classic French fairy tale, he retold it with innumerable little references to Cocteau and his works, which the viewer does not have to know to enjoy the movie on its own delightful terms. It tells of a dying queen who makes her husband promise that if he remarries, it will be only to a woman as beautiful as she. Unfortunately, the only female in the kingdom to live up to that high standard is their daughter. The girl is understandably reluctant, but the king is determined to rewed. After a number of delaying tactics (such as demanding a wedding dress "the color of weather"), she flees in a magic donkey skin. Finally, after many adventures, she meets a handsome prince and contacts her fairy godmother, who makes everything right.

Demy is less serious than Cocteau, and *Donkey Skin* mixes in a bit of camp with its fantasy. The fairy godmother's home is a well-furnished outdoor bower, and she

DONKEY SKIN:

In Jacques Demy's sly *hommage* to Jean Cocteau, Catherine Deneuve is the princess, and Delphine Seyrig (with wand) is her modish fairy godmother.

uses a thoroughly modern telephone to conduct her affairs; the king arrives at his daughter's wedding in a helicopter. But many of the moments echo Cocteau's sorcery, such as the dress "the color of weather," which indeed the king does manage to provide (it's a full gown the fabric of which is the sky, across which drift real clouds). The in-jokes, for lovers of Cocteau, include a reprise of the scene from *Beauty* in a farmyard hung with the family linen set out to dry, and the two lovers drifting down a stream in an ensorcelled boat, puffing on small opium pipes. The major link, however, is the presence of Jean Marais, now the handsomest of kings rather than the handsomest of princes. The beauty of Catherine Deneuve as the princess almost eclipses that of the original Beauty, Josette Day.

The French view of King Arthur appeared in Robert Bresson's *Lancelot of the Lake* (*Lancelot du Lac;* 1975), the quality of which can only be described as *sec.* Deliberately unspectacular, unmagical, unromantic, and rather grubbily realistic, it made its point, particularly in the final shot, which is a scrap heap of armor rusting away in the forest.

Suddenly the Australians began to make an impression with their cinema; one of their first movies to do so was a

MEDEA:

The soprano Maria Callas had made a stir with her interpretation of Cherubini's opera *Medea*. The Italian filmmaker Pier Paolo Pasolini then featured her in a nonoperatic film about the same bloodthirsty lady, loosely based on Euripides and incorporating many of the legend's fantastic elements. The sets and costumes were artistically bizarre. (An alternate and very different Medea can be found in *Jason and the Argonauts.*)

THE LAST WAVE:

This Australian movie was one of the first from the Antipodes to make its mark on the international scene. It was a serious and mysterious story about a modern young lawyer involved in ancient aboriginal magic. It was also the wettest movie since *Moby Dick*.

fantasy dealing with the lore of the Australian aborigine, *The Last Wave* (1977). A young lawyer finds himself involved in a case stemming from the seemingly motiveless murder of an aborigine. It is somehow connected with the native magical rites, which in the dry aboriginal homeland are vitally concerned with water. In fact, this is the *wettest* movie, from overflowing bathtubs to the final vision, a tidal wave that will wipe out "the world." Often mushily metaphysical, the movie still fascinates with its glimpses of the almost totally unknown myths of the Australian natives.

The current vogue in fantasy was started by the popularity of the works of the late J. R. R. Tolkien, notably his trilogy, *The Lord of the Rings.* His stories have fared badly on the screen. The trilogy was made into two movies, *The Lord of the Rings* (1978) and *The Return of the King* (1980), by two entirely different sets of filmmakers, a disaster in itself since it is basically one complete narrative. Despite a disparity in style, however, these films had several things in common. Visually, both relied heavily on comic-strip clichés; narratively, the books were reduced to absurd action thud-and-blunder. Nowhere in either movie was to be found one iota of the poetry and wonder inherent in

Tolkien's great epic. (For the record, it should be noted that *The Hobbit,* which is in a sense the prologue to *The Lord of the Rings* as *Das Rheingold* is a prologue to that other *Ring,* was made into a television movie that was as unfortunate as the other two.)

Nevertheless, true high fantasy did appear on the screen in the 1980s, sometimes successfully. One example is the modest *Dragonslayer* (1981), which concerned itself with the young apprentice to a magician. Galen, the apprentice, is forced by the death of the magician to complete his master's assignment: to destroy a ravaging dragon. This basic story is told on screen with a maximum of seriousness and intelligence and absolutely no quaintness or cuteness whatsoever (excepting, perhaps, Sir Ralph Richardson's usual eccentric performance as the magician). The dragon is fearsome and majestic, and one's feelings about it are those traditionally associated with dragons. There is a moment of terror as its huge claw is first seen emerging from the earth; horror as it is seen finishing off the remains of a princess; and a curious pity as it noses the corpses of its young, slain by Galen. Galen battles it on a lake of fire deep in its lair; it escapes, and its fiery flight over the countryside is awesome.

The dragon, in short, is the star of the movie, and the combination of the seriousness with which it is presented and the excellent special effects by which it is created make *Dragonslayer* the first filmic example of classic high fantasy.

John Boorman's *Excalibur* (1981) attempted to retell the Arthurian legend in contemporary high fantasy style. A laudable attempt, the results were almost pure comic strip. Perhaps because so much of the legend was treated (the film was essentially a biography of Arthur birth to death — Uther to Avalon, as it were), events flashed by with bewildering speed, allowing no time for subtlety or nuance. One was left with the impression of *The Boy's King Arthur* illustrated by a modern comic artist, even to the look of the production: huge, bloody suns lowering behind the horizon; lots and lots of fog; Merlin's enchanted cavern of monumental, Disney-Worldly vulgarity; and chrome-plated knights just off a Detroit assembly line. Matters were not helped by a sound track ladling out rough-cut globs of Orff's *Carmina Burana* and snippets of Wagner.

The traditional animated feature also changed to meet the new public interest in serious fantasy. For instance, *The Last Unicorn* (1982), from Peter Beagle's en-

THE LAST UNICORN:

The unicorn heroine of this animated film undertakes a quest to find the rest of her kind. Here she rescues her companion, an inept magician, from a rather zaftig tree that the magician has inadvertently imbued with a personality, and which has conceived a passion for him.

THE LORD OF THE RINGS:

Elves and hobbits were present in this animated filming of the first half of Tolkien's epic trilogy, but that's about the only resemblance between movie and book. The film contained none of the poetry and wonder of the original, nor did the follow-up, *The Return of the King*.

DRAGONSLAYER:

As is evident, slaying this dragon will be no piece of cake, nor were the special effects in the curiously realistic handling of the classic tale of the untried apprentice who takes on the task of slaying the monster (but only after the princess has been devoured).

EXCALIBUR:

This superb-looking knight with nippled breastplates is director John Boorman's conception of the decadent Mordred, King Arthur's son and archenemy (Robert Addie). Note the resemblance of the mask to Boorman's famous creation, the flying head Zardoz.

CONAN THE BARBARIAN:

Robert Howard, creator of Conan, was the premier American fantasist; his invented mythology drew on the violence and simplicity of the American frontier heritage. Conan, his major hero, long on brawn and battle skills and short on sophistication, was portrayed by Arnold Schwarzenegger; the hero went through many tribulations, but the movie didn't quite capture Howard's vividly primitive sense of fantasy.

chanting novel, kept cuteness at a minimum in dealing with the adventures of a last unicorn who escapes from a carnival, becomes temporarily human, and falls in love with and loses a human prince. Though there are the inevitable songs, the downbeat ending and the inventive artwork made this a distinct change from the pervasive Disney model.

Aside from Tolkien, perhaps the most influential figure in written fantasy of the twentieth century was Robert E. Howard, the prolific writer for pulp magazines. Published in the twenties and thirties, his imaginative works offered a fascinating cultural contrast to those of Tolkien. Howard's fantasies took place in a never-never age (vaguely placed in Earth's pre-

history) of brawling barbarians and decadent kingdoms, liberally laced with sorcerers, fearsome demons, and magic artifacts. While Tolkien's stories reflected the European tradition of folklore, refined and romanticized, Howard's were purely American in style and spirit; straightforward and rambunctious, they were really simple Westerns in exotic dress. (Howard was much influenced by early Hollywood, both Western movies and the great historical spectaculars.)

Despite the crudity of his style, Howard managed to create a mythological world almost single-handedly, and his stories grew slowly but surely in popularity after his tragic early suicide. He influenced a whole generation of fantasy lovers when his stories were put into comic-book form (for which they were well suited). Inevitably, his most famous hero, Conan, came to the screen in *Conan, the Barbarian* (1982); unfortunately, it lacked almost totally Howard's sense of fantasy. Here swords were featured at the expense of sorcery, and the all-important creation of a mythical world was almost entirely fudged. The average viewer assumed that the setting was just over the hill from the low-budget *Hercules* films of the fifties.

THE BEASTMASTER:

Marc Singer is a sort of Dr. Doolittle with muscles in this heroic fantasy. In his adventures in a time of legend, when magic and magical beings were to be encountered around every bend, he is aided by a number of four-footed and feathered friends, including an eagle, two scene-stealing ferrets, and this placid panther. The plot was dispensable, but Singer, the animals, and the marvelous landscapes made the film a visual treat.

KRULL:

In the eye of the beholder. . . . The Princess (Lysette Anthony) beheld by the Beast, who has stolen her on her wedding day. The movie was described as *Star Wars* meets *Excalibur,* but it had charms of its own, primarily an air of fantasy that was lighthearted but not lightheaded. Anthony was a perfect fairy-tale princess.

Also in the American "barbarian fantasy" tradition was *The Beastmaster* (1982); it was more successful than *Conan* in direct proportion to its lesser pretentions. Here a peaceful agricultural village in some mythical, magical time is wiped out by barbarians. The son of the village chief survives to wander in the wilderness; he encounters various fantasy adventures (with winged humanoids and magic rings) until the chance comes to have revenge on the barbarians and wander on, in search of destiny and potential sequels. The gimmick in *The Beastmaster* is that the young hero (played by Marc Singer) has an uncanny rapport with animals; a sort of Muscles Doolittle, he collects fauna the way a ship collects barnacles. The movie suffered from too much length with too little plot, but it was handsomely photographed

(particularly the aerial views through the eyes of a comradely eagle), and the movie was stolen by two ferrets.

Probably the most successful pop fantasy film so far has been *Krull* (1983). Krull, a planet with two suns and a picturesquely medieval culture, is invaded by the Beast and his followers, who arrive on the planet in a sort of peripatetic palace, a gloomy fortress/castle with a habit of shifting to another locale at least once a day. Prince Colwyn and Princess Lyssa, heirs of two of the great kingdoms of Krull, are just in the process of being married (a love match) when the Beast's horde invades the ceremony, kills everyone in sight (including the two kings), kidnaps Lyssa, and decamps.

Colwyn alone survives the massacre. He knows that to rescue Lyssa he must find the traditional magic weapon, in this case a glaive—which technically is a halberd, which technically is a . . . well, it goes on from there. In any case, *this* glaive is a sort of many-bladed jeweled boomerang with magical properties. The real difficulty is in finding the Black Fortress, which keeps wandering around the countryside. And, as one might guess, no timetable for its arrivals and departures has been provided. So there's the quest.

Along the way, Colwyn picks up the usual wise old man, young boy, comic relief (an inept magician), a Cyclops, and an outlaw leader with a heart of gold and outlaws attached. The mixed band zigzags across the landscape in search of various beings with occult powers that might be able to provide a Black Fortress schedule, tangling with representatives of the Beast, enlisting the aid of the Emerald Seer, and braving the hideous widow of the web, an ancient crone who lives in a silken bower held in a huge spider's web. There is, of course, a huge spider to go with it.

The scenario certainly had some originality going for it, and in the production a good deal of style was introduced. Even the scenes *without* special effects have a magical quality; there are quite a few photographed in natural settings. These have been carefully chosen and oh-so-artfully shot, and the viewer is convinced that this is a fantasy landscape. The artificial settings, of course, are more easily given a fantastical air (which is not to imply that there haven't been studio-built settings with all the fantasy of beautiful downtown Paducah). The wedding takes place in a classic fairy-book palace; the Black Fortress interiors are consistently osseous in design—as if built from the skeleton of some huge but delicate sea creature—bringing to mind some of the famous stage settings Isamu Noguchi created for Martha Graham; and the bower, web, and translucent white spider of the widow of the web are very beautiful. Most of the picture is very beautiful, in fact, a neglected quality these days, when it seems to have been forgotten that film is a visual medium.

The visual pleasure extends to the principal actors; Ken Marshall looks like what a handsome prince *should* look like (an updated Errol Flynn who knows how to buckle a swash), and Lysette Anthony is fire, ice, fragility, and intelligence—a true princess.

One special sequence must be cited. The final leg of the journey can only be accomplished on the far-traveling fire mares, which are luckily close at hand to be rounded up (a short rodeo sequence) and which bear a resemblance to the striking but hardly graceful Clydesdales that pull beer wagons. But then they take off; they travel on fire (no, *they're* not on fire; it's the medium on which they travel), on the ground and in the air, and complete a memorable and beautiful journey through the dusk and night.

The Company of Wolves (1984) was greeted with universal bafflement by American reviewers, though the English notices were generally ecstatic. And the attempt to market it in the United States through television and newspaper ads as a sort of werewolf story didn't help matters.

It is indeed an unclassifiable movie, but in an oblique way is probably closer to Cocteau than anything done in modern times. Basically, it's the story of Little Red Riding Hood. She lives in a small village in a great wood with her mother and father. We first see the family at the funeral of her older sister, who has been killed in the forest by a pack of wolves. There is also Granny, who lives in a cottage some distance away in the wood, and is one of those dear old ladies who have down through the ages delighted in frightening the children with gruesome tales that are supposedly cautionary, but in reality perpetrate the bitterness and bleakness of sour old age (hence "old wives' tales").

Three of these stories are dramatized: one of a woman whose husband deserts her to run with the wolves on their wedding night, and then after she remarries returns and changes into a wolf; one of a village girl impregnated by a member of the local aristocracy, who crashes the

THE COMPANY OF WOLVES:

This free adaptation of the children's tale of "Little Red Riding Hood" had many surprises, not the least of which was the wolf that Red Riding Hood (Sarah Patterson) meets on the way to Granny's house. The sexually compelling young man (Micha Bergese) shares her lunch and bets a kiss that he can reach Granny's house first. The psychological symbolism, for once, did not get in the way of the fantasy in this intelligent, intriguing film.

wedding party and changes all the guests into wolves; and one of a local lad who meets the devil in the forest with improbable results. The girl herself tells a story of a wounded she-wolf who becomes a woman and stays among humans for a time.

There is finally the climactic journey to Grandma's house, where indeed Little Red meets a suave stranger in the forest. After a picnic on the contents of the basket meant for Granny, he bets her a kiss that he can get to Granny's cottage before she can. He wins, unpleasant old Granny is satisfactorily (and ungorily) done in, and the final confrontation is thoroughly surprising. Hint — there's not a woodsman in sight.

If one cares to find them, there *are* strong psychological overtones in *The Company of Wolves:* the various wolves throughout are an equation for sexuality,

but hardly negatively (except in Granny's view), and the story is framed as the dream of a modern young girl trembling (as they say) on the brink of adolescence. Luckily, all this doesn't overburden the narrative.

The look of the whole thing is marvelous; this is a true fairy-tale village and wood, the latter alive with wild things aside from the wolves. There are Cocteauesque touches — in the one tale, the devil arrives in a chauffeured Rolls-Royce. One of the man-to-wolf transformations is rather horrifically done, but it's not gratuitously nasty. And the wolves are wonderful, coursing through the forest or emerging suddenly from its moonlit depths.

Ladyhawke (1985) took a very good idea for a movie and stretched it way beyond what the idea could bear. But in these days of continual cloning of ideas, one should be grateful for any attempt at originality, and *Ladyhawke* gets full marks for that.

It's a medieval romance, one that might have — at least one wishes it might have — come from a Provençal troubadour's song. In a Franco-Spanish never-never land in some vague part of the Middle Ages, the beauteous Lady Isabeau loves and is loved by the handsome Etienne, captain of the guards of the city of Aquila. Unfortunately, she is also desired by the all-powerful bishop of Aquila, who, consumed by jealousy, puts a rather malevolent curse on them with the aid of the Powers of Darkness. *She* is to be a hunting hawk by day, and a lady only at night. *He* gets to be handsome Etienne during the day, but a black wolf by night. Right there you can see they have problems.

LADYHAWKE:
Rutger Hauer is the captain of the guard, and that's his lady love on his arm. At night, the hawk regains her normal form (that of Michelle Pfeiffer). Unfortunately, the brave captain becomes a wolf between sunset and dawn. All this is the result of a very unpleasant enchantment.

We learn about all this through the involvement of Phillipe, a young thief and the only prisoner ever to escape the dungeons of Aquila. (There's more than a faint resemblance to the plot of *The Thief of Bagdad* here.) Etienne rescues Phillipe as he is about to be recaptured, and more or less dragoons him into accompanying him (and his hawk) in his wanderings, with the vague purpose of having Phillipe guide him secretly into Aquila.

Phillipe begins to wonder, of course, where Etienne disappears to at night, and who the lovely lady is that keeps appearing nocturnally and disappearing mysteriously. When the hawk is wounded he takes her to a solitary priest, who cures her and explains to Phillipe the circumstances into which he has fallen; it seems that this priest was the unwitting cause of the bishop discovering the love affair.

The renegade priest has predicted that the curse will be lifted when the two lovers confront the bishop in their human forms together, and that this seeming impossibility can be accomplished on a day upcoming soon. The four of them decide to venture into Aquila, Phillipe by the sewer route by which he escaped, the

LEGEND:
Despite the legendary princely good looks, Tom Cruise seemed more at ease in jet plane and crewcut than with sword and sorcery. Mia Sara was a little more relaxed coping with demons and unicorns.

THE PRINCESS BRIDE:

Though Rob Reiner's direction kept nudging you in the ribs, saying, "Aren't we funny and fey," Cary Elwes and Robin Wright, as the hero and heroine, and much of the scenery and photography did manage to capture a fairy-tale quality.

others at night in a cart with Etienne in the form of the wolf. It all ends in a spectacular dustup in the Cathedral itself, which Etienne enters on horseback during services.

Ladyhawke is one hell of a treat for the eyes. The sets (European castles, landscapes, and cathedrals), costumes, and photography are almost overwhelming in their sumptuousness at times. And you couldn't ask for a handsomer lady and captain of the guard than Michelle Pfeiffer and Rutger Hauer (in both their forms — the hawk and wolf are good-looking, too). All these factors are gloriously romantic, forcibly evoking the feeling of a legend, but the dialogue is sometimes jarringly modern. (Historical characters need not always talk in the thee-thou-shouldst-prithee style, but there is a neutral dialogue that isn't laden with anachronisms.) And the movie runs for over two hours; there's just not enough material to keep you glued

to your seat. Thief, lady, captain, priest, hawk, and wolf can only escape, flee, and come close to capture so many times before a certain repetitiousness sets in; the movie concentrates on those four characters' alarums and excursions with almost no relief (even though two of them have two aspects), and you begin to long for something in the way of subplot, or even some new characters. The score is a horror: banal, repetitive, and loud. Nevertheless, *Ladyhawke* is an original and beautiful film, marred only by its extreme length and decibel level.

Legend (1985) reflected the public passion for fantasy of the eighties with many clichés presented in splendid visuals. The plot concerns a romantically rustic couple who replay the Adam and Eve story: he shows her a pair of unicorns disporting in a stream, she through her curiosity is responsible for one of the unicorns being captured by the evil Prince of Darkness.

In the end the hero must save both the unicorn and the girl from the magically powerful villain. This is accomplished with the aid of various companions he has picked up in the classic quest tradition and an ingenious use of a series of mirrors that he uses to beam light into the shadowed lair of the Dark Prince.

Tom Cruise seemed ill at ease as a fairy-tale hero. As is so often the case, the demonic villain — in the person of Tim Curry, made up to look like a cross between Mephistopheles and a satyr — stole the show.

William Goldman's popular novel *The Princess Bride* was an arch exercise in fable, constantly nudging you in the ribs with the knowledge that both author and reader are aware that it is a fairy tale. The movie (1987), directed by Rob Reiner, carried over the same quality to a degree, as it told the story of Princess Buttercup (the name says it all) and her love for the farmboy Westley, who returns from an assumed death at the hands of a bloodthirsty pirate to save her from enforced marriage to the wicked Prince Humperdinck. Here is another case where the visuals project the true fantasy that the script, with its self-parody, does not. The exteriors (real and studio) are colored and styled to resemble a Maxfield Parrish painting (fifty years after *The Blue Bird*).

Robin Wright as Buttercup is eerily like Grace Kelly at times, which immediately says *princess* to the viewer, and Cary Elwes as Westley is an updated, blond Doug Fairbanks, Jr., impossibly handsome but with a Cary Grant wit that the script lacks. Fantasy *per se* is notably sparse: there is a "fireswamp" that Westley and Buttercup must traverse, the floor of which belches flame periodically and which is inhabited by giant rats (none too convincing); Westley is subjected to torture in a Rube Goldbergish machine which "takes years off one's life"; and there is an aged wizard, Miracle Max (performed by Billy Crystal as a Yiddish vaudeville act), who restores Westley to life after the torture machine has taken *all* the years off his life. And there is an appealingly bumbling giant (played by the seven-foot-four André the Giant).

High fantasy took a long time to become acceptable on the movie screen as such. Considering the marvels of which the screen is now capable, it is possible that the wonders will now never cease, and that the screen will show us more things in heaven and Earth than are presently dreamt of.

No matter how mightily a medium strains to repeat success, to safely copy what has pleased an audience before, in short, to make money on a sure thing, there are inevitably mavericks. As we have seen, movies have for the most part used a few basic ideas, well or badly, with which a large audience would be familiar. But there are the odd few science fiction and fantasy movies that don't quite fit into any pigeonhole. The reasons are not necessarily a desire for originality. Some are based on literary classics of unusual theme. Some probably started out as safe, unoriginal ideas and in the convoluted process of filmmaking went off somewhere else. One or two do have the quality of trying for something different.

She, from H. Rider Haggard's famous nineteenth-century novel, had been filmed more than once in the silent days (reportedly seven times, in fact); its first sound incarnation was in 1935. The background ideas are a preposterous mishmash of occultism and reincarnation by today's standards, but it should be noted that such things were taken more seriously in Haggard's day. Ayesha (She-Who-Must-Be-Obeyed), a woman rendered immortal by arcane knowledge and a sacred flame in the heart of an African mountain, has waited more than two millennia for the reincarnation of her lost Greek lover. Leo Vincey, a redoubtable young English explorer, makes it through the wilds to Ayesha's lost city of Kor, and, of course, he turns out to be the spitting image of the long-lost Kallikrates. As can be imagined, complications ensue as the true-blue, Victorian Leo has doubts about becoming Ayesha's lover, much less entering the flame to become immortal.

For reasons best known to themselves, the scriptwriters for the sound version transferred the locale from Haggard's beloved Africa to Canada. But as She, Helen Gahagan (in her only film role) made up in commanding presence what she may have lacked in voluptuousness, which might also partially account for her later career as United States Representative Helen Gahagan Douglas. Audiences for revivals of this version of *She* invariably give a gasp of recognition at one of Her costumes, a black gown with tight-fitting sleeves and hood showing only the face,

crowned with a crystal circlet. It is almost line-for-line that of the Wicked Queen in *Snow White.*

Tribute to all the juvenile serials whose science fictional devices enthralled boyish audiences can be paid through noting the daffy doings of *The Phantom Empire* (1935; aka *Radio Ranch* when cut down to a feature film). Starring the singing cowboy Gene Autry (then a prominent radio star), it had something to do with Autry attempting to broadcast from his ranch, underneath which was the superscientific city of Murania, which did not want to be discovered. The none-too-special effects included a wonderful *moderne* Murania with elevators zipping up and down the cavern in which it lay; the clunkiest robots ever to be shown on film; a great many anticipatory television screens; and a She-like queen with an Elizabethan neck-ruff of monumental proportions. This madness went on for twelve episodes.

Rudyard Kipling's glorious Mowgli stories, the major part of his two *Jungle Books*, concern an Indian boy brought up by the animals of the Indian jungle. The animals are intelligent and speak in their own tongues, but are otherwise of a natural, Rousseauian nobility and beauty. The difficulties of bringing this to the screen are evident. Alexander Korda's 1942 film version solved the problem but lost much of the magic by limiting the animals' speech to a few lines for the snakes, and concentrating mostly on the adolescent Mowgli's problems when first encountering other humans. Nevertheless, the movie was often breathtakingly beautiful,

THE PHANTOM EMPIRE:

Cowboys and robots share equal billing in this twelve-part serial, also seen as a feature film. It had something to do with a futuristic lost civilization that lay in caverns beneath the ranch of cowboy star Gene Autry. Some idea of the advanced technology can be gathered from the spiffy (though dented) robot. Made strictly for Saturday matinees, it can now be viewed as a period delight.

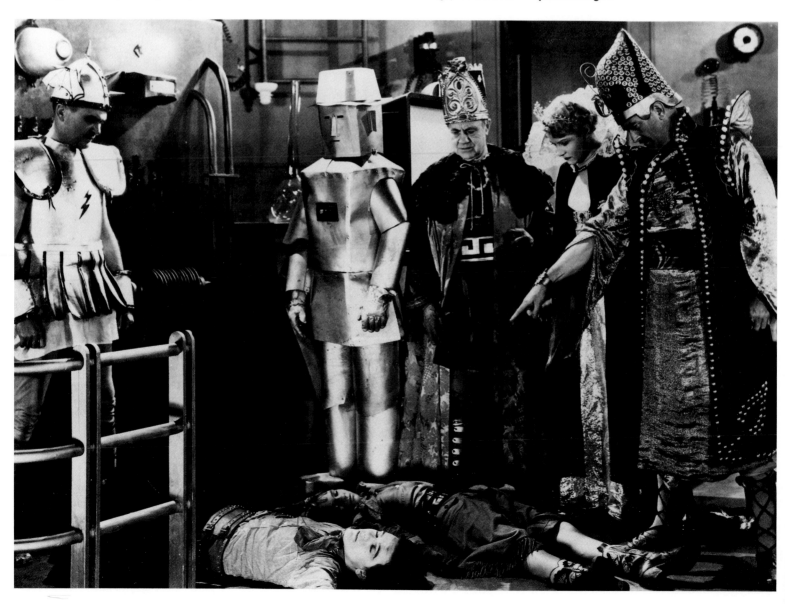

THE JUNGLE BOOK:

especially the scenes filmed in the ruined city lost deep in the jungles, here modeled (with rather shaky ethnic authenticity) on Angkor Wat.

A movie that started out as yet another built around its special effects, *The Incredible Shrinking Man* (1957) became something else again in the hands of writer Richard Matheson. Scott Carey is a perfectly ordinary citizen with a wife, a house, a boat, and a cat. Out on his boat, he is drenched by a mysterious cloud lying on the sea; soon thereafter, he begins to shrink, slowly but inexorably. Doctors are unable to do anything; eventually he is reduced to living in a doll's house, tended by his wife. One day in her absence he is pursued by the cat into the cellar; convinced that he has been eaten by the cat, his wife shuts up the house. The last part of the movie is Scott's struggle to survive in the wilderness of an ordinary cellar; particularly enthralling is an ongoing duel with a predatory spider. What could have been ludicrous is rendered absorbing by a script that is sensible and even poetic (in an ambiguous and moving finale), and the superb handling of the actor (Grant Williams) against the oversized settings and terrifying spider.

In the vogue for Jules Verne started by the success of Disney's *20,000 Leagues,* an oddball entry appeared from Czechoslovakia. *The Fabulous World of Jules Verne* (1958) was very loosely based on Verne's *Face au Drapeau* (which was about a gang of cutthroats seeking to rule the world through a naive inventor's discovery of a superexplosive). It can best be classified as an animated film, but its stylish combination of live action and animation was not quite like anything that had been seen before; the general effect was that of actors moving in animated versions of the steel-point engravings that illustrated Verne's works when they were first published.

Verne's *Journey to the Center of the Earth* was filmed in 1959; it was one of the last of the Verne cycle, and one of the most diverting. The usual Verne expedition (this time including a duck) led by the usual grumpy scientist (here James Mason) descends the vent of an Icelandic volcano, and discovers a great many unlikely things in the caverns below, including giant lizards, giant mushrooms, and the ruins of Atlantis. Their reascent to the surface via Vesuvius, lifted by volcanic gasses, is comically outrageous.

THE FABULOUS WORLD OF JULES VERNE:

The basis was a mélange of Verne novels, incorporating many of Verne's wonders, such as airships, submarines, giant squids, and lots of machinery. Its major charm, however, was the Czech genius for animation, which here combined with live actors to convey the quality of living steel engravings.

THE INCREDIBLE SHRINKING MAN:

Universally agreed to be one of the best science fiction films ever made, this low-budget movie benefited from an evocative script by Richard Matheson that combined thrills and thought and a simply beautiful and beautifully simple production with excellent effects depicting a miniaturized human facing the perils of an ordinary cellar. The affecting ending had Grant Williams escaping the cellar through the mesh of a common screen.

JOURNEY TO THE CENTER OF THE EARTH:

Mushroom omelette, anyone? Pat Boone has just discovered this patch of larger-than-life fungi in a cavern several miles below the surface as he and various companions make their way downward. Getting there was more than half the fun in this jolly adaptation of Verne.

A new production of *She* (1965) was done on a somewhat lower budget than that of thirty years earlier, but it made perhaps a better stab at Haggard's romanticism, helped by returning the action to Africa, whose natural wonders were rivaled by the leads. John Richardson was a Leo worth waiting two thousand years for, and Ursula Andress combined a spectacular face and figure with truly immortal imperiousness.

Richard Lester's *How I Won the War* (1967) was certainly more concerned with making an antiwar statement than amusing its audience with fantasy, but despite that, this story of a fighting platoon in World War II whose members continue even after their deaths (they reappear as "ghosts" colored in distinctly unreal hues) had an odd flavor that impressed critics, if not most of the audience.

HOW I WON THE WAR:

This bizarre, antiwar, black comedy was John Lennon's first solo acting effort. The director was Richard Lester, who had made *A Hard Day's Night* and *Help!* Set in World War II, it baffled most of the audience with the story of a platoon whose defunct members continued to accompany their living associates. Supporting Lennon was Roy Kinnear, a stalwart comic character actor.

SHE (1965):

Thirty years after the original talkie of H. Rider Haggard's famous novel, a remake appeared. Ursula Andress may not have had the commanding presence of Helen Gahagan, but she brought other attributes to the role. Here She is, dominating things as usual. The hero from the outside world is John Richardson (standing against pillar); the high priest (on the stairs) is Christopher Lee.

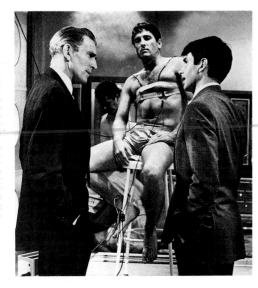

THE POWER:

Power, power, who's got the power? Surely not the gentleman with the painfully squeezed chest, but it just might be Michael Rennie or George Hamilton, members of a scientific research team that someone is manipulating with psi powers and lethal intent. Figuring out who results in an eerie chase with an invisible quarry who could be the hunter.

The Power (1967) was one of the rare films to handle psychic powers in a rational, science fictional way. One of a group of research scientists discovers that another of the group (he doesn't know who) has superior mental powers that are being used for personal power, in ways that include murder. The film develops into a cat-and-mouse chase, with the mouse having no idea who or where the cat is. There is a memorable sequence in which the hero and his friends, who realize that to survive they must remain awake and with other people, crash a dreadful party and stay with it to its awful end. Unfortunately, there's some incoherence in plot and concept, but despite this *The Power* has intelligence and more than its share of suspense.

The Lost Continent (1968) is a film so off-the-wall that one wonders how it ever came to be made. The first half is a fairly tedious "ship-of-fools" exercise, with several misfit characters at sea on a tramp steamer. But suddenly they find themselves enmeshed in the weeds of the Sargasso Sea, with the hulks of many vessels that have been caught there over hundreds of years. Aboard the hulks is a weird culture of survivors who have managed to keep going for generations; there are also sea monsters and giant crabs for good measure.

Night of the Living Dead (1968) became a cult film almost immediately, and for one very good reason. After a decade of tedious technicolor *Frankenstein*s, it managed to scare the audience. Made on the proverbial shoestring (a black-and-white shoestring, in this case), it still had enough polish to make believable the story of a group of disparate people trapped in a lonely farmhouse by a sudden plague of corpses brought to life

NIGHT OF THE LIVING DEAD:

Not the nicest people to have on your front lawn, these animated corpses are besieging a house in which the film's protagonists are trapped. The countryside is alive with them (as it were) because some unidentified plague is reviving the dead as cannibalistic killers. Shots of their eating habits provided the necessary modern grue, but the movie also had some good old-style scary moments that had the audience shrieking.

THE LOST CONTINENT:

A forgotten but oddly intriguing little movie from 1968 started out like *Ship of Fools* and then took its variegated cast into the classic pulp-magazine cliché situation familiar to all readers of boys' adventure novels, the seaweed-choked area of the ocean in which are trapped ships from all eras of navigation history. There are also some rather exotic fauna, such as giant scorpions.

(never fully explained, but there is some peripheral talk of radiation from space). It had been some time since a movie audience actually jumped and screamed at *anything* on screen, but when a host of arms suddenly broke through a boarded-up window, viewers reacted in the good old horror-movie tradition. Special effects were minimal (mostly rather good corpse-white makeup for the animated deceased). A downbeat ending (the sole survivor is thought to be a zombie and is killed by a posse) topped off the movie's disturbing effect, and sociologists by the thousands found all sorts of meanings in it and its popularity.

Savages (1972) is a little-known film from the intellectual production team of Ismail Merchant and James Ivory. It's an out-and-out allegory (which is why it's little known), but the surface story is so outrageously amusing that it transcends inner meaning to become an intriguing fantasy. Essentially, a very grubby tribe of primitives follows a croquet ball onto the grounds of an elegant, deserted mansion and spends the weekend there. In the process, they go through all the processes of civilized evolution, ending up in dinner clothes at a sumptuous banquet. Devolution sets in rapidly, as they become involved in mysticism and pleasure seeking, and grubby as ever, they parody a last game of croquet and follow a wild ball back into the forest.

Raiders of the Lost Ark (1981) is an upmarket tribute to the old downmarket values of juvenile serials (see *The Phantom Empire,* above) and adventure pulp magazines. Basically, it's what those serials might have been had their makers been able to work with the kind of budget Steven Spielberg was able to employ after a series of hit films. The major fantasy element was, of course, the lost Ark (of the Covenant) itself, but what with jungle adventures, lost cities, forgotten treasures, and whatnot, all superbly realized, it was an exercise in the nostalgia of the mindless. One suspects that its immense popularity was due less to craft or nostalgia than to its mindlessness.

RAIDERS OF THE LOST ARK:

This movie caught the public's fancy by reproducing the thrill-a-minute serials of the 1940s, Nazis and all, as they might have been done with the budget of an epic. There seemed to be at least one crisis in every two minutes of running time. Here, in a comparatively small-scaled one, Indiana Jones (Harrison Ford) and bullwhip protect a damsel who doesn't seem to be in all that much distress.

ENVOI

From the delicate and fierce wonder of *La Belle et la Bête* to the harshly beautiful hardware of *Dune,* from the terrors of *Dracula* to the laughing elves of *A Midsummer Night's Dream,* the movies we have talked about here are visions, visions of what is not. Cinema has served many purposes, and will continue to do so; it should not be forgotten that visions have also been of value throughout history. By imagining what is not, men and women the world over have made wonderful realities. The cinema of the fantastic has served a prime purpose in diverting and entertaining us, and giving us laughter and the unique *frisson* that only a sense of wonder brings, but it also has broadened our horizons toward the what-might-be and the what-might-have-been. Don't make the mistake of dismissing fantasy as valueless; an age without imagination is an age without soul, and the movies have, more than anything else, brought an age's imagination to life.

The Abominable Dr. Phibes 1971 [C]. D. Robert Fuest. With Vincent Price, Joseph Cotten

Algol 1920. D. Hans Werckmeister. With Emil Jannings

Alice in Wonderland 1933. D. Norman Z. McLeod. With Charlotte Henry, Cary Grant, Gary Cooper

Alien 1979 [C]. D. Ridley Scott. With Sigourney Weaver, John Hurt

Aliens 1986 [C]. D. James Cameron. With Sigourney Weaver, Carrie Henn, Michael Biehn

Alphaville 1965. D. Jean-Luc Godard. With Anna Karina, Eddie Constantine

Altered States 1980 [C]. D. Ken Russell. With William Hurt, Blair Brown

The Amazing Colossal Man 1957. D. Bert I. Gordon. With Glenn Langan, Cathy Downs

An American Werewolf in London 1981 [C]. D. John Landis. With David Naughton, Jenny Agutter

The Andromeda Strain 1971 [C]. D. Robert Wise. With Arthur Hill, Kate Reid, James Olson

At the Earth's Core 1976 [C]. D. Kevin Connor. With Doug McClure, Peter Cushing, Caroline Munro

L'Atlantide 1932. D. G. W. Pabst. With Brigitte Helm, John Stuart

Back to the Future 1985 [C]. D. Robert Zemeckis. With Michael J. Fox, Christopher Lloyd

Barbarella 1968 [C]. D. Roger Vadim. With Jane Fonda, John Philip Law

Battle of the Worlds 1960 [C]. D. Antonio Margheriti. With Claude Rains, Maya Brent

Beastmaster 1982 [C]. D. Don Coscarelli. With Marc Singer, Rip Torn

The Bed-Sitting Room 1969 [C]. D. Richard Lester. With Ralph Richardson, Rita Tushingham

Bell, Book and Candle 1958 [C]. D. Richard Quinn. With Kim Novak, Jimmy Stewart

La Belle et la Bête (Beauty and the Beast) 1946. D. Jean Cocteau. With Jean Marais, Josette Day

Berkeley Square 1933. D. Frank Lloyd. With Leslie Howard, Heather Angel

Between Two Worlds 1944. D. Edward A. Blatt. With John Garfield, Sidney Greenstreet

The Birds 1963 [C]. D. Alfred Hitchcock. With Rod Taylor, Jessica Tandy

The Bishop's Wife 1947. D. Henry Koster. With Cary Grant, Loretta Young, David Niven

The Black Cat 1934. D. Edgar G. Ulmer. With Boris Karloff, Bela Lugosi

The Black Hole 1979 [C]. D. Gary Nelson. With Anthony Perkins, Maximilian Schell

Black Orpheus 1959 [C]. D. Marcel Camus. With Marpessa Dawn, Breno Mello

Blade Runner 1982 [C]. D. Ridley Scott. With Rutger Hauer, Harrison Ford

Blithe Spirit 1945 [C]. D. David Lean. With Rex Harrison, Constance Cummings

The Blob 1958 [C]. D. Irvin S. Yeaworth, Jr. With Steve McQueen, Aneta Corseaut

Blood on Satan's Claw 1970 [C]. D. Piers Haggard. With Patrick Wymark, Linda Hayden

The Blue Bird 1940. D. Walter Lang. With Shirley Temple, Gale Sondergaard

Brainstorm 1983 [C]. D. Douglas Trumbull. With Natalie Wood, Christopher Walken

Brazil 1985 [C]. D. Terry Gilliam. With Jonathan Pryce, Robert De Niro, Kim Greist

The Bride 1985 [C]. D. Franc Roddam. With Sting, Jennifer Beals, Clancy Brown

The Bride of Frankenstein 1935. D. James Whale. With Boris Karloff, Elsa Lanchester

Brigadoon 1954 [C]. D. Vincente Minnelli. With Gene Kelly, Cyd Charisse, Van Johnson

Buck Rogers 1979 [C]. D. Daniel Haller. With Gil Gerard, Pamela Hensley

Burn Witch, Burn 1962. D. Sidney Hayers. With Janet Blair, Peter Wyngarde

The Cabinet of Dr. Caligari 1919. D. Robert Wiene. With Werner Krauss, Conrad Veidt

Camelot 1967 [C]. D. Joshua Logan. With Vanessa Redgrave, Richard Harris

The Canterville Ghost 1944. D. Jules Dassin. With Charles Laughton, Margaret O'Brien

Carnival of Souls 1962. D. Herk Harvey. With Candace Hilligoss, Herk Harvey

Carousel 1956 [C]. D. Henry King. With Shirley Jones, Gordon MacRae

The Cat People 1942. D. Jacques Tourneur. With Simone Simon, Kent Smith

Charly 1968 [C]. D. Ralph Nelson. With Cliff Robertson, Claire Bloom

A Clockwork Orange 1971 [C]. D. Stanley Kubrick. With Malcolm McDowell, Patrick Magee

Close Encounters of the Third Kind 1977 [C]. D. Steven Spielberg. With Richard Dreyfuss, François Truffaut

Cocoon 1985 [C]. D. Ron Howard. With Don Ameche, Gwen Verdon, Hume Cronyn

Colossus: The Forbin Project 1970 [C]. D. Joseph Sargent. With Eric Braeden, Susan Clark

The Company of Wolves 1984 [C]. D. Neil Jordan. With Angela Lansbury, David Warner

Conan the Barbarian 1982 [C]. D. John Milius. With Arnold Schwarzenegger, Sandahl Bergman

Crack in the World 1965 [C]. D. Andrew Marton. With Dana Andrews, Kieron Moore

Creation of the Humanoids 1962 [C]. D. Wesley E. Barry. With Don Megowan, Erica Elliott

Creature from the Black Lagoon 1954. D. Jack Arnold. With Richard Carlson, Julia Adams

Curse of the Cat People 1944. D. Robert Wise, Gunther V. Fritsch. With Simone Simon, Kent Smith

The Damned 1961. D. Joseph Losey. With Mac-Donald Carey, Shirley Ann Field

The Dark Crystal 1982 [C]. D. Jim Henson, Frank Oz

The Day After 1983 [C]. D. Nicholas Meyer. With Jason Robards, John Cullum

The Day of the Triffids 1963 [C]. D. Steve Sekely. With Howard Keel, Nicole Maurey

The Day the Earth Caught Fire 1962. D. Val Guest. With Edward Judd, Janet Munro

The Day the Earth Stood Still 1951. D. Robert Wise. With Michael Rennie, Patricia Neal

Death Takes a Holiday 1934. D. Mitchell Leisen. With Fredric March, Evelyn Venable

Deluge 1933. D. Felix E. Feist. With Sidney Blackmer, Peggy Shannon

Demon Seed 1977 [C]. D. Donald Cammell. With Julie Christie, Fritz Weaver

Le Dernier Combat (The Last Battle) 1982. D. Luc Besson. With Pierre Jolivet, Jean Bouise

Destination Moon 1950 [C]. D. Irving Pichel. With John Archer, Warner Anderson

The Devil-Doll 1936. D. Tod Browning. With Lionel Barrymore, Maureen O'Sullivan

Dinosaurus 1960 [C]. D. Irvin S. Yeaworth, Jr. With Ward Ramsey, Paul Lukather

Donkey Skin (Peau D'Ane) 1971 [C]. D. Jacques Demy. With Catherine Deneuve, Jean Marais

Down to Earth 1947 [C]. D. Alexander Hall. With Rita Hayworth, Larry Parks

Dr. Cyclops 1940 [C]. D. Ernest Schoedsack. With Albert Dekker, Janice Logan

Dr. Jekyll and Mr. Hyde 1932. D. Rouben Mamoulian. With Fredric March, Miriam Hopkins

Dr. Jekyll and Mr. Hyde 1941. D. Victor Fleming. With Spencer Tracy, Ingrid Bergman

Dr. Phibes Rises Again 1972 [C]. D. Robert Fuest. With Vincent Price, Valli Kemp, Beryl Reid

Dr. Who and the Daleks 1965 [C]. D. Gordon Flemyng. With Peter Cushing, Jennie Linden

Dracula 1931. D. Tod Browning. With Bela Lugosi, David Manners

Dracula 1979 [C]. D. John Badham. With Frank Langella, Laurence Olivier

Dracula's Daughter 1936. D. Lambert Hillyer. With Gloria Holden, Otto Kruger

Dragonslayer 1981 [C]. D. Matthew Robbins. With Peter MacNicol, Ralph Richardson

Dune 1984 [C]. D. David Lynch. With Kyle MacLachlon, Francesca Annis, Linda Hunt

The Dunwich Horror 1969 [C]. D. Daniel Haller. With Dean Stockwell, Sandra Dee

E.T. The Extra-Terrestrial 1982 [C]. D. Steven Spielberg. With Dee Wallace, Henry Thomas, Peter Coyote

The Emperor's Nightingale 1947 [C]. D. Jiří Trnka.

The Empire Strikes Back 1980 [C]. D. Irvin Kershner. With Mark Hamill, Harrison Ford, Carrie Fisher

Excalibur 1981 [C]. D. John Boorman. With Nigel Terry, Nicholas Clay, Cherie Lunghi

The Exorcist 1973 [C]. D. William Friedkin. With Ellen Burstyn, Linda Blair, Max Von Sydow

The Fabulous World of Jules Verne 1958. D. Karel Zeman. With Lubor Tokos, Arnost Navratil

Fahrenheit 451 1966 [C]. D. François Truffaut. With Oskar Werner, Julie Christie

Fantasia 1940 [C].

Fantastic Planet 1973 [C]. D. René Laloux.

Fantastic Voyage 1966 [C]. D. Richard Fleischer. With Stephen Boyd, Raquel Welch

The Fearless Vampire Killers 1967 [C]. D. Roman Polanski. With Roman Polanski, Sharon Tate

First Men in the Moon 1964 [C]. D. Nathan Juran. With Edward Judd, Lionel Jeffries

Five Million Years to Earth 1968 [C]. D. Roy Ward Baker. With Andrew Keir, James Donald

Flash Gordon 1936. D. Frederick Stephani. With Buster Crabbe, Charles Middleton

Flash Gordon 1980 [C]. D. Mike Hodges. With Sam J. Jones, Melody Anderson, Timothy Dalton

Forbidden Planet 1956 [C]. D. Fred M. Wilcox. With Leslie Nielsen, Walter Pidgeon, Anne Francis

Frankenstein 1910. D. J. Searle Dawley. With Charles Ogle, Augustus Phillips, Mary Fuller

Frankenstein 1931. D. James Whale. With Boris Karloff, Colin Clive

Fright Night 1985 [C]. D. Tom Holland. With Chris Sarandon, William Ragsdale

From the Earth to the Moon 1958 [C]. D. Byron Haskin. With Joseph Cotten, George Sanders, Debra Paget

Gertie the Dinosaur 1909. With Winsor McCay

The Ghost and Mrs. Muir 1947. D. Joseph Mankiewicz. With Rex Harrison, Gene Tierney

The Ghost Goes West 1936. D. Rene Clair. With Robert Donat, Jean Parker, Eugene Pallette

Godzilla, King of the Monsters 1954. D. Inoshiro Honda. With Raymond Burr, Akihiko Hirata

Gorgo 1959 [C]. D. Eugene Lourie. With Bill Travers, William Sylvester

The Green Slime 1968 [C]. D. Kinji Fukasaku. With Robert Horton, Richard Jaeckel

The Haunting 1963. D. Robert Wise. With Julie Harris, Claire Bloom

Heartbeeps 1981 [C]. D. Allan Arkush. With Bernadette Peters, Andy Kaufman

Highlander 1986 [C]. D. Russell Mulcahy. With Christopher Lambert, Sean Connery

Homunculus the Leader 1916. D. Otto Rippert. With Olaf Fonss, Aud Egede Nissen

The Horn Blows at Midnight 1945. D. Raoul Walsh. With Jack Benny, Alexis Smith

How I Won the War 1967 [C]. D. Richard Lester. With Michael Crawford, John Lennon

The Hunger 1983 [C]. D. Tony Scott. With Catherine Deneuve, David Bowie

I Married a Monster from Outer Space 1958. D. Gene Fowler, Jr. With Tom Tryon, Gloria Talbott

I Married a Witch 1942. D. René Clair. With Fredric March, Veronica Lake

I Walked with a Zombie 1943. D. Jacques Tourneur. With Francis Dee, Tom Conway

The Illustrated Man 1968 [C]. D. Jack Smight. With Rod Steiger, Claire Bloom, Robert Drivas

The Incredible Shrinking Man 1957. D. Jack Arnold. With Grant Williams, Randy Stuart

The Innocents 1961. D. Jack Clayton. With Deborah Kerr, Pamela Franklin

Invasion of the Body Snatchers 1978. D. Philip Kaufman. With Donald Sutherland, Brooke Adams

The Invisible Man 1933. D. James Whale. With Claude Rains, Gloria Stuart, Una O'Connor

The Island of Dr. Moreau 1977 [C]. D. Don Taylor. With Michael York, Burt Lancaster

Island of Lost Souls 1932. D. Erle C. Kenton. With Charles Laughton, Richard Arlen, Bela Lugosi

It's a Wonderful Life 1946. D. Frank Capra. With James Stewart, Donna Reed, Lionel Barrymore

Jason and the Argonauts 1963 [C]. D. Don Chaffey. With Todd Armstrong, Gary Raymond, Honor Blackman

Je T'Aime, Je T'Aime 1968 [C]. D. Alain Resnais. With Claude Rich, Olga Georges-Picot

Journey to the Center of the Earth 1959 [C]. D. Henry Levin. With Pat Boone, James Mason, Arlene Dahl

The Jungle Book 1942 [C]. D. Zoltan Korda. With Sabu, Joseph Calleia, Rosemary De Camp

Just Imagine 1930. D. David Butler. With El Brendel, Maureen O'Sullivan

King Kong 1933. D. Merian C. Cooper, Ernest Schoedsack. With Fay Wray, Bruce Cabot

King Kong 1976 [C]. D. John Guillermin. With Jessica Lange, Jeff Bridges

Krull 1983 [C]. D. Peter Yates. With Ken Marshall, Lysette Anthony

Labyrinth 1986 [C]. D. Jim Henson. With David Bowie, Jennifer Connelly

Ladyhawke 1985 [C]. D. Richard Donner. With Rutger Hauer, Michelle Pfeiffer

Lancelot of the Lake 1975 [C]. D. Robert Bresson. With Luc Simon, Laura Duke Condominas

Land that Time Forgot 1975 [C]. D. Kevin Connor. With Doug McClure, Susan Penhaligon

The Last Man on Earth 1964. D. Ubaldo Ragona. With Vincent Price, Giacomo Rossi-Stuart

The Last Unicorn 1982 [C]. D. Arthur Rankin, Jr., Saul Bass.

The Last Wave 1977 [C]. D. Peter Weir. With Richard Chamberlain, Olivia Hamnett

Legend 1985 [C]. D. Ridley Scott. With Tom Cruise, Mia Sara, Tim Curry

Logan's Run 1976 [C]. D. Michael Anderson. With Michael York, Jenny Agutter, Peter Ustinov

Lord of the Rings 1978 [C]. D. Ralph Bakshi.

The Lost Continent 1968 [C]. D. Michael Carreras. With Eric Porter, Hildegarde Neff

Lost Horizon 1937. D. Frank Capra. With Ronald Colman, Jane Wyatt, Sam Jaffe

The Lost World 1925. D. Harry O. Hoyt. With Wallace Beery, Bessie Love

The Lost World 1960 [C]. D. Irwin Allen. With Claude Rains, Michael Rennie, Jill St. John

The Luck of the Irish 1948. D. Henry Koster. With Tyrone Power, Anne Baxter, Cecil Kellaway

The Man in the White Suit 1951. D. Alexander Mackendrick. With Alec Guiness, Joan Greenwood

The Man Who Fell to Earth 1976 [C]. D. Nicholas Roeg. With David Bowie, Rip Torn, Candy Clark

The Man Who Haunted Himself 1970 [C]. D. Basil Dearden. With Roger Moore, Hildegard Neil

Mannequin 1987 [C]. D. Michael Gottlieb. With Andrew McCarthy, Kim Cattrall, Meshach Taylor

Mary Poppins 1964 [C]. D. Robert Stevenson. With Julie Andrews, Dick Van Dyke

The Masque of the Red Death 1964 [C]. D. Roger Corman. With Vincent Price, Hazel Court

Master of the World 1961 [C]. D. William Witney. With Vincent Price, Charles Bronson

A Matter of Life and Death 1946 [C]. D. Michael Powell, Emeric Pressburger. With David Niven, Kim Hunter, Roger Livesey

Medea 1970 [C]. D. Pier Paolo Pasolini. With Maria Callas, Massimo Girotti

Metropolis 1926. D. Fritz Lang. With Brigitte Helm, Alfred Abel, Gustav Frohlich

A Midsummer Night's Dream 1935. D. Max Reinhardt, William Dieterle. With James Cagney, Mickey Rooney, Ian Hunter

A Midsummer Night's Dream 1959 [C]. D. Jiří Trnka. With Richard Burton (narrator)

Million Dollar Legs 1932. D. Edward Cline. With W. C. Fields, Lyda Roberti, Jack Oakie

The Miracle on 34th St. 1947. D. George Seaton. With Edmund Gwenn, John Payne, Maureen O'Hara

Miranda 1948. D. Ken Annakin. With Glynis Johns, Googie Withers

Moon Zero Two 1969 [C]. D. Roy Ward Baker. With James Olson, Catherine Von Schell

Mothra 1961 [C]. D. Inoshiro Honda. With Frankie Sakai, Emi and Yumi Ito

Mr. Peabody and the Mermaid 1948. D. Irving Pichel. With Ann Blyth, William Powell

The Mummy 1932. D. Karl Freund. With Boris Karloff, Zita Johann

Night in Paradise 1946 [C]. D. Arthur Lubin. With Merle Oberon, Turhan Bey, Gale Sondergaard

Night Life of the Gods 1935. D. Lowell Sherman. With Alan Mowbray, Florine McKinney

Night of the Living Dead 1968. D. George Romero. With Judith O'Dea, Russell Streiner, Karl Hardman

Nightflyers 1987 [C]. D. T. C. Blake. With Catherine Mary Stewart, Michael Praed

1984 1956. D. Michael Anderson. With Edmond O'Brien, Michael Redgrave

No Blade of Grass 1970 [C]. D. Cornel Wilde. With Nigel Davenport, Jean Wallace

Nosferatu 1922. D. F. W. Murnau. With Max Schreck, Alexander Granach

The Omega Man 1971 [C]. D. Boris Sagal. With Charlton Heston, Rosalind Cash

On the Beach 1959. D. Stanley Kramer. With Gregory Peck, Ava Gardner, Fred Astaire

On the Comet 1970 [C]. D. Karel Zeman. With Emil Horvath, Magda Vasarykova

One Million B.C. 1940. D. Hal Roach, Hal Roach, Jr. With Victor Mature, Carole Landis

One Million Years B.C. 1966 [C]. D. Don Chaffey. With Raquel Welch, John Richardson

One Touch of Venus 1948. D. William A. Seiter. With Robert Walker, Ava Gardner

Orphée (Orpheus) 1950. D. Jean Cocteau. With Jean Marais, Maria Casares, François Perier

Outland 1981 [C]. D. Peter Hyams. With Sean Connery, Frances Sternhagen

Pandora and the Flying Dutchman 1950 [C]. D. Albert Lewin. With Ava Gardner, James Mason

Panic in Year Zero 1962. D. Ray Milland. With Ray Milland, Jean Hagen, Frankie Avalon

Paris Qui Dort (The Crazy Ray) 1923. D. René Clair. With Albert Préjean, Henri Rollan

The People that Time Forgot 1977 [C]. D. Kevin Connor. With Patrick Wayne, Sarah Douglas, Doug McClure

The Phantom Empire 1935. D. Otto Brower, B. R. Eason. With Gene Autry, Frankie Darro, Dorothy Christy

Phase IV 1973 [C]. D. Saul Bass. With Nigel Davenport, Michael Murphy

The Picture of Dorian Gray 1945. D. Albert Lewin. With Hurd Hatfield, George Sanders

Planet of the Apes 1968 [C]. D. Franklin J. Schaffner. With Charlton Heston, Roddy McDowall, Kim Hunter

Poltergeist 1982 [C]. D. Tobe Hooper. With Jobeth Williams, Craig T. Nelson

Portrait of Jennie 1948. D. William Dieterle. With Jennifer Jones, Joseph Cotten

The Power 1967 [C]. D. Byron Haskin. With George Hamilton, Suzanne Pleshette

The Princess Bride 1987 [C]. D. Rob Reiner. With Cary Elwes, Robin Wright, Mandy Patinkin

Privilege 1967 [C]. D. Peter Watkins. With Paul Jones, Jean Shrimpton

The Purple Rose of Cairo 1985 [C]. D. Woody Allen. With Mia Farrow, Jeff Daniels

Quintet 1979 [C]. D. Robert Altman. With Paul Newman, Vittorio Gassman, Bibi Andersson

Raiders of the Lost Ark 1981 [C]. D. Steven Spielberg. With Harrison Ford, Karen Allen, Denholm Elliott

Re-Animator 1985 [C]. D. Stuart Gordon. With Jeffrey Combs, Bruce Abbott

Return of the Jedi 1983 [C]. D. Richard Marquand. With Harrison Ford, Carrie Fisher, Mark Hamill

The Return of the King 1980 [C]. D. Arthur Rankin, Jr., Jules Bass.

The Road Warrior 1981 [C]. D. George Miller. With Mel Gibson, Bruce Spence

Robinson Crusoe on Mars 1964 [C]. D. Byron Haskin. With Paul Mantee, Adam West, Vic Lundin

Rocketship X-M 1950. D. Kurt Neumann. With Lloyd Bridges, Osa Massen, John Emery

Rollerball 1975 [C]. D. Norman Jewison. With James Caan, John Houseman, Maud Adams

Rosemary's Baby 1968 [C]. D. Roman Polanski. With Mia Farrow, John Cassavetes, Ruth Gordon

Savages 1972 [C]. D. James Ivory. With Louis J. Standlen, Anne Francine

Seconds 1966. D. John Frankenheimer. With Rock Hudson, Salome Jens

The Seven Faces of Dr. Lao 1964 [C]. D. George Pal. With Tony Randall, Tony Randall, Tony Randall, etc.

The Seventh Seal 1956. D. Ingmar Bergman. With Max Von Sydow, Gunnar Bjornstrand

She 1935. D. Irving Pichel, Lancing C. Holden. With Helen Gahagan, Randolph Scott

She 1965 [C]. D. Robert Day. With Ursula Andress, Peter Cushing

Silent Running 1971 [C]. D. Douglas Trumbull. With Bruce Dern, Cliff Potts, Ron Rifkin

Siren of Atlantis 1947 [C]. D. Gregg C. Tallas. With Maria Montez, Jean-Pierre Aumont

Sleeper 1973 [C]. D. Woody Allen. With Woody Allen, Diane Keaton, John Beck

Snow White and the Seven Dwarfs 1937 [C]

Solaris 1972 [C]. D. Andrei Tarkovsky. With Donatas Banionis, Natalya Bondarchuk

Something Wicked This Way Comes 1983 [C]. D. Jack Clayton. With Jason Robards, Jr., Jonathan Pryce

Somewhere in Time 1980 [C]. D. Jeannot Szwarc. With Christopher Reeve, Jane Seymour

Son of Frankenstein 1939. D. Rowland V. Lee. With Basil Rathbone, Boris Karloff, Bela Lugosi

The Sorceress 1956. D. André Michel. With Maria Vlady, Maurice Ronet

Soylent Green 1973 [C]. D. Richard Fleischer. With Charlton Heston, Edward G. Robinson

Star Trek – The Motion Picture 1979 [C]. D. Robert Wise. With William Shatner, Leonard Nimoy

Star Trek II: The Wrath of Khan 1982 [C]. D. Nicholas Meyer. With William Shatner, Leonard Nimoy, Ricardo Montalban

Star Trek IV: The Voyage Home 1986 [C]. D. Leonard Nimoy. With William Shatner, Leonard Nimoy, James Doohan

Star Wars 1977 [C]. D. George Lucas. With Mark Hamill, Carrie Fisher, Harrison Ford

The Student of Prague 1913. D. Stellan Rye. With Paul Wegener, Lyda Slamanova

Superman 1978 [C]. D. Richard Donner. With Christopher Reeve, Marlon Brando

Svengali 1931. D. Archie Mayo. With John Barrymore, Marian Marsh

The Sword and the Dragon 1956 [C]. D. Alexander Ptushko. With Boris Andreyev, Andrei Abrikosov

The Sword in the Stone 1963 [C]. D. Wolfgang Reitherman.

The Tales of Hoffman 1951 [C]. D. Michael Powell, Emeric Pressburger. With Moira Shearer, Robert Rounseville

Tarantula 1955 [C]. D. Jack Arnold. With John Agar, Mara Corday, Leo G. Carroll

Teenage Caveman 1958. D. Roger Corman. With Robert Vaughn, Leslie Bradley

The Tenth Victim 1965 [C]. D. Elio Petri. With Marcello Mastroianni, Ursula Andress

The Terminator 1984 [C]. D. James Cameron. With Arnold Schwarzenegger, Michael Biehn

Them! 1954. D. Gordon Douglas. With James Whitmore, James Arness, Edmund Gwenn

The Thief of Bagdad 1924. D. Raoul Walsh. With Douglas Fairbanks, Sr., Julanne Johnston

The Thief of Baghdad 1940 [C]. D. Michael Berger, Ludwig Powell, Tim Whelan. With Sabu, Conrad Veidt, June Duprez, John Justin

The Thing 1951. D. Christian Nyby. With Kenneth Tobey, Margaret Sheridan

Things to Come 1936. D. William Cameron Menzies. With Raymond Massey, Ralph Richardson

This Island Earth 1954 [C]. D. Joseph M. Newman. With Jeff Morrow, Rex Reason, Faith Domergue

THX 1138 1971 [C]. D. George Lucas. With Robert Duvall, Donald Pleasence

Time after Time 1979 [C]. D. Nicholas Meyer. With Malcolm McDowell, David Warner

Time Bandits 1981 [C]. D. Terry Gilliam. With Sean Connery, David Warner, Ralph Richardson

Time Flies 1944. D. Walter Forde. With Felix Aylmer, Leslie Bradley

The Time Machine 1960 [C]. D. George Pal. With Rod Taylor, Yvette Mimieux, Alan Young

The Time Travelers 1964 [C]. D. Ib Melchior. With Preston Foster, Phil Carey, John Hoyt

Topper 1937. D. Norman McLeod. With Roland Young, Cary Grant, Constance Bennett

Trancers 1985 [C]. D. Charles Band. With Tim Thomerson, Helen Hunt

Transatlantic Tunnel 1935. D. Maurice Elvey. With Richard Dix, Madge Evans, George Arliss

A Trip to Mars 1910.

A Trip to the Moon 1902. D. Georges Méliès. With George Méliès, Bleuette Bernon

Tron 1982 [C]. D. Steven Lisberger. With Jeff Bridges, Bruce Boxleitner, David Warner

Turnabout 1940. D. Hal Roach. With Carole Landis, John Hubbard

20,000 Leagues Under the Sea 1907. D. Georges Méliès.

20,000 Leagues Under the Sea 1954 [C]. D. Richard Fleischer. With Kirk Douglas, James Mason, Paul Lukas

Twilight Zone – The Movie 1983 [C]. D. Spielberg et al. With John Lithgow, Albert Brooks, Vic Morrow

2001: A Space Odyssey 1968 [C]. D. Stanley Kubrick. With Keir Dullea, Gary Lockwood, William Sylvester

2010 1984 [C]. D. Peter Hyams. With John Lithgow, Helen Mirren, Roy Scheider

Ugetsu 1954. D. Kenji Mizoguchi. With Machiko Kyo, Mitsuko Mito

Ulysses 1955 [C]. D. Mario Camerini. With Kirk Douglas, Silvana Mangano, Anthony Quinn

The Undying Monster 1942. D. John Brahm. With John Howard, Heather Angel, Bramwell Fletcher

The Uninvited 1944. D. Lewis Allen. With Ray Milland, Gail Russell, Ruth Hussey

The Valley of Gwangi 1969 [C]. D. Jim O'Connolly. With James Franciscus, Gila Golan, Richard Carlson

Vampyr 1932. D. Carl Dreyer. With Julian West, Henrietta Gerard

Victor Frankenstein 1977 [C]. D. Calvin Floyd. With Leon Vitali, Per Oscarsson, Nicholas Clay

Village of the Damned 1960. D. Wolf Rilla. With George Sanders, Barbara Shelley

Voyage to the End of the Universe 1964 [C]. D. Jindrich Polak. With Zdenek Stepenak, Dana Merdricka

The War Game 1965. D. Peter Watkins.

War of the Worlds 1953 [C]. D. Byron Haskin. With Gene Barry, Ann Robinson, Les Tremayne

Werewolf of London 1935. D. Stuart Walker. With Henry Hull, Valerie Hobson, Warner Oland

Westworld 1973 [C]. D. Michael Crichton. With Richard Benjamin, James Brolin, Yul Brynner

When Worlds Collide 1951 [C]. D. Rudolph Mate. With Richard Derr, Barbara Rush, Peter Hansen

Where Do We Go from Here? 1945 [C]. D. Gregory Ratoff. With Fred MacMurray, June Haver, Joan Leslie

The White Reindeer 1952. D. Eric Blomberg. With Mirjami Kuosmanen, Kalervo Nissila

The Wicker Man 1972 [C]. D. Robin Hardy. With Edward Woodward, Christopher Lee

The Wizard of Oz 1939 [C]. D. Victor Fleming. With Judy Garland, Frank Morgan, Ray Bolger

The Wolf Man 1941. D. George Waggner. With Lon Chaney, Jr., Evelyn Ankers, Claude Rains

Woman in the Moon 1929. D. Fritz Lang. With Gerda Maurus, Willy Fritsch

World Without End 1955 [C]. D. Edward Bernds. With Hugh Marlowe, Nelson Leigh, Nancy Gates

Young Frankenstein 1974. D. Mel Brooks. With Peter Boyle, Gene Wilder, Marty Feldman

Zardoz 1973 [C]. D. John Boorman. With Sean Connery, Charlotte Rampling

All of these sources were of great help, but particular mention should be made of Walt Lee's trailblazing *Reference Guide To Fantastic Films,* still unparalleled in some areas.

Benson, Michael. *Vintage Science Fiction Films, 1896–1949.* McFarland & Co., (Jefferson, N.C., and London), 1985.

Brosnan, John. *Future Tense.* St. Martin's (New York), 1978.

Cocteau, Jean. *Beauty and the Beast: Diary of a Film.* Dover (New York), 1972.

Finch, Christopher. *The Art of Walt Disney.* Abrams (New York), 1973.

Halliwell, Leslie. *The Filmgoer's Companion.* Avon (New York), 1978.

Halliwell, Leslie. *Halliwell's Film Guide.* Scribner's (New York), 1983.

Kael, Pauline. *5001 Nights at the Movies.* Holt, Rinehart & Winston (New York), 1982.

Katz, Ephraim. *The Film Encyclopedia.* Putnam's (New York), 1979.

Lee, Walt. *Reference Guide to Fantastic Films,* 3 vols. Chelsea-Lee (Los Angeles), 1972–74.

Lentz, Harris M., III. *Science Fiction, Horror & Fantasy Film Credits,* 2 vols. McFarland & Co. (Jefferson, N.C.), 1983.

Maltin, Leonard (ed.). *TV Movies 1988.* Signet (New York), 1987.

Menville, Douglas, and R. Reginald. *Things to Come.* Times Books (New York), 1977.

———. *Future Visions.* Newcastle Pub. Co. (North Hollywood), 1985.

Meyers, Richard. *S-F 2.* Citadel (Secaucus, N.J.), 1984.

Naha, Ed. *Horrors from Screen to Scream.* Avon (New York), 1975.

Nicholls, Peter. *Fantastic Cinema.* Ebury Press (London), 1984.

Schickel, Richard. *The Disney Version.* Simon & Schuster (New York), 1968.

Shipman, David. *A Pictorial History of Science Fiction Films.* Hamlyn (London), 1985.

Stanley, John. *The Creature Features Movie Guide.* Warner (New York), 1984.

Taylor, Deems; Marcelene Peterson; and Bryant Hale. *A Pictorial History of the Movies.* Simon & Schuster (New York), 1950.

Willis, Donald C. *Horror and Science Fiction Films: A Checklist.* Scarecrow Press (Metuchen, N.J.), 1972.

———. *Horror and Science Fiction Films II.* Scarecrow Press (Metuchen, N.J.), 1982.

———. *Horror and Science Fiction Films III.* Scarecrow Press (Metuchen, N.J., & London), 1984.

Willis, Donald (ed.). *Variety's Complete Science Fiction Reviews.* Garland (New York & London), 1985.

INDEX

All references are to page numbers; text references appear in roman type, illustrations in *italic*.

CREDITS

Photo Credits Courtesy of the Academy of Motion Picture Arts and Sciences: 7, 11, 12, 21, 39, 51, 62 below, 63, 66, 71, 77, 79, 82, 85, 86, 88, 95, 99, 105, 106 below, 114, 117, 137, 138 below, 139, 142, 146, 152, 162–65, 168 below, 173 below, 182–83, 187, 188–90, 192, 205, 220. The Kobal Collection: 17 below, 24, 29, 31–34, 36–37, 44–45, 61, 65, 68, 69, 72–73, 89, 93, 96–97, 100–101, 124–25, 128–29, 130, 133, 147 above, 154–55, 181, 207 below, 210 above, 211 above, 212, 224. Phototeque: 175. Jerry Vermilye: 14, 16 above, 19 below, 26, 40, 53 below, 54 below, 55 below, 64 below, 87, 91 below, 94, 111 below, 112, 126 above, 148 above, 171–72, 178, 179 above, 191, 197–98, 200 below, 203 below, 208, 211 below, 222 above, 227.

Film Copyrights 1: *Fantasia*, 1940, © Walt Disney Productions. 2 above: *Star Trek II: Wrath of Kahn*, 1982, Copyright © by Paramount Pictures Corporation. All rights reserved. Courtesy of Paramount Pictures. 2: *Star Wars*, 1977, © Lucasfilm Ltd. (LFL) 1977. All rights reserved. 2 below: *King Kong*, 1976, © Dino de Laurentiis Corporation. 3: *She*, 1965, ABP/Hammer, Great Britain. 4: *The Incredible Shrinking Man*, 1957, Copyright © Universal Pictures, a Division of MCA Communications, a Division of MCA Communications, Inc. Courtesy of MCA Publishing, a Division of MCA Communications, Inc. 5: *Superman*, 1978, © Warner Bros., Inc. Courtesy of Warner Bros. Inc./Alexander Salkind. 7: *Mary Poppins*, 1964, © Walt Disney Productions. 9: *One Million Years B.C.*, 1966, Hammer. 11: *A Trip to the Moon*, 1902, Star, France. 12: *The Woman in the Moon*, 1929, UFA Films, Germany. 13: *Flash Gordon*, 1936, Copyright © Universal Pictures, a Division of Universal City Studios, Inc. Courtesy of MCA Publishing, a Division of MCA Communications, Inc. 14: *Rocket Ship X-M*, 1950, © Lippert Pictures, Inc. 15 above: *Destination Moon*, 1950, Copyright © Universal Pictures, a Division of Universal City Studios, Inc. Courtesy of MCA Publishing, a Division of MCA Communications, Inc. 15 below: *When Worlds Collide*, 1951, Copyright © by Paramount Pictures Corporation. All rights reserved. Courtesy of Paramount Pictures. 16 above: *From the Earth to the Moon*, 1958, © Warner Bros., Inc. Courtesy of Warner Bros., Inc. 16 below: *First Men in the Moon*, 1964, Copyright © Columbia Pictures Industries, Inc. Courtesy of Columbia Pictures, a Division of Columbia Pictures Industries, Inc. 17 above: *Forbidden Planet*, 1956, © 1956 Loew's Incorporated. 17 below: *Robinson Crusoe on Mars*, 1964, Copyright © by Paramount Pictures Corporation. All rights reserved. Courtesy of Paramount Pictures. 18: *Voyage to the End of the Universe*, 1963, American International Pictures/Orion Pictures. 19 above: *Dr. Who and the Daleks*, 1965, © British Lion/Regal/Aaru, Great Britain. 19 below: *Battle of the Worlds*, 1960, Courtesy Topaz Film Corporation. 20: *Barbarella*, 1968, Copyright © by Paramount Pictures Corporation. All rights reserved. Courtesy of Paramount Pictures. 21: *The Illustrated Man*, 1968, © Warner Bros., Inc. Courtesy of Warner Bros., Inc. 22–23: *Moon Zero Two*, 1969, © Warner Bros., Inc. Courtesy of Warner Bros., Inc. 24: *2001: A Space Odyssey*, 1968, Copyright 1968 Metro-Goldwyn-Mayer, Inc. 25: *2010*, 1984, © 1984 Metro-Goldwyn-Mayer, Inc./United Artists Associated, Inc. 26: *Silent Running*, 1971, Copyright © Universal Pictures, a Division of Universal City Studios, Inc. Courtesy of MCA Publishing, a Division of MCA Communications, Inc. 28: *Fantastic Planet*, 1973, New World Pictures. 29 above: *Star Wars*, 1977, © Lucasfilm Ltd. (LFL) 1977. All rights reserved. 29 below: *The Black Hole*, 1979, © Walt Disney Productions. 30: *Flash Gordon*, 1980, © E.M.I./Famous/Starling/Dino de Laurentiis. 31: *Outland*, 1981, © Warner Bros., Inc. Courtesy of Warner Bros., Inc./The Ladd Company. 32: *Star Trek: The Motion Picture*, 1979, Copyright © by Paramount Pictures Corporation. All rights reserved. Courtesy of Paramount Pictures. 33: *The Empire Strikes Back*, 1980, © Lucasfilm Ltd. (LFL) 1980. All rights reserved. 34: *Return of the Jedi*, © 1983 Twentieth Century Fox Film Corporation. 35: *Nightflyers*, 1987, © New Century/Vista Films Co. 36: *The Dark Crystal*, 1982, Copyright © Universal Pictures, a Division of Universal City Studios, Inc. Courtesy of MCA Publishing, a Division of MCA Communications, Inc./AFD/ITC. 37: *Dune*, 1984, © Dino de Laurentiis Corporation. 39: *Berkeley Square*, 1933, © 1933 Twentieth Century Fox Film Corporation. 40: *Where Do We Go from Here?*, © 1945 Twentieth Century Fox Film Corporation. 41: *World Without End*, © 1955 Allied Artists Pictures Corporation. 42: *The Time Machine*, © 1960 Metro-Goldwyn-Mayer, Inc./Galaxy. 43: *The Time Travelers*, 1964, American International Pictures/Orion Pictures. 44: *Time After Time*, 1979, © Warner Bros., Inc. Courtesy of Warner Bros., Inc./Orion Pictures. 45: *Somewhere in Time*, 1980, Copyright © Universal Pictures, a Division of Universal City Studios, Inc. Courtesy of MCA Publishing, a Division of MCA Communications, Inc. 46: *Time Bandits*, 1981, Handmade Films. 47: *Back to the Future*, 1985, Copyright © Universal Pictures, a Division of Universal City Studios, Inc. Courtesy of MCA Publishing, a Division of MCA Communications, Inc. 48: *The Terminator*, © 1984, Orion Pictures. 49: *Star Trek: The Voyage Home*, 1986, Copyright © by Paramount Pictures Corporation. All rights reserved. Courtesy of Paramount Pictures. 51: *Metropolis*, 1926, UFA Films, Germany. 52: *Just Imagine*, © 1930 Twentieth Century Fox Film Corporation. 53 above: *The Tunnel*, © 1935 Gaumont British Picture Corporation of America. 53 below: *Things to Come*, 1936, London Films. 54 above: *Teenage Caveman*, 1958, American International Pictures/Orion Pictures. 54 below: *1984*, 1955, Holiday. 55 above: *The Creation of the Humanoids*, 1962, Emerson Film Enterprises. 55 below: *On the Beach*, 1959, © United Artists Associated, Inc. 56 above: *The Day the Earth Caught Fire*, 1961, Copyright © Universal Pictures, a Division of Universal City Studios, Inc. Courtesy of MCA Publishing, a Division of MCA Communications, Inc. 56 below: *The Day of the Triffids*, © 1963 Metro-Goldwyn-Mayer, Inc./United Artists Associated, Inc. 56 center: *Panic in Year Zero*, 1962, American International Pictures/Orion Pictures. 57: *The Last Man on Earth*, 1964, American International Pictures/Orion Pictures. 58 above: *Alphaville*, 1965, Chaumiane/Film Studio, France, Italy. 58 below: *The Tenth Victim*, 1965, Embassy International Pictures. 59: *Planet of the Apes*, 1968, © 1967 Apjac Productions, Inc., and Twentieth Century Fox Film Corporation. All rights reserved. Courtesy Twentieth Century Fox Film Corporation. 60: *Fahrenheit 451*, 1966, Rank/Anglo Enterprise/Vineyard. 61: *Privilege*, 1967, Copyright © Universal Pictures, a Division of Universal City Studios, Inc. Courtesy of MCA Publishing, a Division of MCA Communications, Inc. 62 above: *The Bed-Sitting Room*, 1969, © United Artists Associated, Inc. 62 below: *No Blade of Grass*, © 1970 Metro-Goldwyn-Mayer, Inc. 63: *The Omega Man*, 1971, © Warner Bros., Inc. Courtesy of Warner Bros., Inc. 64 above: *A Clockwork Orange*, 1971, © Warner Bros., Inc. Courtesy of Warner Bros., Inc./Polaris. 64 below: *THX 1138*, 1969, © Warner Bros., Inc. Courtesy of Warner Bros., Inc. 65 above: *Sleeper*, 1973, © 1973 Jack Rollins and Charles H. Joffe Productions. 65 below: *Zardoz*, © 1973 Twentieth Century Fox Film Corporation. 66: *Westworld*, © 1973 Metro-Goldwyn-Mayer, Inc. 67: *Rollerball*, 1975, © 1975 United Artists Associated, Inc. 68 above left: *Soylent Green*, © 1973 Metro-Goldwyn-Mayer, Inc. 68 below right: *Buck Rogers in the 25th Century*, 1979, Copyright © Universal Pictures, a Division of Universal City Studios, Inc. Courtesy of MCA Publishing, a Division of MCA Communications, Inc. 69: *Logan's Run*, © 1976 Metro-Goldwyn-Mayer, Inc. 70: *Quintet*, © 1979 Twentieth Century Fox Film Corporation. 71: *Heartbeeps*, 1981, Copyright © Universal Pictures, a Division of Universal City Studios, Inc. Courtesy of MCA Publishing, a Division of MCA Communications, Inc. 72: *The Road Warrior*, 1981, Kennedy, Miller Entertainment. 73: *Blade Runner*, 1982, © Warner Bros., Inc. Courtesy of Warner Bros., Inc./The Ladd Company/Blade Runner Partnership. 74: *The Day After*, 1983, © American Broadcasting Companies, Inc., Television Network. 75: *Brazil*, 1985, Arnon Milchan, Great Britain. 77: *Frankenstein*, 1910, © Edison. 78: *The Cabinet of Dr. Caligari*, 1919 Twentieth Century Fox Film Corporation. 79: *Paris Qui Dort (The Crazy Ray)*, 1923, Films Diamant. 80: *Frankenstein*, 1931, Copyright © Universal Pictures, a Division of Universal City Studios, Inc.

Courtesy of MCA Publishing, a Division of MCA Communications, Inc. 81: *Svengali*, 1931, © Warner Bros., Inc. Courtesy of Warner Bros., Inc. 82: *Dr. Jekyll and Mr. Hyde*, 1932, Copyright © Universal Pictures, a Division of Universal City Studios, Inc. Courtesy of MCA Publishing, a Division of MCA Communications, Inc. 83 above: *Island of Lost Souls*, 1932, Copyright © Universal Pictures, a Division of Universal City Studios, Inc. Courtesy of the Kobal Collection. 83 below: *The Invisible Man*, 1933, © Universal Pictures, a Division of Universal City Studios, Inc. Courtesy of MCA Publishing, a Division of MCA Communications, Inc. 84: *The Bride of Frankenstein*, 1935, Copyright © Universal Pictures, a Division of Universal City Studios, Inc. Courtesy of MCA Publishing, a Division of MCA Communications, Inc. 85 above: *The Black Cat*, 1934, Copyright © Universal Pictures, a Division of Universal City Studios, Inc. Courtesy of MCA Publishing, a Division of MCA Communications, Inc. 85 below: *Son of Frankenstein*, 1939, Copyright © Universal Pictures, a Division of Universal City Studios, Inc. Courtesy of MCA Publishing, a Division of MCA Communications, Inc. 86: *Dr. Cyclops*, 1940, Copyright © by Paramount Pictures Corporation. All rights reserved. Courtesy of Paramount Pictures. 87: *Dr. Jekyll and Mr. Hyde*, © 1941 Metro-Goldwyn-Mayer, Inc. 88: *The Man in the White Suit*, 1951, Ealing. 89 above: *The Tales of Hoffman*, 1951, British Lion/London/Michael Power, Emeric Pressburger. 89 below: *20,000 Leagues Under the Sea*, © Walt Disney Productions. 90: *The Amazing Colossal Man*, 1957, American International Pictures/Orion Pictures/Malibu. 91 above: *The Damned*, 1961, Copyright © Columbia Pictures Industries, Inc. Courtesy of Columbia Pictures, a Division of Columbia Pictures Industries, Inc. 91 below: *Master of the World*, 1961, American International Pictures/Orion Pictures/Alta Vista, Great Britain. 92: *Crack in the World*, 1965, Copyright © by Paramount Pictures Corporation. All rights reserved. Courtesy of Paramount Pictures. 93: *Fantastic Voyage*, 1966, © 1966 Twentieth Century Fox Film Corporation. All rights reserved. 94: *Seconds*, 1966, © by Paramount Pictures Corporation. All rights reserved. Courtesy of Paramount Pictures. 95 above: *Colossus: The Forbin Project*, 1970, Copyright © Universal Pictures, a Division of Universal City Studios, Inc. Courtesy of MCA Publishing, a Division of MCA Communications, Inc. 95 below: *Charly*, 1968, © Selmur/Robertson Associates. 96: *The Abominable Dr. Phibes*, 1971, American International Pictures/Orion Pictures. 97: *Dr. Phibes Rises Again*, 1972, American International Pictures/Orion Pictures. 98: *Young Frankenstein*, 1974, © 1974 Twentieth Century Fox Film Corporation. 99 above: *Demon Seed*, © 1977 Metro-Goldwyn-Mayer, Inc. 99 below: *The Island of Dr. Moreau*, 1977, American International Pictures/Orion Pictures. 100: *Altered States*, 1980, © Warner Bros., Inc. Courtesy of Warner Bros., Inc. 101: *Tron*, 1982, © Walt Disney Productions/Lisberger-Kushner. 102: *Brainstorm*, 1983 Metro-Goldwyn-Mayer, Inc./United Artists Associated, Inc. 103 above: *Re-Animator*, 1985, Empire Pictures. 103 below: *The Bride*, 1985, Copyright © Columbia Pictures Industries, Inc. Courtesy of Columbia Pictures, a Division of Columbia Pictures Industries, Inc. 105 above: *The Lost World*, 1925, © Warner Bros., Inc. Courtesy of Warner Bros., Inc. First National Pictures. 105 below: *Gertie the Dinosaur*, 1909, © Windsor McCay Pictures. 106 above: *King Kong*, 1933, © RKO General Pictures, Inc. 106 below: *One Million B.C.*, 1940, Hal Roach Studio. 107: *The Creature from the Black Lagoon*, 1954, Courtesy of Universal Pictures, a Division of Universal City Studios, Inc. Courtesy of MCA Publishing, a Division of MCA Communications, Inc. 108: *Godzilla, King of the Monsters*, 1954, Toho. 109 above: *Tarantula*, 1955, Copyright © Universal Pictures, a Division of Universal City Studios, Inc. Courtesy of MCA Publishing, a Division of MCA Communications, Inc. 109 below: *Them!*, 1954, © Warner Bros., Inc. Courtesy of Warner Bros., Inc. 110: *Gorgo*, © 1959 Metro-Goldwyn-Mayer, Inc. 111 above: *Dinosaurus*, 1960, Copyright © Universal Pictures, a Division of Universal City Studios, Inc. Courtesy of MCA Publishing, a Division of MCA Communications, Inc. 111 below: *The Lost World*, 1960, Courtesy Twentieth Century Fox Film Corporation. 112: *Mothra*, 1961, Copyright © Columbia Pictures Industries, Inc. Courtesy of Columbia Pictures, a Division of Columbia Pictures Industries, Inc. 113 above: *One Million Years B.C.*, 1966, Hammer. 113 below: *The Valley of Gwangi*, 1968, © Warner Bros., Inc. Courtesy of Warner Bros., Inc. 114 above: *At the Earth's Core*, 1976, Courtesy Amicus, Great Britain. 114 below: *Land That Time Forgot*, 1975, Courtesy Amicus, Great Britain. 115: *King Kong*, 1976, © Dino de Laurentiis Corporation. 117: *Algol*, 1920, UFA Films, Germany. 118: *The Day the Earth Stood Still*, 1951, © 1951 Twentieth Century Fox Film Corporation. All rights reserved. 119: *The Thing*, 1951, Courtesy RKO General Pictures, Inc. 121 above: *The War of the Worlds*, 1953, Copyright © 1952 by Paramount Pictures Corporation. All rights reserved. Courtesy of Paramount Pictures. 121 below: *This Island Earth*, 1954, Copyright © Universal Pictures, a Division of Universal City Studios, Inc. Courtesy of MCA Publishing, a Division of MCA Communications, Inc. 122: *The Blob*, 1958, Tonylyn/Jack J. Harris. 123 above: *I Married a Monster from Outer Space*, 1958, Copyright © by Paramount Pictures Corporation. All rights reserved. Courtesy of Paramount Pictures. 123 below: *Village of the Damned*, © 1960 Metro-Goldwyn-Mayer, Inc. 124: *The Andromeda Strain*, 1971, Copyright © Universal Pictures, a Division of Universal City Studios, Inc. Courtesy of MCA Publishing, a Division of MCA Communications, Inc. 125: *The Man Who Fell to Earth*, 1976, British Lion, Great Britain. 126 above: *Five Million Years to Earth*, 1968, © Warner Bros., Inc. Courtesy of Warner Bros., Inc. 126 below: *The Green Slime*, © 1968 Metro-Goldwyn-Mayer, Inc. 127: *Phase IV*, 1973, Copyright © by Paramount Pictures Corporation. All rights reserved. Courtesy of Paramount Pictures. 128–29: *Close Encounters of the Third Kind*, 1977, Copyright © 1977, 1980 Columbia Pictures Industries, Inc. Courtesy of Columbia Pictures, a Division of Columbia Pictures Industries, Inc. 130: *Invasion of the Body Snatchers*, 1978, Courtesy Allied Artists/Walter Wanger. 131: *Superman*, 1978, © Warner Bros., Inc. Courtesy of Warner Bros., Inc./Alexander Salkind. 132: *Alien*, 1979, © 1979 Twentieth Century Fox Film Corporation. 133 above: *E.T.: The Extra-Terrestrial*, 1982, Copyright © Universal Pictures, a Division of Universal City Studios, Inc. Courtesy of MCA Publishing, a Division of MCA Communications, Inc. 133 below: *Cocoon*, © 1985 Twentieth Century Fox Film Corporation. 134, 135: *Aliens*, 1986, Courtesy Twentieth Century Fox Film Corporation. 137 above: *Alice in Wonderland*, 1933, Copyright © Universal Pictures, a Division of Universal City Studios, Inc. Courtesy of MCA Publishing, a Division of MCA Communications, Inc. 137 below: *Million Dollar Legs*, 1932, Copyright © Universal Pictures, a Division of Universal City Studios, Inc. Courtesy of MCA Publishing, a Division of MCA Communications, Inc. 137 above: *The Ghost Goes West*, 1935, London Films. 138 below: *Night Life of the Gods*, 1935, Copyright © Universal Pictures, a Division of Universal City Studios, Inc. Courtesy of MCA Publishing, a Division of MCA Communications, Inc. 139: *Topper*, © 1937, renewed 1964 Metro-Goldwyn-Mayer, Inc. 140 above and below: *The Wizard of Oz*, 1939, © 1939 Loew's Incorporated. Renewed 1966 Metro-Goldwyn-Mayer, Inc. 141: *I Married a Witch*, 1942, © United Artists Associated, Inc. 142 above: *The Canterville Ghost*, 1944, Courtesy Metro-Goldwyn-Mayer, Inc. 142 below: *Blithe Spirit*, 1945, Two Cities/Cineguild. 143: *The Horn Blows at Midnight*, 1945, © Warner Bros., Inc. Courtesy of Warner Bros., Inc. 144 above: *It's a Wonderful Life*, 1946, Courtesy RKO General Pictures, Inc. 144 below: *A Matter of Life and Death*, Copyright 1946. 145: *Night in Paradise*, 1946, Copyright © Universal Pictures, a Division of Universal City Studios, Inc. Courtesy of MCA Publishing, a Division of MCA Communications, Inc. 146 above: *The Bishop's Wife*, 1947, Samuel Goldwyn. 146 below: *The Ghost and Mrs. Muir*, © 1947 Twentieth Century Fox Film Corporation. 147 above: *Down to Earth*, 1947, Copyright © Columbia Pictures Industries, Inc. Courtesy of Columbia Pictures, a Division of Columbia Pictures Industries, Inc. 147 below: *Miracle on 34th Street*, 1947, © 1947, renewed 1974 Twentieth Century Fox Film Corporation. 148 above: *One Touch of Venus*, 1948, Copyright © Universal Pictures, a Division of Universal City Studios, Inc. Courtesy

of MCA Publishing, a Division of MCA Communications, Inc. 148 below: *The Luck of the Irish*, © 1948 Twentieth Century Fox Film Corporation. 149 above: *Miranda*, 1948, GFD/Gainsborough, Great Britain. 149 below: *Mr. Peabody and the Mermaid*, 1948, Copyright © Universal Pictures, a Division of Universal City Studios, Inc. Courtesy of MCA Publishing, a Division of MCA Communications, Inc. 150: *Portrait of Jennie*, 1948, David O. Selznick. 151: *Carousel*, © 1956 Twentieth Century Fox Film Corporation. 152: *Bell, Book and Candle*, 1959, © Columbia Pictures Industries, Inc. Courtesy of Columbia Pictures, a Division of Columbia Pictures Industries, Inc. 153: *Mary Poppins*, 1964, © Walt Disney Productions. 154: *Seven Faces of Dr. Lao*, © 1964 Metro-Goldwyn-Mayer, Inc./George Pal. 155: *Twilight Zone: The Movie*, 1983, © Warner Bros., Inc. Courtesy of Warner Bros., Inc. 156: *Poltergeist*, 1982 Metro-Goldwyn-Mayer, Inc. 157: *The Purple Rose of Cairo*, © 1985 Orion Pictures/Jack Rollins-Charles H. Joffe. 158: *Labyrinth*, 1986 © Tri-Star/Eric Rattray, George Lucas. 159: *Mannequin*, © 1987 Twentieth Century Fox Film Corporation. 161: *Dracula*, 1931, Copyright © Universal Pictures, a Division of Universal City Studios, Inc. Courtesy of MCA Publishing, a Division of MCA Communications, Inc. 162: *Nosferatu*, 1922, Prana, Germany. 163: *The Mummy*, 1932, Copyright © Universal Pictures, a Division of Universal City Studios, Inc. Courtesy of MCA Publishing, a Division of MCA Communications, Inc. 164: *Vampyr*, 1932, Tobis Klangfilm/Carl Dreyer, Germany, France. 165: *The Werewolf in London*, 1935, Copyright © Universal Pictures, a Division of Universal City Studios, Inc. Courtesy of MCA Publishing, a Division of MCA Communications, Inc. 166: *Dracula's Daughter*, 1936, Copyright © Universal Pictures, a Division of Universal City Studios, Inc. Courtesy of MCA Publishing, a Division of MCA Communications, Inc. 167: *The Wolf Man*, 1941, Copyright © Universal Pictures, a Division of Universal City Studios, Inc. Courtesy of MCA Publishing, a Division of MCA Communications, Inc. 168 above: *Cat People*, 1942, Courtesy RKO General Pictures, Inc. 168 below: *I Walked with a Zombie*, 1943, Courtesy RKO General Pictures, Inc. 169: *The Uninvited*, 1944, Copyright © by Paramount Pictures Corporation. All rights reserved. Courtesy of Paramount Pictures. 170: *The Picture of Dorian Grey*, 1945, © 1945 Loew's Inc. Renewed 1972 Metro-Goldwyn-Mayer, Inc. 171: *The Innocents*, © 1961 Twentieth Century Fox Film Corporation. 172: *The Haunting*, © 1963 Metro-Goldwyn-Mayer, Inc. 173 above: *Burn, Witch, Burn*, 1962, American International Pictures/Orion Pictures. 173 below: *The Birds*, 1963, Copyright © Universal Pictures, a Division of Universal City Studios, Inc. Courtesy of MCA Communications, Inc. 175: *The Masque of the Red Death*, 1964, American International Pictures/Orion Pictures/Alta Vista, Great Britain. 176: *The Fearless Vampire Killers*, © 1967 Metro-Goldwyn-Mayer, Inc./Cadre Films/Filmways. 177 above: *The Dunwich Horror*, 1969, American International Pictures/Orion Pictures. 177 below: *Rosemary's Baby*, 1968, Copyright © 1968 by Paramount Pictures Corporation. All rights reserved. Courtesy of Paramount Pictures. 178: *Blood on Satan's Claw*, 1970, Tigon-Chilton, Great Britain. 179: *The Man Who Haunted Himself*, 1970, ABP, Great Britain. 179 above: *The Wicker Man*, 1972, British Lion, Great Britain. 180: *The Exorcist*, 1973, © Warner Bros., Inc. Courtesy of Warner Bros., Inc. 181: *Dracula*, 1979, Copyright © Universal Pictures, a Division of Universal City Studios, Inc. Courtesy of MCA Publishing, a Division of MCA Communications, Inc. 182: *An American Werewolf in London*, 1981, Polygram/Lycanthrope. 183: *The Hunger*, © 1983 Metro-Goldwyn-Mayer, Inc./United Artists Associated, Inc. 184: *Something Wicked This Way Comes*, 1983, © Walt Disney Productions/Bryna. 185: *Highlander*, 1986, © E.M.I./Highlander. 187: *The Thief of Bagdad*, 1924, © United Artists Associated Inc. 188: *Death Takes a Holiday*, 1934, Copyright © Universal Pictures, a Division of Universal City Studios, Inc. Courtesy of MCA Publishing, a Division of MCA Communications, Inc. 189: *A Midsummer Night's Dream*, 1935, © Warner Bros., Inc. Courtesy of Warner Bros., Inc. 190: *Lost Horizon*, 1937, Copyright © 1937. Renewed 1965 Columbia Pictures Corporation of California, Ltd. Courtesy of Columbia Pictures, a Division of Columbia Pictures Industries, Inc. 191: *Snow White*, 1937, © Walt Disney Productions. 192 above: *The Thief of Baghdad*, 1940, London Films. 192 below: *The Blue Bird*, © 1940 Twentieth Century Fox Film Corporation. 193: *Fantasia*, 1940, © Walt Disney Productions. 194: *Between Two Worlds*, 1944, © Warner Bros., Inc. Courtesy of Warner Bros., Inc. 195 above: *La Belle et la Bête (Beauty and the Beast)*, 1946, © Discina Films-Lopert, United Artists Associated, Inc., Janus Films. 195 below: *The Curse of the Cat People*, 1944, Courtesy RKO General Pictures, Inc. 196 above: *Siren of Atlantis*, 1947, © United Artists Associated, Inc. 196 below: *Orpheus*, 1950, © Janus Films. 197: *Pandora and the Flying Dutchman*, 1950, Romulus. 198: *Ugetsu*, 1953, Daiei, Japan. 199: *Ulysses*, 1954, © Warner Bros., Inc. Courtesy of Warner Bros., Inc. 200 above: *The Seventh Seal*, 1956, Swensk Filmindustri, Sweden. 200 below: *The Sorceress*, 1955, © Iena Productions/Ellis Films. 201: *The Sword and the Dragon*, 1956, Valiant Films Corp. 202: *Brigadoon*, © 1953 Metro-Goldwyn-Mayer, Inc. 203 above: *A Midsummer Night's Dream*, 1959, Showcorporation. 203 below: *Black Orpheus*, 1959, Dispatfilm/Gemma/Tupan, France, Italy, Brazil. 204: *Jason and the Argonauts*, 1963, Copyright © Columbia Pictures Industries, Inc. Courtesy of Columbia Pictures, a Division of Columbia Pictures Industries, Inc. 205: *The Sword in the Stone*, 1963, © Walt Disney Productions. 206: *Camelot*, © 1967 Warner Bros. Inc.—Seven Arts. 207 above: *Medea*, 1970, San Marco/Number One/Janus Films, Italy, France, Germany. 207 below: *Donkey Skin*, 1971, Park Film—Marianne. 208: *The Last Wave*, 1977, Ayer/MacElroy/Derek Power, Australia. 209 above: *The Last Unicorn*, 1982, © Jenson Farley/ITC Films. 209 below: *The Lord of the Rings*, 1978, © United Artists Associated, Inc. 210 above: *Dragonslayer*, 1981, © Walt Disney Productions/Courtesy of Paramount Pictures. 210 below: *Excalibur*, 1981, © Warner Bros., Inc. Courtesy of Warner Bros., Inc./Orion Pictures (John Boorman). 211 above: *Conan the Barbarian*, 1982, © Dino de Laurentiis/Edward R. Pressman. 211 below: *The Beastmaster*, © 1982 Metro-Goldwyn-Mayer, Inc. 212: *Krull*, 1983, Copyright © Columbia Pictures Industries, Inc. Courtesy of Columbia Pictures, a Division of Columbia Pictures Industries, Inc./Ted Mann—Ron Silverman, Great Britain. 214: *The Company of the Wolves*, 1984, ITC/Palace, Great Britain. 215 above: *Legend*, © 1985 Twentieth Century Fox Film Corporation. 215 below: *Ladyhawke*, 1985, © Warner Bros., Inc. Courtesy of Warner Bros., Inc. 216: *The Princess Bride*, © 1987 Twentieth Century Fox Film Corporation. 219: *She*, 1935, © Mascot Serial. 221: *The Jungle Book*, 1942, © Walt Disney Productions. 222 above: *The Fabulous World of Jules Verne*, 1958, © Warner Bros., Inc. Courtesy of Warner Bros., Inc. 222 below: *The Incredible Shrinking Man*, 1957, Copyright © Universal Pictures, a Division of Universal City Studios, Inc. Courtesy of MCA Publishing, a Division of MCA Communications, Inc. 223: *Journey to the Center of the Earth*, © 1959 Twentieth Century Fox Film Corporation. 224: *She*, 1965, ABP/Hammer, Great Britain. 225: *How I Won the War*, 1967, © United Artists Associated, Inc. 226 above: *The Power*, © 1967 Metro-Goldwyn-Mayer, Inc. 226 below: *Night of the Living Dead*, 1968, Image Ten. 227: *The Lost Continent*, 1968, Hammer, Great Britain. 229: *Raiders of the Lost Ark*, 1981, © 1981 Lucasfilm Ltd. (LFL). All rights reserved. Courtesy Lucasfilm Ltd

About the Jacket Finished art for the front and back jacket collages was created by Creative Imaging Design using their digital paint system. Black-and-white photographs were scanned to magnetic tape on a Hell rotary drum scanner and input to the Quantel Graphic (high resolution) Paintbox. The elements were isolated, composed in position, and colorized using digital watercolor, paint, and airbrush. The final piece was once again recorded on magnetic tape, and the data drove lasers that exposed ektachrome transparency film using a Hell CPR 403 digital transparency recorder. The final transparencies, or Digital Originals, were then used as shooting art for color separations.